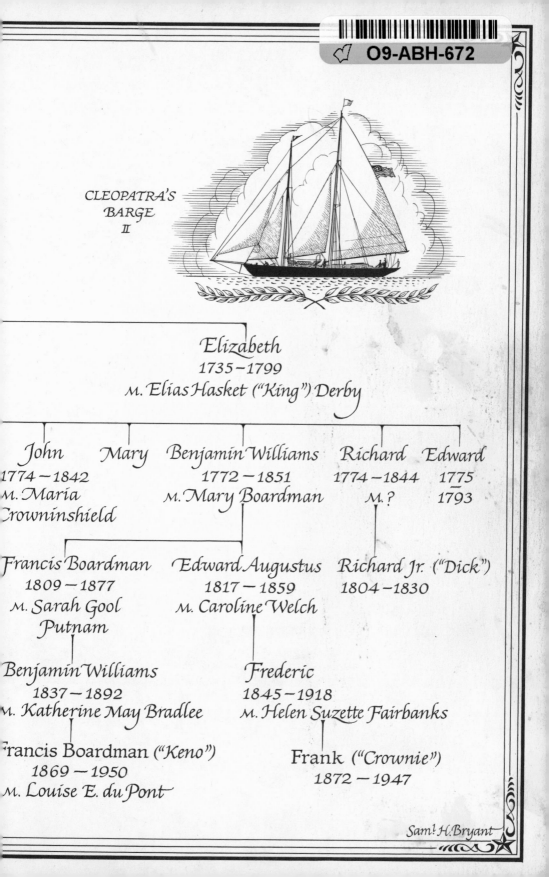

CLEOPATRA'S
BARGE
II

Elizabeth
1735–1799
M. Elias Hasket ("King") Derby

John
1774–1842
M. Maria
Crowninshield

Mary

Benjamin Williams
1772–1851
M. Mary Boardman

Richard
1774–1844
M.?

Edward
1775
1793

Francis Boardman
1809–1877
M. Sarah Gool
Putnam

Edward Augustus
1817–1859
M. Caroline Welch

Richard Jr. ("Dick")
1804–1830

Benjamin Williams
1837–1892
M. Katherine May Bradlee

Frederic
1845–1918
M. Helen Suzette Fairbanks

Francis Boardman ("Keno")
1869–1950
M. Louise E. du Pont

Frank ("Crownie")
1872–1947

Sam! H. Bryant

CLEOPATRA'S BARGE

The Crowninshield
Story

by David L. Ferguson

CLEOPATRA'S BARGE

LITTLE, BROWN AND COMPANY
BOSTON · TORONTO

FIRST EDITION

T 09/76

For permission to reprint previously unpublished materials, the author is grateful to:

Harold Ober Associates, Inc., for the F. Scott Fitzgerald letter on p. 210.

The Houghton Library, Conrad W. Oberdorfer and G. d'Andelot Belin, Trustees under the Will of Amy Lowell, for excerpts from Amy Lowell letters on pp. 212–213.

The Houghton Library and Nancy T. Andrews, for the E. E. Cummings letter on pp. 214–215.

The excerpts from *Mrs. De Peyster's Parties and Other Lively Studies from The New Yorker* by Geoffrey Hellman are reprinted by permission of Macmillan Publishing Co., Inc. Copyright 1948, © 1963, renewed © 1976 by Geoffrey Hellman. This material originally appeared in *The New Yorker.*

LIBRARY OF CONGRESS CATALOGING IN PUBLICATION DATA

Ferguson, David L
  Cleopatra's barge.

  Bibliography: p.
  Includes index.
  1. Crowninshield family. 2. Cleopatra's Barge (Yacht) 3. United States—Genealogy. I. Title.
CS71.C9563 1976 929'.2'0973 76-16491
ISBN 0-316-27895-5

Designed by Janis Capone

*Published simultaneously in Canada
by Little, Brown & Company (Canada) Limited*

PRINTED IN THE UNITED STATES OF AMERICA

I will tell you.
The barge she sat in, like a burnish'd throne,
Burn'd on the water: the poop was beaten
*   gold;*
Purple the sails, and so perfumed that
The winds were love-sick with them; the oars were
*   silver,*
Which to the tune of flutes kept stroke and made
The water which they beat to follow faster,
As amorous of their strokes. For her own person,
It beggar'd all description: she did lie
In her pavilion, cloth-of-gold of tissue,
O'er-picturing that Venus where we see
The fancy outwork nature: on each side her
Stood pretty dimpled boys, like smiling Cupids,
With divers-colour'd fans, whose wind did seem
To glow the delicate cheeks which they did cool,
And what they undid did.

Shakespeare, *Antony and Cleopatra*
Act II, Scene ii

Contents

CLEOPATRA'S BARGE

Prologue

—◄●►—

The Caribbean is the last anchorage this side of oblivion for great American pleasure craft. To this sea they come finally, after yet another name by yet another owner — both, as some have it, of progressive vulgarity. Be this as it may, some bounty has in one way or another been blighted, most usually (and most acceptably) by the gatherer of taxes in life and in death. Here, off the Windwards and the Grenadines, these seagoing splendors, having been banished forever from Bar Harbor, Newport, and Marblehead by anxious trustees and unsmiling executors, sail for the last time. Reprieve, customarily under a Panamanian flag, is conditional; in exile, as never before, the ocean queens must earn their keep.

Among these yachts, one could probably choose no better than *Janeen*, whose home port is St. Vincent and whose captain is an agreeable Canadian named Boudreau. The blue-hulled schooner and her master are about the same age — sixty. And together they are everything expected of expensive cruising anywhere. *Janeen* (she is named after the captain's wife) is large and luxurious, her crew attentive to one's every need, the food and drink excellent, the staterooms spacious, even plush. And she is fast. Sheets started, rail awash, the yacht easily makes a speed as great as that of the America's Cup contenders tacking to and fro in the swirl of Rhode Island Sound, where indeed in years gone by she was a frequent visitor. Moreover, as Captain Boudreau is not slow to confide, his ship is in great demand and so his clients (he prefers to call them guests) can be few, even select.

Obviously the captain knows a great deal about sailing ships and

3

about his own most of all. His *Janeen* has no specification, no trait and no nuance of which he is not keenly aware. Clearly his knowledge is of the happiest kind, giving pleasure to himself and to others and disturbing no one. But for all the halcyon, sunny West Indian days spent among congenial guests on his much-loved ship, Captain Boudreau does have his troubles. The most worrisome in recent years has been the replacement of the yacht's mainmast. This was a problem requiring considerable thought and effort, and an upward glance tells why: *Janeen*'s mast reaches as high as a thirteen-story building, almost lost in the blue of the Lesser Antilles. A new mast, specially constructed of aluminum, was stepped only after the greatest difficulty (it was hard to find facilities for the purpose); the job consumed a year of the captain's time and nearly fifty thousand of his dollars. But now he is certain that his vessel will sail on for many more years — more years than those left him.

As attractive as the yacht is, there are of course other magnificent sailing ships available for charter in the Caribbean. Some of these, surely, although the captain does not like to think so, possess an equal purity of design — staterooms of matched Circassian walnut painstakingly crafted by Scotch carpenters, perhaps even a spanking new aluminum mast. But in one respect Captain Boudreau need brook no rival. Of all the yachts in the Caribbean, none is as compellingly evocative of history as *Janeen;* Captain Boudreau's charter boat is the last Crowninshield ship afloat.

Once scores of Crowninshield vessels were sent to roam the world by a family who for nearly three hundred years lent an extraordinary and varied presence to American life. For much of this time they went upon one sea or another for a livelihood, to gain great riches, to make war, for reasons not easily explained in a few words, and — in the end — for pleasure alone. Like their ships, the Crowninshields are gone now. An exhausted male line is survived only by collaterals in whom the blood is so diffused as to be irrelevant — a few middle names to be found around Boston, New York and Washington, and, inevitably, a fraud or two.

4

They have never bothered to compile a formal history of the sort endlessly pleasing to old New England families, in which some Samuel amid his stony acres and infrequent gills of rum begets Becky, another Samuel, little Sarah (she had that trouble with her ears), Ebenezer, and Oliver, and then constructs for himself a cane of hickory, and dies admired by all. Mercifully this kind of thing has been left to generations of antique Crowninshield females whose tireless pinnings-together of pinnings-together of amiable and mindless jottings are forever redeemed by never finding their way into print. Yet their story is as deserving of being told as any other.

Captain Boudreau, good sailor by day and now in the short, soft twilight a personable host, moves easily among his guests with stories of his own. Alongside in the sea a small saffron plastic bottle gleams and bobs as merrily as a toy. Beyond, in silence and desiccation, lies the island of St. Kitts. Too long leached by the sugar cane, too long echoing to the melancholy wail of the conch shell summoning slave to toil, too long in the very trade winds, St. Kitts's sere and useless grasses seem to plead for final abandonment, to be allowed to brood always, whisper alone forever. Over cocktail glasses in which ice shifts and is shifted, muted pleasantries shift and are shifted. Far out at sea a great fish leaps. Long seconds later the slap of his return is heard. At any moment now Captain Boudreau may sit beside you and talk of the day's sail, maybe tell you more of the trouble he has had with his mast.

And with masts perhaps any Crowninshield story ought to start. For long ago the Crowninshields too had difficulty with masts. In that difficulty was the beginning.

ONE

The King's Broad Arrow and a Chinaman's Map

George Crowninshield (1734–1815)

In a small museum a few miles north of Boston lies a map of North America compiled some hundred and seventy-five years ago by a nameless cartographer. The continent is depicted with care on fragile parchment: a truly huge Mississippi precisely bisects the land mass, and although the maker has reduced the Great Lakes in number, their importance has been assured by his drawing them much larger and of the same shape. At first glance the work might almost be taken for the classroom exercise of a child to be crayoned, displayed and compared with those of his fellows, and forgotten — all within the hour. But the careful inking, the imperative symmetry of east and west coastlines, suggest that this cartographer was moved less by a model than by something inestimably more important to him: a view of life which no American child will ever have. Apart from this, certainly no child, when he came to label his map, would deny existence to New York, omit Canada entirely, and instead, in sweeping letters from the Mississippi to the Atlantic print the word SALEM, leaving all else the haunt of barbarians too unimportant even to name. The map is the work of an Asian, probably a Chinese, around 1800 and it was intended as a serious and indispensable guide to Orientals wishing to be better informed about the United States.

How came this earnest and long-dead man of the Middle Kingdom to so extraordinary an understanding? The answer is that he was impelled to it by a handful of Americans, some named Crowninshield.

The name itself has an odd ring, putting one somehow in mind of a not particularly large, yet fairly prosperous, brewery located some-

9

where in the Midwest — possibly in St. Louis. Yes, that must be it. One does not hear much about it because its product is sold regionally and is not nationally advertised. Or maybe it was a family firm with a so-so dividend record assimilated by a competitor and now forgotten.

Such speculation would have appalled the slight, dark, and very serious immigrant who stepped ashore in the New World at Boston late in 1684. He was, as he carefully informed the English custom-house authorities, none other than Johannes Kaspar Richter von Kronenscheldt, scion of a long since ennobled Saxon family. And, he added equably — in passable English sprinkled with Latin — he was a doctor and a surgeon, as certain documents he carried would surely attest. His English, always courteous, had been learned in the course of his travels in England and Ireland, where the impressive medical education so graciously now at the disposal of His Majesty's subjects in Massachusetts had been greatly improved.

To these stark disclosures Dr. Kronenscheldt added nothing, thereby inspiring three centuries of conjecture which have added little more. So careful a reticence gave rise to considerable speculation, most of it unfavorable to the little German nobleman. Said variously to have left Saxony on account of gambling debts, to have killed a man in a duel, and to have been expelled from both England and Ireland for dark, nameless doings, the Doctor made no attempt to deny such rumors. Instead he was content to let them grow and swirl about him, and there were times when it seemed he even cultivated them.

Why did the Doctor never silence his detractors? Whatever stories were told about him, none imperiled — but rather all enhanced — his aristocratic origins. Here, perhaps, lies the key. Is it possible that the truth, had it been told, was even less acceptable than slander? What is certainly known is that curiosity among his descendants reached a fever pitch around the turn of this century, when some of the best genealogists in Europe were employed at great expense to burrow among the tombstones and fusty tithing books without finding the faintest indication that any Kronenscheldt family had ever existed. In reporting their failure to the blue-blooded Boston ladies who employed

10

them, and whom they did not entirely understand, some of them were at pains to point out that the "scheldt" ending was in all probability once "schild" and that surely something of interest would be learned about the founding father if only further research (suitably financed, of course) were restricted to certain Jewish families. No suitable funding was forthcoming, and since then the first Crowninshield has been allowed the repose of oblivion.

But no one can blame the Doctor, if such he was, for ennobling himself, however carelessly, en route to the New World. Consider the intensely homogeneous religious character of New England at the time of his arrival and long after. Some notion of this is gained when one understands that a century or so later the presence of half a dozen Catholics in a Massachusetts township could cause grave unease and suspicion. If Catholics could scarcely be conceded to be Christians, what indeed were the prospects of an ambitious German Jew and one who wanted to practice medicine in 1684?

Whatever the Doctor's antecedents, the Crowninshields did not have the ordinary origins of New England families. It is happily so. Dr. Kronenscheldt's descendants have always been atypical of New England; none was ever very religious, much less troubled by any Puritan conflict between piety and the desire to get ahead in the world. Except among the women, and then not always, they have cared little for the social conventions of their times. Closely knit they were not; each went his or her way without thinking very much about what the others may have thought. To picture any gathering of Crowninshield generations agreeably exchanging familial amenities under one roof at Christmastime is absurd. None was ever very self-conscious; not a few were, in money matters, ostentatious in a manner quite inconsistent with that of New England peers.

Many Crowninshields have had the delightful trait of not taking themselves or anyone else too seriously. All have profoundly distrusted government in any form, especially that with which they were most intimately connected. Some Crowninshields, one feels, would have preferred no government at all, whether of English kings or American presidents. A few wished no restraints of any kind.

11

Of Dr. Kronenscheldt's appearance nothing much is remembered. He was short for the time, probably something less than five feet. His ministrations in Boston, which then had a population of about seven thousand, were instantly characterized by what was by any standards an extraordinary litigiousness. These squabbles, prosecuted and defended with equal adroitness, uniformly involved the debtor-creditor relationship, clearly one to which he was no stranger.

In 1690 the Doctor wandered north of Boston to the village of Lynn and its still-wild countryside. Wolves were everywhere; the catamount's unearthly cry filled dark forests of oak and pine; and wild pigeons wheeled for hours overhead in whose millions there was neither beginning nor ending, length nor breadth, and when they alighted in the trees, their weight broke off large limbs whose crashing fall was heard at a great distance. The hard, acidulous soil and its bog iron were grubbed by consumptive Puritans, whose funerals — watched sullenly by derelict Indians — were so drunken they came to be forbidden on the Sabbath. Endless feasts and prayers were offered for deliverance from the birds, insects, and cankerworms that devastated the thin yield of field and orchard. When ritual failed, the inhabitants had recourse to measures more worldly. They voted "that every householder . . . should, some time before the fifteenth day of May next, kill or cause to be killed twelve blackbirds, and bring the heads of them, at or before the time aforesaid, to Ebenezer Stocker's . . . and if any householder shall refuse or neglect to kill and bring in the heads of twelve blackbirds as aforesaid, every such person shall pay three pence for every blackbird that is wanting."

More worldly yet were specially appointed townsmen who roamed what passed for streets, warning off strangers whether rich or poor, lest they tarry and become objects of charity. The little German was not warned off. In an age of appalling home remedies, physicians, who treated man and animal alike, were scarce. In no time, the Doctor, his saddlebags full of electuaries of sow bugs ground with vinegar, perhaps a "Somniferous Bolus" or two, and probably crowned with an eelskin peruke, became known as a sound man. Although admittedly not

12

the equal of the boastful "doctker prescott," who with a single stroke of his "lancit" easily relieved a patient of "several gallons of Corruption," he was almost certainly above such practitioners as Thomas Andrews, who thrust a large burning pipe of tobacco into the anus of a sick mare, whereupon "thar arose a blaze . . . which seem . . . to cover the butocks of the said mear. The blaze went up towards the roof of the barn and in the roof of the barn there was a grate crackling . . . and said mear fell downe dade."

But whether Dr. Kronenscheldt (or for that matter the great "doctker prescott") could have much improved on Thomas Andrews's treatment may be doubted, for the mare had been stricken by a plague worse than that of any blackbirds. It was 1692, a time chosen by the Prince of Darkness, who had three hundred witches at his command and the prospect of recruiting more, to unloose himself on the countryside. Cows ran amuck and drowned themselves in ponds; blue boar darted electrifyingly among the legs of oxen. Soon men themselves were bewitched. Giles Corey was seen walking about with a pair of turtles clinging to his coat; whereupon he "open his bosom . . . and gave them suck." Obviously, and "contrary to the peace of Reginae Gulielmi & Mariae Angliae," Corey had been nourishing agents of the Devil. But, as the Doctor reminded himself, other cases were subtler. The slightest wart or excrescence could be a "Witches tit," and he, like his colleagues, must allay or confirm suspicion by a critical test. After blindfolding the patient, he probed the growth with a needle. If there was no sign of pain, the diagnosis was clearly bewitchment and the patient's urine was boiled, preferably with nails, as a countercharm. Yet the Doctor never acquired the sinister reputation of his contemporary, one Grigges, who regularly diagnosed the most humdrum of ailments as yet another case of witchcraft, sometimes with horrifying results.

Even Dr. Kronenscheldt's good friend, the large-nosed, terrible Puritan Divine and demonologist, the Reverend Cotton Mather, although he had discovered that caressing the naked stomachs of young girls was apt to confound the "Prince of Lies," had sometimes to confess himself unequal to so formidable an adversary. The more worldly

13

remedy of course lay elsewhere: a few pressings to death — Giles Corey was so dispatched — some selected hangings; and within months the affair passed as had the blackbirds.

Dr. Kronenscheldt's practice appears to have prospered and in 1694 he was called to the sickbed of one Elizabeth Allen, who lay dangerously ill, probably of some scorbutic or pulmonary affliction. A cure was effected, whereupon the Doctor, who was then about fifty years of age, married his much younger patient.

A few years later, to accommodate the children born yearly of Elizabeth, the Doctor managed to acquire some twenty acres "neer a certain pond called the Spring Pond" from his mother-in-law, for which he agreed to furnish among other things "sufficient cordwood at her door, convenient for one chimney, winter and summer."

But some of his trees, usually the tallest and straightest pines, would never go to satisfy his legal obligation toward his mother-in-law. These had cut into them at about the height of a man's head three deep slashes resembling a barbed arrow, the hatchetings of men who roamed the forests of the east coast of North America, usually with an armed guard or two, at the bidding of timber-starved English kings. The pine of America was needed to hold aloft the swelling canvases of His Majesty's men-of-war. As early as 1668, the diarist Samuel Pepys noted among his tumbled, bureaucratic agitations his anxiety that the masts of royal vessels had to be constructed in pieces rather than of a single log. It was, he complained, "a business I understand not." Masts of Massachusetts pine, the Lords of the Admiralty were not amiss in concluding, would last three times as long as those of Norway pine and, happily, would not have to be paid for. Moreover, if His Majesty were to seize the heavier timber of his American subjects, their dependence was further assured: they could build no large ships of their own. So considered an arrangement was to last more than a century and a half, and trees thus marked were said to carry the "King's Broad Arrow." It mattered nothing on whose land they grew; men who dared touch them did so at their peril.

But this was of no consequence to Dr. Kronenscheldt, who had wood aplenty for his mother-in-law, summer and winter, and for English kings too. Besides, he was now a kind of country gentleman; he liked

14

to plant apple trees and to sit by Spring Pond on summer evenings, when its surface was illumined by millions of fireflies. And he loved to entertain. The place had a sulphur spring to which his friend Cotton Mather, although he thought Kronenscheldt maybe a "little Atheistical," came frequently to bask in the ambience he was so fond of creating for others, unmindful that such preachments in all probability condemned his affable little host to sulphur and flame forever.

Johannes Kaspar Richter von Kronenscheldt fell ill and died in 1711, leaving behind him Elizabeth and five children. His testament, on the finest paper, impressively sealed and holographically laden with the legalisms he so loved in life, gave "Imprimus" his soul to God, his estate to Elizabeth for her lifetime, then to those of his children unable to "shift for themselves." God alone — perhaps — benefited; the Doctor died broke.

Within four months Elizabeth remarried and departed New England (probably for the South) never to be heard of again, leaving some of her children behind. One of these very quickly learned to shift for himself. About fifteen at the time of his father's death, the boy, John, seems to have been almost immediately apprenticed to a Salem ropemaker whose hemp he found uncongenial, and shortly became a sailor in the coastal schooners fishing for cod.

As was true of his parents, no likeness or physical description of John has survived, and it is unlikely that any ever existed. The few portraits of the period are those of the great, among whom he was not, and in early eighteenth century America, physical characteristics, unless striking or of extreme deformity or disability, were not much thought on. He was called, and indifferently signed himself (he was scarcely literate), Grouncell, Groungsell, sometimes Cronchel. Gone were the titular pretensions of his father, which later generations were to revive with such unexpected results. John was probably called a great many other things as well, for his manners were fit only for the sea, and in this tough, irreverent young sailor it is very hard to see the child who had sat at the ecclesiastical feet of the Reverend Cotton Mather only a few years before in his father's house in Lynn.

Good-humored, hard-drinking and not without guile, John Groun-

cell was a solitary sort who preferred to fish for the cod alone, sometimes far out at sea, sometimes even to the Georges Bank with its
howling gales. Although time has shrouded much of his life, there
are glimpses of him spreading his catch — "Poor Jack" destined
for West Indian slaves — along the rocky beaches of Marblehead and
Salem to dry in the sun amid clouds of insects and the plover's slurred
whistle.

He was the first Crowninshield to turn to the sea, the first to own a
vessel — and the first of many to marry money. In 1722 he sued for
the hand of Anstiss Williams, who was in no way repelled by her
manly young suitor's crudity in which her father may have seen certain qualities suited for the quarterdeck if not for the parlor. In 1727
in Salem, John built a frame house with a great central fireplace; the
structure (in which their ten children were born) still stands.

Grouncell prospered. He became a merchant and "Shipp'd by the
Grace of God, in good Order and well Condition'd" upon schooners
"by God's Grace bound for the Leeward Islands" many a barrel of
"Mackrell." But although the world was opening up, that is as far
as he went. The brigs, ketches and sloops of his New England were
small vessels of from forty to ninety tons and prey to pirates, to coasts
unbuoyed and unlighted, to every peril named and unnamed. But
what really inhibited him and others like him was an English colonial
policy that shut New England off from its natural markets. In London,
it was out of the question for one English enterprise to compete with
another, and on the Thames lay the most powerful fleet in the world.
Yankees like Grouncell were simply not invited to share in the prosperity of London shipowners; the proper stance of colonials lay in their
ready recognition of their inferiority.

But what could one do if English kings, not content with marking
trees, enforced the will of the English mercantile class on their American subjects? John did what he could and died in 1761 at the age of
fifty-eight, a first-rate smuggler and, some thought, a pirate of no
little distinction. His estate, worth a very respectable fifteen hundred
pounds, included a "Case Wt. Drawers," "8 framed Picktures carved,"
"a blew Bed Quilt," another of "Callico," a few pieces of inelegant

silver, and "a Negro Man" who was valued at thirty-six pounds, thirteen shillings, fourpence. Beyond inventory and any probate was the settled hatred of England and all things English that Grouncell bequeathed to his heirs.

Of John's sons, the most able and ambitious was George, born in 1734, to whom today's prolonged adolescence was unknown. Before his death in 1815, eighty-one years later, he had witnessed with some amusement the wrangling of the proposers of a United States naval academy about the age of those to be admitted — they finally decided that candidates must be "full eleven years of age." At George's eleventh birthday he had been at sea for three years; in those days men were considered as competent at twenty as they ever would be, and at forty they were lucky if they were still alive. In Salem museums, among the beautiful copperplate writings of children, one finds none by George Crowninshield, for his was another school.

Sometime after his father's death, George "Grouncell" became Crowninshield and the name has so remained. We do not know what George looked like except that he was not thought a handsome man. A harsh disciplinarian at sea, all his life he found it difficult to omit profanity from his simplest sentence. Early he excelled in evading the British Navigation Acts by false registrations and in the West Indies made his little sloops English, French, Spanish or Dutch as the case required. Nonetheless, his vessels were from time to time seized and then condemned by British admiralty courts, which were frequently so corrupt that their unsalaried judges would condemn a colonial vessel merely to ensure that they be paid a percentage of its value. By the time he was thirty, George had been more than once found guilty of "rioting against the King's Peace," a habit he was to cultivate all his life.

In 1757, at twenty-three, George married Mary Derby, the sister of Elias Hasket Derby, a Salem merchant. Mary was quiet, even-tempered and full of charm, all qualities conspicuously lacking in her husband. At about the same time George's sister, the very beautiful Elizabeth, married Elias Hasket Derby, who came to be called "King"

Elias Hasket Derby. From a miniature portrait. Artist unknown. Courtesy of the Essex Institute, Salem

Elizabeth Crowninshield Derby. From a miniature portrait. Artist unknown. Courtesy of the Essex Institute, Salem

Derby. Visitors to his splendid farm in Danvers with its spacious greenhouses of lemons, strawberries and geraniums were certain to be led to a bark hut sheltering a wooden hermit clothed in brown serge. At the manikin's feet lay a crust of bread and a jug of water, and it held an open book in which was written in large letters, "Give me neither poverty or riches."

Its owner had himself preferred great riches. Tall, stately, of uncommon presence, "King" Derby had the manners and viewpoint of the old English gentry. Like his father, he was a successful merchant before the Revolution. During it he became the most successful of American privateers at a time when George Crowninshield could scarcely afford such ventures. By war's end, his fortune had many times doubled and his eyes, one blue and one black, gazed beyond the old colonial trade routes to the unrestricted seas.

Hurriedly the Derby vessels were converted from privateers and put to sea in a frantic search for new trade goods, new markets. Derby's *Light Horse* was the first American ship to go directly to Russia. (The sugar it carried did not sell well and to Russia no Derby ship ever returned again.) The "King" demanded profits of not less than one hundred percent on his ventures and he usually got them. In 1785, his former privateer *Grand Turk* was outfitted for the Indian Ocean, long the exclusive bailiwick of England's Honorable East India Company. The voyage was enormously profitable, and was the first of Derby's countless East Indian ventures.

Derby's ship captains found him a tyrant: he was acutely cost-conscious and insisted that they engage, in the course of a voyage, in enough trading, on the side as it were, to pay for all costs without regard to the profits in Salem, which were at times upward of seven hundred percent. The "King" questioned a ten-dollar expense and one of a hundred thousand with equal outrage. Everyone in Salem took note of his "Sir Roger de Coverly coat and small-clothes," his ample vest, his diamond buckles, the "Washingtonian gait" and the imperious wave of his gold-headed cane. He was America's first millionaire.

Those who thought the Derby-Crowninshield marriages portended a powerful alliance of old money and new ambition were wrong. Elizabeth set about spending her husband's money as ostentatiously as possible and she was to insist that he build a costly and imposing mansion in which he had not the slightest interest. In those days one died at home and Elizabeth had a horror of being carried downstairs dead with either her head higher than her feet, or her feet higher than her head. She was also a virago. The "King" thought it best to placate her, and so it came about that the black-marble stairs of her new house were seven feet in width.

But Elias Hasket Derby had been less accommodating toward his brother-in-law, whom he regarded as a fortune hunter. George, he made it clear, would be allowed to serve in Derby ships, perhaps captain them, and that would be quite enough. And George had done so, as would, in time, his sons. From the beginning he regarded the "King" with the most implacable of human hatreds, envy, and the object of that hatred was yet to fully realize that George Crowninshield was like the badger of proverb: he never bit but what he made his teeth meet.

The children of George and Mary surviving infancy were Sarah, George Jr., Jacob, John, Mary, Benjamin, Richard, and Edward (who was born in 1775). Their early years are almost entirely a blank. We know they skated on the frozen ponds of Salem with "Holland" skates and that the boys preferred to "potter," a game that involved running upon broken ice without falling into the water. "Graydoes" (marbles) and kites were popular among them. None of George's sons inherited his stamina; they were all slight and uncommonly sickly. Yet far more congenial to them than "pottering" was a scrap, be it a fistfight, a rock fight or any other kind of set-to. Failing a suitable enemy, they fought one another. Their education was nearly as limited as that of their father. As far as George was concerned it was enough for his sons to learn navigation and go to sea, the sooner the better. They were required as well to write patriotic ditties. One has survived, inspired by a Baptist hymn:

> *Jacob Crowninshield is My Name*
> *New England is My Station*
> *Salem is My Dwelling Place*

21

Christ is My Salvation
When I am Dead in My Grave
And all My Bones are Rotten
This you sea to Remember Me
That I might Not be Forgotten

Jacob, who wrote this pious poem at the age of fourteen, was very slight, with a long droopy nose; he was considered the most alert of the boys. Cross-eyed Richard had the worst temper. John, blue-eyed, blond and the handsomest, tended to dream. Benjamin was the most dutiful, the most equanimous and the least audacious. Edward, the youngest, tended, to his father's disgust, to be introverted and timorous. The eldest, George, seemed oddly childlike far past adolescence. All that is known of the two young daughters is that Sarah had some problem at school. The difficulty has never been explained; only that she was withdrawn from the school, her father enjoining the schoolmaster to silence.

Years later a guest recalled a breakfast at the Crowninshield house: "Irritated at the different wants as regarded food and particularly in the beverages [George], one day on finding that hardly any two of his eight children wanted the same thing to drink, after asking what each wanted, ordered the servant to bring a large bowl. Then reiterating his question, 'George, what do you want?' 'Tea, sir.' He poured some tea into the bowl. 'Jacob, what do you want?' 'Milk, sir.' And in turn, coffee, water, chocolate, etc., all were poured in. He then took a spoon stirred it up pushed it into the middle of the table, and said, 'Now children help yourselves.' "

All readily acquiesced to the stony will of their father, and to the day he died they obeyed him explicitly. They always addressed him as "Sir" and referred to him by that title long after his death. For Edward, compliance with paternal wishes ended badly. Following his older brothers to sea in 1793, when he was eighteen, he was brutalized by the ship's captain in whose charge George had placed him. At Guadeloupe, Edward could bear no more and killed himself. Nothing much was ever said of the affair; the boy was simply a loss at sea.

By 1790 George had acquired, by a diligence which had not failed to exploit his Derby connections, two or three large ships of his own; no more would he be "Derby's boy." If his brother-in-law could become rich beyond the Cape of Good Hope, so could George Crowninshield. And he did.

The west coast of Sumatra is one of the most beautiful in the world. Today, the long green swells of the Indian Ocean beat upon white sands unbroken by alien cairns that lie just beneath the surge. Polyp-encrusted, the habitat of brilliant fishes that dart to and fro, these piles of stone are the speckled granite of Cape Ann, Massachusetts — the ballast of Crowninshield ships — and the foundation of an American fortune.

Sumatra, once part of a great Indonesian state of Islamic origins, had long since been shattered by the impact of Europeans seeking its principal source of wealth and sorrow — pepper. After the British and the Dutch came the Crowninshields.

The pepper trade was no easy business, involving as it did a voyage of fourteen thousand miles at an average speed not much greater than a well-conditioned man can walk in an hour's time. Once there, the traders found the beautiful pepper coast harborless, a long and sullen surf washing shores riddled with dysentery, malaria, cholera, and pirates of every ingenuity. Little wonder that in Salem it was sung:

> *For the coast of Sumatra, now I'm bound*
> *Pepper to get if there's any to be found.*
> *From thence for Europe if the Lord spares my life,*
> *And back again to Beverly to get a pretty wife.*

Should some sailor be already married, his wife's lot could be as difficult as that of a young woman who wrote:

DEAR HUSBAND   I set down to inform you that the first day of this month you had A Son. i cant say a grate Boy but there is room a nuf to grow and if you want to now who he looks like you must Look in the glass. I am very Week indeed and have been this four months but hope with the blessing of god i shall soon gett my health And Streght. I have moved out of Mr. Safford house into Mr. Preston for i was disconted. I want able to pay him but a very littel and he has treated me in a Shameful [m]aner. I am not Able to write more. all the folks Desires to be rembered to you. it apears to me if you every Live to get home I shall bee to happy But i am afraed that your Boy will say father first. Write every oppertunity And make yourself Easy on my account.

Yours til Death

Elizabeth Nichols

Fearful of the American competition on the pepper coast, the British did all they could to suppress it. Each ship captain employed every wile to persuade the Malays to deliver pepper to him alone, thereby generating enmity and every kind of deceit. At times American vessels came very close to loosing their cannon on one another. Sumatran officials (local rajahs who despised each other) were as corrupt as any in the world. There was much cheating, and however carefully guarded, the scales used for weighing the pepper were apt to be loaded with lead or mercury. Almost always the natives attempted, in one way or another, to adulterate the sale, usually with sand.

Among other endemic problems was the Malays' refusal to accept anything other than cash; they insisted on Carolus or Ferdinandus "pillared" Spanish reals, difficult for New Englanders to obtain, especially if one needed twenty thousand to fifty thousand of them. Too frequently the natives would accept these from one party, sell to another, and vanish. It was all business as usual in Sumatra, and once home, all one might find for one's pains was a glutted market and a pressing need to repay the "pillared" dollars one had had to borrow in the first place.

But for all this the Crowninshield successes were spectacular, almost miraculously unattended by losses of the sort every shipowner expected. In 1801, two Crowninshield ships alone brought home over a million pounds of pepper. In these early days of the trade the duties payable in Salem were roughly equivalent to the value of the ship and the specie sent out with her. Some idea of the enormous profit is gained when it is understood that the cargo usually sold for five times the amount of the duties.

Among the first Americans on the pepper coast was John, George's third (and only literary) son, who, aboard *America III*, wrote: "July 2, 1801. . . . There was perhaps 4 or 500 natives on the beach, some drawing a net, others in small parties &c. all with there creases [krises] & some with long broad swords & the whole of them laughing at us. We proceeded up to the Rajahs . . . where I had to wait some time before could see him they told me he was ingaged on business from home when he came he carried me up in a little cock loft (in a square incloser of trees several guns & swivels mounted all round without any kind of regularity) it appeared as if he wished to be in secret as only two of the natives were admitted he could not speak nor understand a word of English — one of his men could make out with a few signs &c. He asked 11$ per pickall 133⅓ lb. for pepper. I find that here is plenty of it. I told him I did not like the place to load as we could not fill our ship in two months & in such a wild readstead the risk is too great & that I must go further down the Coast & look for a better harbour. He then offered me pepper at 8$."

But the harbor was too dangerous. John sailed further down the coast to Maca, where there was plenty of pepper, and a bargain was struck. To solemnize the agreement, he filled a handkerchief with pepper and eight dollars as "a prooff of the bargain untill all is finished." By way of an even more solemn contractual precaution the principal Malays were conducted on board *America III* and shown the lighted matchsticks lying near the sixteen cannon, which would be trained on the beach night and day for the duration of the agreement. Yet another form of insurance lay in John's conclusion that although some natives wore "poisoned creases elegantly set off with gold and silver . . . they are from so many defferent towns & so many defferent interests to consult I have my doubts if they could form a union strong enough to cut us off."

Now *America III* was loaded at a frantic pace with pepper packed in sail bags, and at times there were more than a thousand natives scurrying about the beach. On July 15, John was given a "present of a Buffalow . . . and [we] were 3 hours last night killing the Buffalow they bruised his head all to pieces & could not hurt him & finally was obliged to heave him down & cut his throat."

In a moment of leisure John noted another execution, that of a confessed pepper thief by drowning. John had suggested a whipping instead. The *lemonagee* or chief prosecutor had a very different view of the matter: "Suppose his father come — mother sisters brothers & all come beg pray & will give one thousand dollars no can catch him what for let thief live suppose let go he will make steel again & nothing more bad more better for drown him God give him let God take him back again." So it was. The man was forthwith lashed to a board, which was overturned in the river, and two men sat on it for an hour.

Although Crowninshield still kept his cannon trained on the Malays, he came to admire them. Were they really so cruel and warlike? He liked their hospitality. What if they were infidels? One day a native refused payment for some "sugar cain" he gave to the ship's doctor. Was this the behavior of people supposed to be worse than the pirates of Algeria?

America III was now nearly loaded and the natives chose the moment to enlist the Americans against a local enemy, the "Acheens." But Crowninshield parried: "I should make them my enemies as allso create a disterbance between themselves — & that tomorrow it might be the reverse with me & I might inadvertantly offend them both without doing myself any real service & making it disagreeable for any others who should come after me & leave them enemies amongst themselves."

By now every crevice of the ship was jammed. Pepper was everywhere, even on the gundeck. In some parts of the vessel there was only room for a man to crawl on all fours.

It was time to sail. "God bless tham what money they have had from us will be the means of much gambling (& perhaps war) fighting cocks for dear life — I returned them the handkerchief of pepper which we had for a muster . . . all is finished contract fulfilled we are square as they say."

In John's diary may be seen the reasons why within two years the Crowninshields could coolly refer to the island of Sumatra as "our pepper gardens"; they had acquired a virtual monopoly of the trade. Never did they treat the natives, who were long used to European arrogance, on any other than a basis of perfect equality. Nor did any

Crowninshield ever for a moment interfere in their local affairs, much less fuel their incessant wars. And just as important, the Crowninshields paid cash and kept clear of Sumatran women. An atmosphere of perfect trust evolved and it is said that the Malays, who had a well-deserved reputation for bloodiness, wept whenever a Crowninshield vessel, usually the first to be loaded and never molested, took its leave.

It was much the same in India.

Pepper made George decide that his sons had been long enough at sea. One by one they were recalled and a partnership, George Crowninshield & Sons, was formed. He had better things for them to do than captain merchant vessels in the Indian Ocean. Represented in France by John, in New York by Richard, and in Salem by George Jr., Benjamin and Jacob, business rapidly expanded; more and more ships were acquired.

The next few years were years of unparalleled success in trading, and for a time the firm was spared the terrible losses merchants usually suffered in the course of business. Salem was thriving as never before. After pepper had come coffee, and something of the local jubilation comes through in a letter Benjamin wrote to his brother John in Bordeaux: "Coffee, coffee is the stuff. . . . Salem rolls in riches with every tide, & every ship plank is bound to India."

That we know so much about the Crowninshields and the Salem of this period is largely due to the remarkable Reverend William Bentley. Graduated from Harvard in 1773, Bentley gravitated to Salem six years later, where the first words said to him were "Beware of George Crowninshield." The last words Bentley, who was the master of twenty languages, spoke thirty-six years later were a bit of gossip for the ear of a Crowninshield, in the course of which he dropped dead. But in the interval, his truly omnivorous interest in everything that went on around him is reflected in his diaries. Here nothing is omitted: whether death and disaster, a strange fish cast ashore on Marblehead Neck, his quarrels with his predecessor, his salary arrears, some curious coin from China, his struggles with his father, who dunned him endlessly for money, or the "Humming Bird . . . caught by flying into a House"

The Reverend William Bentley. Copy made in 1828 by Charles Osgood after the original portrait by James Frothingham, 1818–1819. Courtesy of the Essex Institute, Salem

(while it was "thus confined, the other humming birds came and sat on a line opposite making notes of complaint, to which it answered"). At times the tiny scrawl became tinier — he liked to save paper — and sometimes, to exercise himself linguistically — and lest his diary be discovered — the indiscretions of Salem are recorded in Latin and French.

"Beware George Crowninshield" — that had been the warning. But Bentley had been heedless. No sooner had he taken up his ministry than he approached George for a charitable contribution. To understand what then occurred, one must know something of a certain Benjamin Thompson, later Count Rumford, whom George had known when Thompson had been an apprentice ironmonger in Salem. At the time of the Revolution, Thompson, a Tory, left the country. In Europe, as a newly minted aristocrat, he invented a variety of stoves for which he became famous; one of these must be called the first "soup kitchen." The Count, with his Toryism, his clever stoves — the notion of ingenuity and pretended nobility dedicated to the feeding of paupers — was the subject of the most sardonic glee to Crowninshield all his life.

In Bentley's words, "we called upon [Crowninshield] & it was the first & only refusal we had. . . . After telling us that he instructed Count R[umford] in making chimnies, that he had set on foot a charity for the poor of the Town of 2000 D. & several other rousers, he declined tho' he had before given every encouragement." The Reverend Bentley came away from his first encounter with George Crowninshield, his leg pulled and not a dime to show for it. In the future he was to conclude that his parishioner, Crowninshield, was of "habitual indiscretion," whose conduct was "the most impudent to be imagined." But mostly the Parson contented himself with characterizing Crowninshield as "a son of nature" with "powers employed only in seafaring concerns."

No prude and no ascetic but a sturdy trencherman five feet high and almost as wide, he battled all his life — without zeal and without success — against obesity. He relished a pint of ale or two at "Mother Morse's" and regretted, without sorrow, that he came to find the taking

29

of wine with meals indispensable. Bentley was the sort of man who could with perfect equanimity write of a stingy deceased parishioner that "her mother and surviving sisters have been blessed in her life and in her death." Once, irritated by the Reverend Joshua Spaulding, Bentley wrote:

> *A Fool throughout in every motion*
> *Heaven, once on earth has wrought perfection.*

Bentley played politics and got his fingers burned; and although busy giving the back of his Unitarian hand to Quakers, Shakers, Hopkinsians, Roman Catholics, Baptists, all those for whatever reason predestined, and the deplorable "New Lights," not to mention certain Unitarians with whom he disagreed, he still had a moment or two for a purely temporal concern. It would "have one false & moveable bottom of a wood least apt to warp, & entering on the side opposite to the trough, on account of the dovetailed bottom . . . this false bottom, shall be covered on all sides by a Groove cut into the sides, which shall be of greater thickness on that account. The false bottom shall not rest on the true bottom, but shall play into the groove made for it. The trough shall enter on one side, & the frame in which the trough commonly is placed, shall be removed at pleasure on the other, being formed like a larger trough, & resting upon the true bottom, having a groove upon its open side in the cage to receive the end of the false bottom at the height of the groove made in the inner part of the immovable sides. The top of this frame in which the holes are made for a communication with the trough, shall also slide in & out, at the side in which the frame enters."

The Reverend William Bentley had designed for himself a birdcage.

About him there was something of balance, of measured humanity, as is exemplified in his account of the death of Caesar, a poor, blind black, in the Salem Charity House on December 29, 1804: "The last fear of this poor creature was that he should not get well soon enough for new years day. He had a surprising memory by which he got a decent support while his health lasted & which he retained with-

30

out losing it, so as to bring it to a common size till his death. He employed it soberly upon one subject, the ages of persons, & no example have I ever known for such retention on this favorite subject. Twenty years ago I gave him the age of my parents & kindred of three generations with the promise of a reward upon every notice of their birthday. I have never known that he lost one or confounded it with any other. I shall save my pennies & miss Caesar. Tho' often at my door, he never was troublesome. In the close Liquor easily overpowered him but did not enslave him. He was peaceable & disposed to behave well, he never meant to be intoxicated."

And there was "Old Grandame Whitefoot, above one hundred years old, being christened in 1690, among other children of the same parents, & then not the youngest. She was very small of stature, small face, quick temper, but soon reconciled. Always singing & dancing, not modest in her conversation, & aimed at jocose wit. Her whole habit was thin, & nothing made a deep impression on her mind. She was addicted to smoking which easily intoxicated her, & rendered her troublesome. She went abroad till nearly the time of her death, & she sunk away in insensibility. She was a woman who neglected reading altogether, & for many years public worship, but never professed an aversion, but a carelessness." Here is Bentley at his best. Although one doesn't know everything about Caesar and Grandame Whitefoot, one knows as much about them as will ever be known — and much more about the writer.

On March 29, 1819, Bentley wrote of a Crowninshield wedding: "This day I passed through the most interesting scene of my life. . . . As soon as Hanna . . . was of age for instruction she was put into my care. She has rewarded it with her virtues & accomplishments. This day I delivered her in marriage to an officer of the Navy (Lieut. James Armstrong). He is from Virginia, but to me unknown. What the prospects are I cannot guess. The event is not from my wishes or at my will. The sympathy was beyond description. The hundred I have united never gave such emotions. I know nothing contrary to the hopes of the young man & that is the evil, that even this consolation is not borrowed from the ample means to render it happy, being rather my

ignorance than my observation. The branches of the family were represented on the occasion & after the ceremonies H. retired to her Father's
in Danvers. . . . The questions were Will she go to Virginia? . . . Thus
after nearly 30 years all our hopes are unknown. Why did not so accomplished a girl find a bosom friend in Salem. . . . All the domestic
relations were not such as ambition could desire. I hope H. will be
happy. It will be my happiness. My best wishes attend her." Bentley
had expressed the sentiments of a father.

Bentley could hate as well. In 1803, when Harvard refused to accept a young Crowninshield he had tutored, he was to write, "My
connections with Cambridge cease." At sixty, he did accept an honor-
ary degree from Harvard, but with little pleasure; too long had the
college at Cambridge neglected his merits. Besides, the honor was attended by the ominous words of Dr. Bowditch: "Prepare to die, for
Degrees are usually fore runners as they are given to the Aged when
their course is finished." Bowditch had been right. Within weeks the
once-indefatigable Bentley was complaining of "affections of the head
& breast" and found himself "obliged to employ . . . much caution in
walking," always a favorite pastime. Worse yet, the old gossip had
become deaf.

Christmas of 1819 drew near and Bentley, the gourmand, was
stirred by the abundance of poultry, turkey and the "excellent pork to
be had at 6 cents pr. lb." For another page or so the gossip rambles
on and then stops at last. The inattentions of Harvard College were
remembered in his will, and by it not a single volume of his library,
second only to that of Thomas Jefferson, found its way to the banks of
the Charles River. When he had first come to Salem, there had been
times when he had despaired: "Am I unlike the world, & unfit for it,
that it looks so to me?" The Reverend William Bentley need not have
worried.

As the century closed, in the great two-storied house with its porch-
like gallery enclosed with Chinese latticework and its cupola sur-
mounted by the elaborately carved figure of a merchant in the garb of
the Revolutionary period and dominating Salem Harbor, George

Crowninshield-Bentley House, 120–126 Essex Street, Salem. Photograph taken in 1964. Courtesy of the Essex Institute, Salem

Crowninshield, now over sixty, was less than happy. His discontent was one of the most grievous that afflict men. His struggles with the sea, with the English and the French, his own government and his Yankee competitors, had left him nearly exhausted. Yet these astonishing victories and his wealth had failed to gain his family the measure of social acceptance he desperately wanted and which all the riches of the Indies had not purchased.

The cleavage was evident from his cupola. Codfish aristocracy (led by his brother-in-law) tended to live in the western part of Salem along Chestnut Street, then, as now, one of the most beautiful streets in the world. The Crowninshields had erected no less stately mansions in the eastern section of town, until recently a noisome neighborhood of tanyards and ropewalks. The eastern section was largely beautified by the Crowninshields, who took a special pride in the park: "Our Common looks Beautifully & mortifies the West-end quite exceedingly." Although George might scorn Chestnut Street as "Statequo," it was in the end the "right" part, and the barb of the anonymous poet who had addressed himself to the Crowninshields stung:

> *Ye say, base Plebians, none respect your merit,*
> *So I believe, for where the Devil is it?*
> *In what does it consist, ye Vulgar Race,*
> *Ye Sons of Pride, but in a shameless Face?*

The established mercantile aristocracy of Derbys, Pickmans, Grays, and Ornes — the old rich, the educated and the articulate, into whose hands all power had long since been consolidated — had never included the Crowninshields. George's marriage had done him little good. Then he had been regarded in Derby circles as an upstart and now they looked on him as a parvenu. His newly acquired riches, his wharf, his warehouses, his houses and other properties, his very ambition, had merely galled the ancien régime, confirmed it in its rejection. Codfish aristocracy would never forget that he and his sons had for years been "Derby's boys." To make things worse, sea captains could not be regarded as gentlemen until they had retired from the sea. For his part, George had long felt that his relationship with his in-laws was designed to prolong his inferiority and that of his sons. They had impeded his rise whenever possible, and he had done what he could to defeat them, and he had not.

Nor had the gulf been narrowed by a certain infidelity in Crowninshield's manner. Always acerbic, he had paid little attention to what others thought of him. As to his sons, even a loyal female relative admitted that she knew of "no . . . Crowninshield . . . distinguished for intellect or piety. They were all marked by haughtily knit brows and intense hauteur of Manners." Moreover, the Crowninshields liked to brag and they had a great deal to brag about.

But most of all, Crowninshield popularity had been lacerated by an incident which was to have the most profound effect on the ancien régime and the nouveau riche alike. In the summer of 1798, George and his sons had outraged the Salem oligarchy in an evidently treasonous refusal to contribute one cent toward the construction of the frigate *Essex* then being built for use against the French.

To understand the enormity of their decision, it is necessary to go back a few years. During the War of Independence, the French, by way of discomfiting their ancient enemy at no great expense, deemed it prudent to assist the Americans after the latter's victory at Saratoga. This aid, accepted with the alacrity of the truly desperate, turned on the understanding that the United States would help the French should England and France go to war. Fifteen years later, in 1793, hostilities between the two commenced. France reminded President Washington of his obligation, whereupon Washington deemed it prudent to renege. The neutrality he wanted seemed to require a better relationship with Great Britain. John Jay was dispatched thither to soothe certain antagonisms left over from the Revolution: unpaid bills owing to British merchants, compensation for the American confiscation of Loyalist property, and the troublesome presence of the few redcoats remaining on the western frontier.

When the Jay Treaty was ratified in 1795, Crowninshield eyes fell with horrified disbelief on its thirteenth article. Here, the British had cunningly stipulated, at the instigation of the East India Company, that American cargoes from India would have to be carried directly, without stopping, to American ports. Heretofore, Salem merchants, including George and his sons, had carried manufactured goods to India and sold them for rice and cotton goods. These in turn were traded elsewhere in the Indian Ocean for products — like pepper and coffee — more marketable in the United States and Europe. To the Crowninshields, the Jay Treaty meant they would have to trade in India with cash only. Equally pernicious, they could no longer coast from one Indian port to another trading as flexibly and profitably as they wished. Clearly, the "damned British Treaty" was nothing more than the old English greed. What, they asked, had the American Revolution been all about? Was it possible Yankee ships on the Indian Ocean were still subject to John Bull? The Crowninshield salad days, which they had imagined were only beginning, had ended in the East Indies. It was the King's Broad Arrow all over again.

Angrier yet were the French. To assuage them, President Adams sent envoys to Paris in 1797, where their opposite numbers (creatures of Monsieur Talleyrand, the foreign minister) suggested that George Washington's sin would best be expiated by a large loan to France. By the way, could Adams's emissaries doubt that Monsieur Talleyrand himself had been inconvenienced? However, a quarter of a million American dollars would probably restore the spirits of the French foreign minister. Mais oui? When the bribe was refused, one of the most obscure of American wars broke out.

Now the United States was begging for warships to use against the French in a contest that ill met George's concept of patriotism. When in Salem the hat was passed around to collect money to build the frigate *Essex*, George's eye fell upon his armed ships *America* and *Belisarius*, idling at Crowninshield Wharf with furled sails. With this war they would idle yet longer, a prospect which gnawed at his soul more deeply than did the war. If the United States government wanted some warships, perhaps he could be in the way of furnishing a couple if the price was right. Besides, *America* at 645 tons, which had been picked up in France a few months earlier, drew too much water for Salem Harbor, and he was damned if he would build another wharf

36

for her. As for *Belisarius*, she was one of his finest ships, but unfortunately on her most recent voyage, a question of seaworthiness had arisen. If the government was poor and could not buy them outright, he was willing to lease them for an appropriate figure, transferring the burden of maintenance to the Navy Department for the duration.

In August 1798, George's offer to sell or charter the two ships to the navy was rejected by Secretary of the Navy Benjamin Stoddart. Once more the proposition was renewed in a petulant letter of outraged virtue to President Adams in September. But it was not to be. Thereafter, the Crowninshields refused to give one cent toward the building of the *Essex*. Beggars, allowed George, could not be choosers.

The whole subject of the *Essex*, which he derided as "our frigate," amused him. His special scorn (apart from his feelings about the very conception of the vessel) revolved around financial difficulties, the cumbersome committees that supervised its stagnated construction, and their endless disputes. They were amateurs, blockheads. To George Crowninshield's delight there was even a shotmaker, the loquacious Seymour, who, instead of making shot, wrote enigmatic letters. Such stupidity, such waste, would never attend the construction of a Crowninshield vessel; let "King" Derby spend his money.

Derby did so, and finally the United States frigate *Essex*, ceremoniously launched, sailed from Salem Harbor with *Belisarius* under George's mocking gaze. To his son John, George scribbled: "The Belisarius Sailed Sunday last in Company with our Famous Frigate & with a fare Tryall the BS [Belisarius] Beet her." Old George had arranged the trial but that was all. Once out at sea, the two separated; for the Crowninshields, it was to be business as usual during the French war.

For this defiance of public opinion, for mercantile self-interest, Anglophobia, and general contrariness, the Crowninshields were loudly denounced. But there was more to the affair than met the eye. In truth, the Crowninshields had sensed a strange new tide lapping at the piers and wharves of Salem. And they had never been slow to seize a propitious breeze or turn a current to advantage.

The "great people" of George Crowninshield's New England, the aristocrats who had rejected him, had always been, after the fashion of George Washington and Alexander Hamilton, Federalists, whose aim was to protect the prosperity of the upper classes. As Samuel Eliot Morison wrote: "Sired by Neptune out of Puritanism, the teacher of its youth was Edmund Burke. Washington, Hamilton, and Fisher Ames formed the trinity of its worship. Timothy Pickering was the kept politician of New England Federalism, Harrison Gray Otis its spell-binder, Boston its political and Hartford its intellectual capital, Harvard and Yale the seminaries of its priesthood. New England Federalism believed that the main object of government was to protect property, especially commercial and shipping property; and they supported nationalism or states' rights according as the federal government protected or neglected these interests of maritime New England. It aimed to create and maintain in power a governing class, of educated, well-to-do men."

In Salem, all power had long been gathered into Federalist hands. Federalists owned the banks, the marine insurance companies; controlled the press, the collection of revenues, the militia; and they ran the town meetings with a heavy hand.

To Federalists no one could be more dangerous or more incomprehensible than Thomas Jefferson, with his strange persuasions of the rights of man, his peculiar vision of a democracy of affluent and honest yeomen supported by slaves. The gangling rheumatic figure in his coat of red laced with gold, who blathered of Arcadia in the accents of Virginia and was said to sleep with the more attractive of his female blacks, was anathema to New England mariners who looked only to the sea. More dismaying yet, Jefferson was professedly against the building of any navy to protect their Indiamen. To them, he was all Jacobinism and heresy; they wanted none of him.

But heresy or no, the Crowninshields, like many other American families to come, had soon recognized that parvenus without a political base remain parvenus. For years they had been despised and impeded by a society which was to them inseparable from Federalism. Wholeheartedly they embraced a political philosophy ostensibly at war with

38

their economic interest out of a wish to destroy and supersede the Old Guard, and out of the conviction that once they acquired power they would be sufficiently adroit to protect, perhaps even enhance, their property.

It was the twenty-nine-year-old Jacob who had been selected as the best foot forward. Slim, handsome, the most polished of George's sons, the debonair Jacob seemed to partake more of the charm of his Derby mother than did the others. And although he suffered badly from having no education, he was easily the most gifted son.

As a child Jacob Crowninshield had been sickly, plagued with a weakness of the lungs. This had not however prevented him from being one of the most aggressive of what were called the Wapping boys. Codfish aristocracy then tended to live in a section of the town called St. James, and the lowest level of society inhabited an area known as Knocker's Hole. Between them lay Wapping — Crowninshield turf. Jacob and his brothers' frequent invitations to the young gentlemen of St. James for a fight were almost always declined and so the battles were fought with the young ruffians of Knocker's Hole who were ready enough to oblige.

In 1787, old George, fearing for the seventeen-year-old Jacob's health, sent him to the East Indies. His condition improved, and three years later he assumed command of *Active* on a voyage to Europe. At twenty-one he commanded ships for "King" Derby on voyages to India, and after the last of these, his accounts were challenged by Derby in a vitriolic dispute. Thereafter no Crowninshield ever sailed for Derby again.

Imaginative and with a flair for the unusual, Jacob brought the first elephant to this country in 1796. The elephant was, according to Bentley, "of large Volume, his skin black, as though lately oiled." On exhibition in Salem, the animal repeatedly shook off its keeper, drew the corks from two dozen bottles of porter and drank them, and picked the pockets of the delighted spectators, who were charged a twenty-five-cent admission fee. When novelty and fees abated and fears for its health arose, Jacob sold it for $10,000 to an out-of-towner.

Jacob Crowninshield. Oil port
by Robert Hinkley. Courtesy of
Peabody Museum of Salem

John Crowninshield. Courtesy
the Peabody Museum of Salem

Jacob began the struggle for the social and political domination of Salem in 1799, when he ran for the Massachusetts senate and was soundly beaten by the Old Guard. He had received only forty-seven votes. In 1800 he was trounced again for the same office in April, and in October was beaten in the contest for the United States Congress. But the Crowninshields were learning. They acquired a newspaper (all Crowninshield shipping advertisements were channeled to it) to extol Jacob's virtues, which were those of "Adams Federalists," "Republican Federalists," and "Anti-Federalists." (The word "Jeffersonian" was as yet too hot to handle.) The newspaper, called the *Impartial Register*, carried a column in which the Reverend William Bentley reported the news of the day with the appropriate political bias. Before long, the *Impartial Register* dropped the "Impartial" from its banner, and the Parson went after Crowninshield opponents with a will. In turn, the Salem *Gazette* labeled him "the Wise-Man of the East" and "Jefferson's Toad-Eater," and assured its readers that "the Board of Health, if they do their duty, will take care of such filthy fellows."

By 1801, it was becoming apparent that Thomas Jefferson would be elected President of the United States: the Crowninshields had correctly gauged the new tide. But in an election for state senator in April 1802, Jacob was put down by the establishment once again.

The following November he faced Timothy Pickering, who had been in politics since the Revolution. Pickering was thought to be unbeatable, and alongside him Crowninshield was considered "no more than a twinkling of a fire bug to the blaze of the meridian sun." Besides, was it not notorious that the Crowninshields had tried to cheat the government with *America* and *Belisarius* a few years before? Jacob was a Jacobin (the puns were endless), a "Social leveler" bent on revolution, and he had no education; he was ignorant; he was the only candidate the Anti-Federalists could ever find. Jacob, said Pickering, was like "a piece of old rope, the more you try to splice it, the worse it grows."

But to the readers of the *Register*, Timothy Pickering was an Anglophile in the pay of the British. The Crowninshields, one was as-

41

THE
Elephant,

ACCORDING to the account of the celebrated BUFFON, is the moſt reſpectable Animal in the world. In ſize he ſurpaſſes all other terreſtrial creatures; and by his intelligence, he makes as near an approach to man, as matter can approach ſpirit. A ſufficient proof that there is not too much ſaid of the knowledge of this animal is, that the Proprietor having been abſent for ten weeks, the moment he arrived at the door of his apartment, and ſpoke to the keeper, the animal's knowledge was beyond any doubt confirmed by the cries he uttered forth, till his Friend came within reach of his trunk, with which he careſſed him, to the aſtoniſhment of all thoſe who ſaw him. This moſt curious and ſurpriſing animal is juſt arrived in this town, from Philadelphia, where he will ſtay but a few weeks.——————————He is only four years old, and weighs about 3000 weight, but will not have come to his full growth till he ſhall be between 30 and 40 years old. He meaſures from the end of his trunk to the tip of his tail 15 feet 8 inches, round the body 10 feet 6 inches, round his head 7 feet 2 inches, round his leg. above the knee, 3 feet 3 inches, round his ankle 2 feet 2 inches. He eats 130 weight a day, and drinks all kinds of ſpiritous liquors; ſome days he has drank 30 bottles of porter, drawing the corks with his trunk. He is ſo tame that he travels looſe, and has never attempted to hurt any one. He appeared on the ſtage, at the New Theatre in Philadelphia, to the great ſatisfaction of a reſpectable audience.

A reſpectable and convenient place is fitted up at Mr. VALENTINE's, head of the Market, for the reception of thoſe ladies and gentlemen who may be pleaſed to view the greateſt natural curioſity ever preſented to the curious, and is to be ſeen from ſun-riſe, 'till ſun-down, every Day in the Week, Sundays excepted.

☞ The Elephant having deſtroyed many papers of conſequence, it is recommended to viſitors not to come near him with ſuch papers.

☞ Admittance, ONE QUARTER OF A DOLLAR.——Children, NINE PENCE.

Boſton, Auguſt 18th, 1797.

BOSTON: Printed by D. Bowen, at the COLUMBIAN MUSEUM Preſs, head of the Mall.

Broadside: "The Elephant," 1797. Courtesy of the Peabody Museum of Salem sured, had saved the country from war with the Bey of Algiers and his Barbary pirates in 1800, when Pickering, then Secretary of State, had dishonestly diverted some $78,000 intended as United States tribute. The Bey, a forthright man given to remarking, "You bring me tribute, you are my slaves," had been furious and threatened war. Fortunately, the Crowninshield ship *Brutus* had been in the Mediterranean at the time and had dropped off $40,000 in cash for the Bey, thereby saving the day out of pure patriotism. What was more, Pickering was indifferent to the impressment of American seamen; and in the Revolution, Pickering's regiment of militia had dallied at Lexington. Had it been cowardice or British influence? A reader of the *Register* could take his choice.

On election day, every Crowninshield crony, every employee and dependent, was marched to the polls, be he sailmaker, pumpmaker, cordwainer, shipwright, or wharfinger. The crew of *America*, recently arrived in Salem from the Indies and not a little drunk, were herded en masse to the polls to vote Crowninshield. Men of ninety were borne in on stretchers under the impression that their votes would eject George III and the Tories. Jacob was elected.

The family had played rough to win and they were not to be magnanimous in victory — as the editor of the *Gazette*, one Cushing, discovered. A week after the election two of Jacob's brothers, Richard and Benjamin, paid him a call to say they would shoot him in the dark if they could not in the daytime. Now the *Gazette* could only lament: "It is now proved that 'our family' can do what they please in this town."

The *Gazette* was correct. Power had been wrenched from the old order. With the election, the Crowninshields were quick (with suitable addresses to Jefferson) to exploit the spoils system and many an old score was soon settled.

Old George, although he had propelled "our family" into politics and financed the venture, kept clear of the electioneering. He had no feel for the business and he knew it. In point of fact, he cared nothing for Federalism or Republicanism. Although he hated and feared the

British, he also hated the French, the Dutch, the Irish and the Spanish. As for the United States government, he neither liked nor understood it, nor did he wish to. He did know that he hated his in-laws, the Derbys. Since they were at hand, unlike the British and the French, a battleground to George's taste lay within a short stroll.

Salem Harbor had always been shallow, its narrow channel subject to silting. As trade with the East Indies boomed, the waterfront became more crowded than ever. The merchants pushed their piers further and further out, not only to accommodate their own vessels, but to attract other trading vessels and to forestall rivals. In 1791, "King" Derby, then in the plenitude of his influence, had packed a town meeting, which pushed through a regulation ensuring that his wharf (the longest and the most apt to attract business) would not be troubled with competition. Five years later he sued George Crowninshield, alleging that the length of the latter's wharf was causing the shipping channel to silt up. The "King" won, and George was ordered by the state supreme court to shorten his wharf by twelve feet.

Not long afterwards, George came down to his truncated pier to find that a fence had been built overnight to block access to it. The question of who owned the land abutting Crowninshield Wharf had long been in doubt. A certain Widow Ward had claimed it as hers, while George had argued that it was common land to which he was entitled access. He promptly summoned his workmen and had the fence chopped to pieces. The *Gazette* was exultant: the widow's fence was "a victim to the leveling rage of Jacobinism." It now emerged that the Widow Ward was the niece of Elias Hasket Derby, Jr., who had paid for the construction of the fence. George was brought to court and a Derby-inspired jury indicted him for inciting a riot.

Still stuck with *America*, which the ungrateful United States had refused to accept in 1798, George built a mooring far out in the deepest waters of the harbor to accommodate the ship. At first the structure attracted little notice, but then slowly George began to connect it with the land, and by 1802 India Wharf, as he called it, was the most imposing and most prosperous of all. Again the Derbys sued, this time on the grounds that the new structure had caused the silting of their own facilities and that the Crowninshields did not own the land to which the wharf had been connected. Once more George was ordered to shorten a wharf. Immediately the Derbys sued him again. This time the silting ploy was dropped; Crowninshield, they said, was now obstructing navigation. And so the dispute raged on with extraordinary animosity until 1806, when George was ordered to remove forty feet of India Wharf.

But the Derby triumphs were transitory. Both families had been buying up all the available vacant land in sight for speculative purposes. The Crowninshields were now making a killing in house lots, while much of the Derby land lay across an unbridged river and attracted fewer buyers. Finally, in 1805 the Derbys sought town permission to build a bridge at their own expense in order to exploit their holdings. Sensing that their own land might be cheapened, the Crowninshields managed to defeat the Derby proposal at the first town meeting. But they gilded the lily. Where the bridge had been planned, they caused a building (perhaps in emulation of the Widow Ward's fence) to be hurriedly thrown up to block access to the site. The jerry-built structure generated a backlash of sympathy for the Derbys and at a second town meeting they got their bridge.

Realizing it would take years (providing he was suitably impeded) for Derby to span the river, the Crowninshields next decided to acquire as much town-owned land as possible with a view to profitable resale. Congressman Jacob came to Salem from Washington; all the family's new clout was exercised to counter the argument that legal title lay not in the town but in the heirs of long-gone "town proprietors." Nonsense, retorted the Crowninshields; the old proprietors had themselves stolen the land from the Indians. How could it be returned to them? Clearly, as everyone could see, the only appropriate thing to do would be to let the Crowninshields have it. In a way they would never have succeeded in doing only a dozen years before, "our family," which had learned a thing or two about packing town meetings, carried the day. Their real estate profits swelled anew.

Within a year of Jacob's election, the Crowninshields were leveling the bastions of the ancien régime. They founded a new bank, the

Mechanics Bank, to rival the Federalist Essex Bank; no more would they have to deal with those who had most obstructed their rise. In January 1803, to the anguish of Elias Hasket Derby, Jr., the Salem Regiment, until then his plaything, was infiltrated by Crowninshield adherents. The office of Collector of the Customs had already fallen to the upstarts. And no more would Crowninshield ladies worry about exclusion from the Salem Dancing Assembly or the more prestigious Court Ball; they gave their own parties and entertainments, and after 1802 held their own Fourth of July celebration parade and their own Washington's Birthday ceremonies.

"Our family's" triumphs over old enemies had been greatly facilitated by the death of "King" Derby in August of 1799. He had been predeceased by his wife, Elizabeth, who, true to her wish, had been carried down the great marble steps of the Derby mansion on an even keel. Both stately funerals were unattended by George and his family "in consequence of a disaffection of long standing," as Bentley put it. (The Parson found it prudent, on the occasion of Elizabeth's death, to attend the funeral of an old "french prisoner" from the Salem Charity House.)

Perhaps no great American family declined as rapidly as that of the country's first millionaire, and the saying "from shirtsleeves to shirtsleeves in three generations" might have been coined with the House of Derby in mind. Behind him, the "King" left upwards of a million dollars and two sons who partook of his bounty, but certainly not of his character. Indeed, the elder son, Elias Hasket Derby, Jr., had so angered his father by his enormous and foolish debts that the "King" had once locked him into a kind of cell, such that the young man was unable to speak to anyone for a fortnight. His meals were passed, in silence, through an opening constructed for the purpose.

Undismayed, young Elias had emerged to engineer, among those fearful of his father's influence, his own election to the command of the Salem militia. Under its new chieftain, "General Derby," the reviews of the regiment were characterized by a few ragged volleys and a speedy withdrawal to the nearest tavern, where General Derby's

46

health was drunk at his expense. During elections, Elias Hasket Derby, Jr., forsook his military ambitions to brawl drunkenly in the streets; his Federalist admirers could not restrain him and invariably he was beaten in the fistfights they could not prevent. Once he attended a funeral oration in which the speaker had alluded to "riches" that "take to themselves wings & fly away." Afterwards, thinking the reference was to him, he reprimanded the minister, who within two years was to remark that "the names of Pickman & Derby no longer stand pre-eminent in the business & navigation of the Town."

In fact, some Derbys were already thinking of folding their tents when the late Elizabeth's daughter, to the delight of her Uncle George, afforded Salem the best of fireworks. Named after her mother, something of young Elizabeth is seen in a bitter complaint she lodged against some association from which she angrily resigned after it had printed an alphabetical list of its members. She had married Nathaniel West and had been furious that her name had been listed last. On another occasion she quit a female association for the relief of poor children when it failed to name her "Directress."

In November 1806, Elizabeth brought a libel of divorce against West, from whom she had lived apart for several months while she entertained a series of colorful visitors. Bentley wrote: "This day began the hearing of the case of West & West before the Judges of the Supreme Judicial Court in Salem in plea of divorce. Capt. Nathaniel West is descended from W. West an honest citizen, by his wife who was a daughter of Deacon Beckford, who lived to a great age. He was an enterprising seaman with no uncommon advantages of education or nature, but his ambition led him to address the eldest d[aughter] of the late E. H. Derby, the first merchant in his time. The mother of Elizabeth was a Crowninshield and well known for vanity which she exposed to constant & deserved ridicule. E. possessed the rigid temper of her father, with all the weakness of her mother, & contrary to the will of her father & friends persisted in marrying West." Bentley was reminded of Dr. Johnson's words: "When a man marries a fortune it is not all that he marries."

Elizabeth, with the assistance of her brother, "General Derby," who had a private quarrel to avenge, drummed up a couple of dozen whores from Boston, Salem, Marblehead and Cape Ann as participants in West's infidelity. Charges and countercharges flew about with incredible malignity and Bentley tells us that the public mind grew "disquiet" and that no man was "safe in his reputation after such proceedings." It was "darkness indescribable."

The other of Elizabeth's brothers, Hersey, was somewhat younger than Elias Hasket Derby, Jr., but he too possessed qualities that practically guaranteed extinction. Early in 1806, he led a midnight break-in of the Salem Town Hall with a view to embarrassing the Crown-inshields. On the books of the selectmen he found the entry "Brundy" opposite a figure of money. Next day he bruited it about that the town fathers — mainly Crowninshield partisans — spent their time and the public money swilling brandy. When it became known that "Brundy" was the name of a workman employed upon a perfectly legitimate municipal purpose, Hersey joined his brother and sister as the laughingstocks of the town.

The final Derby humiliation took place at an election meeting in May 1806 to choose a certain number of Federalist and Crowninshield delegates for the November congressional elections. In the crowded courthouse where the meeting was held, there appeared no accurate way to count the mob, whereupon a Federalist proposed that both factions go outside and stand on opposite sides of the street to be counted. At this a Crowninshield man moved that both parties line up on the same side of the street to the left and right of a certain point, the Federalists to be on the right. This proposal, it happened, would have required the anti-Crowninshields to be stretched across a very narrow and rickety footbridge over the South River. The Federalists, among them Elias Hasket Derby, Jr., objected, fearing that once their file was strung over the bridge, the Crowninshield forces would not wait to be counted and bolt en masse for the courthouse, lock the doors and proceed to do as they liked. To settle the matter, the moderator ordered both parties outside, to be counted on the way out. Derby and his allies refused to leave the building. The Crowninshield forces obeyed the order, were counted, and the Federalists were disenfranchised. At this General Derby jumped up shrieking, "Mr. Moderator, Mr. Moderator, I . . . protest your proceedings!" But it was no good. The Crowninshields carried the day; the General left the courthouse in hysteria and what little residual prestige he had carried into it was gone forever.

Four years later, the Reverend Bentley took his last view of the "best finished, most elegant, & best constructed House" he had ever seen. Its stucco, its rotundo, its carvings and the black-marble steps of Elizabeth's design were being razed because no Derby heir could afford to keep it and the "convenience of the spot for other buildings brought a sentence of destruction."

By 1811, the same year in which General Derby respectfully requested that his real property taxes be abated by twenty dollars, his father's marvelous library was advertised for sale. Riches had, indeed, taken wings to themselves and flown away.

The General left Salem forever. Within a few years the possessions of the House of Derby, even the splendid farm with its greenhouses of lemons and strawberries of which old Derby had been so proud were in the hands of the Crowninshields. Now the little wooden hermit in his hut of bark would be shown to the guests of those who cared even less for the sentiments inscribed on his book than did the man who had caused their inscription.

When Congressman Jacob Crowninshield arrived in the rutted, muddy town of Washington in 1803, the place was astir with the news of the Louisiana Purchase. Federalists wondered whether it was France's to sell (had Spain really ceded it?). If so, just how much land was involved and where? There were also some constitutional questions. The Louisiana Purchase caused the most intense debate and party struggle since the election of Jefferson. Characteristically, Jacob swept such nice questions aside and in his maiden speech enthused over the Purchase as a "Cheap bargain" in which he saw enormous advantage for America and for Crowninshield shipping. Also, as he caused Bentley to point out in the Salem press, the territory contained a mountain of salt one hundred and fifty miles in diameter.

It was up to the Eighth Congress to vote the necessary money to pay Napoleon. The agreed-upon price of $15,000,000 seemed fair enough, but certain shipowners had claims amounting to $3,750,000 against France, who had seized their vessels in the late naval war. These claims, known as spoilation certificates, were negotiable, freely traded about, and by 1803 practically worthless. Would Napoleon ever honor them? When it became apparent, on October 30, 1803, that the Louisiana Purchase would become a reality and that henceforth spoilation claims would be payable by the United States Treasury at face value, Jacob decided to turn the late war to account. Frantically he wrote to his brother John in Bordeaux, urging him to buy up all the certificates he could at below par. A very swift ship carried his letter to a Europe ignorant of the value of the claims; "our family" reaped a handsome profit from a war to which they had refused to contribute a cent. The "Great Salt Mountain" never was.

In spite of the coup, old George had grave misgivings. He feared war with Great Britain and advised his sons: "War Seams the Order of the Day Let us Sea how we Stand. . . . I know that Nation (the Eng) Having Know them 5 or 6 wares & they Do & Mean to Make all Pretence for Plunder when they Can." Although war did not come, the order of the day for the East India Company was to cannonade Maca in Sumatra. Soon John Crowninshield's old friends on the pepper coast were scattered or dead, and where he had negotiated for pepper, an English fort now stood. "Our pepper gardens" were no more.

And George worried about his sons. Neither money nor common interest seemed to hold them together; he could not understand it. Jacob in Washington was doing all he could, to be sure. But in Salem the next ablest, Benjamin, was sick day after day. In New York, Richard seemed to be dealing mostly on his own account and was unresponsive to such paternal inquiries as this:

SON RICHARD
All on the wing to know what is the Matter of You & from your Quarter No Letters Since the date of 2 Instant & how to account for Same we Cannot one Says R is Sick one Says he killed him Self . . . & the Mother

50

Says he Must be Dead She knows & She has Sarrched all the N. York
Paper to find in the Lists of Death wither your Name is there.

To Richard Crowninshield's silence was added another propensity
which made the old man uneasy. Richard bragged that he could pass
off the confusing currency and bills of exchange of the time to whom-
ever he chose. John? He was too far away in France. As for George
Jr., he was energetic enough on the wharves, yet his abilities were not
all they ought to be. What was old George to do?

In November of 1804 he proposed dissolution of the partnership:
"I think is rather rong My Notion which we begun with was by Unit-
ing we Should stand & by Dividing we may be hurt which I fear will
happen & which I think we feal all ready." It troubled him that "our
Property should be So Scattred & oute of our Command." Moreover,
"I feal I Gro old fast & I allso feel . . . it would be Best to settle our
firme & Put Me *a one side* . . . My Self Good for nothing." Regretfully
he added, "I was in hopes we Should have Stayed togather to I had
bid you all a Good night & Left you fat and full . . . Rich Very Rich
in Deed."

But to his sons the profits beyond the Cape of Good Hope were irresistible, and Richard spoke for all his brothers when he wrote,
"India voyages must be our aim; & there our fortune lies." The partnership continued as before but for the moment profit lay in quite another direction.

Easily reelected in November 1804, Jacob had proceeded to stun
his Republican colleagues by joining the Federalists in vehemently
denouncing an administration proposal to stop the brisk American
trade to the West Indian island of Santo Domingo, which was then
blockaded by French warships seeking to starve out the black insur-
gent Dessalines. Under pressure from Bonaparte, Jefferson publicly
deplored Americans who engaged in the trade and who frequently
fought with the blockading French men-of-war. These Americans
were, he complained, engaged in a "private war." In Congress, Jacob
first fought the administration's proposal and failing that tried to

51

water down its sanctions. But Jefferson and the French were adamant; all trade must cease. Once again Jacob took the floor, this time to equate American trade with Santo Domingan independence, with black freedom. Should commerce be halted, surely these blacks would become vagabonds, pirates; worse yet, they would become pawns of Great Britain.

At these words Federalists in Salem had a field day and the *Gazette* was in ecstasy. For Crowninshield had not only embarrassed Republicanism, he had openly parted with the Republican principles in whose name he had been elected. Particularly evocative of the *Gazette*'s scorn was Jefferson's earlier condemnation of those who conducted "a private war"; after all, it said, "we have the high example of Captain [Jacob] Crowninshield . . . who is deeply engaged in it." To friends and enemies alike it appeared that he had run up his true colors: the white crown on a shield of blue.

And it was true. Among those most forward in conducting "the private war" were George Crowninshield & Sons, and they were doing so in uninsured ships so heavily armed they resembled men-of-war. By the end of 1804, *Telemachus* and *John* had brought to Salem 430,000 pounds of coffee netting a profit of $30,000.

Angry that it was thought he would so readily exchange party loyalty for what was in his words only "a good four months job," he turned to the British. Would no one understand that the nonstop provision of the Jay Treaty had made profitable trading in India impossible?

This embarrassment notwithstanding, President Jefferson offered Jacob the post of Secretary of the Navy late in 1804. Jacob wavered; in letter after letter he discussed the offer with his wife, Sally, who had remained behind in Salem. She did not want him to take the appointment. Jefferson renewed his soft persuasions and Sally's objections grew stronger in a letter dated February 9, 1805:

MY DEAR FRIEND,

I had hoped you would decide the point without waiting for another letter from me. I feel so incompetent with regard to writing — certainly my letters are not correct enough to show to Mr. Jefferson. . . . Tis no burden to you to write to me tis a hard task — and the children want to be with me so much I find it difficult to leave them for any length of time. . . . If you could have the appointment and reside in Boston or even New York . . . if it was only to mortify . . . the other side this would have some weight with me to let them know you are of consequence than they would wish you to be. . . . I do not like to express myself stronger than I did in my former letters I think I could not be so happy in W. . . . I have wrote the last part in haste and tomorrow I will endeavor to write one a little more correctly at least you shall determine which is the best one, do not if you can help it show either of them to Mr. Jefferson.

Against this, Jefferson could not prevail; Jacob declined the post he had so badly wanted, and the "other side" was not mortified.

In Congress Jacob was at first very popular and was able to rig the election (in recognition of his services as editor of the *Register*) of the Reverend William Bentley to the chaplainship of the House, an offer which the Parson wisely refused. But the congressman was to grow more and more bellicose. In 1803, when Britain had declared war on Napoleonic France, Jacob had asserted that "war will help our voyages, if our ships get home in safety." But by September 11, 1805, Jacob concluded otherwise in a letter to President Jefferson: "England contemplated the destruction of our whole carrying trade; [soon we must] look the British Lyon full in the face." He argued for commercial sanctions against Britain and now he could restrain himself no more: "I would not hesitate to meet her in war." The Vermont and Massachusetts militia would, he promised, easily conquer Quebec and Nova Scotia; it would be glorious.

The hot-tempered John Randolph of Virginia led the attack against Crowninshield. "Great Britain was," he declared, "the only bulwark of the human race against universal [Napoleonic] dominion." And then he turned directly to the "Yazoo man," as he called Crowninshield. "I am not surprised to hear men advocate these wild opinions, to see them, goaded on by a spirit of mercantile avarice, straining their feeble strength to excite the nation to war, when they have reached this stage of infatuation that we are an overmatch for Great Britain on the ocean.

It is mere waste of time to reason with such persons. They do not deserve anything like serious refutation."

Crowninshield, Randolph cried, was a countinghouse politician who needed "a strait-waistcoat, a dark room, water gruel, and depletion." Moreover, shouted the Virginian, his business was a mushroom; it was unfair; it was a fungus; and to follow Crowninshield's advice would be to "plunge into the water in a mad contest with the shark!" And now the choleric southern aristocrat, perspiring and glaring at Jacob, shrieked: "God help you, if these are your ways and means for carrying on war; if your finances are in the hands of such a chancellor of the exchequer! Because a man can take an observation and keep a log-book and a reckoning, can navigate a cock-boat to the West Indies or the East, shall he aspire to navigate the great vessel of state, — to stand at the helm of public councils? *Ne sutor ultra crepidam!*"*

Jacob took the floor again some days later; he would fight until "the last drop of blood," however weak the United States Navy might be, and he had no objection to meeting "France, Spain, or England . . . all collectively if necessary." In Salem, the *Gazette* claimed he was mad and suggested that the Reverend Bentley become his guardian. Even his loyal Republican supporters were aghast at the saber rattling, for in truth there was no saber. Jacob wanted the strongest measures against Great Britain in the hope that they would provoke her into war. Although the Jay Treaty lay immediately behind his rantings, their origin was in an earlier time — that of Johannes Kaspar Richter von Kronenscheldt. To Jacob, Chinaman's map or no, the King's Broad Arrow was still upon the land.

On May 19, 1807, Jacob's wife Sally, always fragile, died after a prolonged and painful illness and without complaint in Salem. After Jacob returned to Washington in the spring of 1808, thoughts of death were always with him. When he received a letter sealed with a black wafer, he would hold it for many minutes before opening it. In Congress he railed against the British once more and for the last time. He spat blood, collapsed, was racked with "mercurial" fever, and could eat nothing but raw chocolate and oysters. His brothers Benja-

* Let the cobbler stick to his last — Pliny.

54

min and John hastened to the capital and they did not undeceive him when he felt himself to be improving. The doctors quit dosing him with mercury and bled him instead, but from the emaciated arm they could get only about three spoonfuls. It was mid-April; the peach trees were in blossom and he slept fitfully, dreamed of India, and died.

Mr. Albert-Horatio of the Washington *Chronicle* wrote these lines on Jacob's death:

> *Shall sounding flatt'ry prostitute the Muse?*
> *Shall worth, unnotic'd, pass like morning dews?*
> *Like fallen leaves, the sport of every wind*
> *Nor leave a trace of what they were behind?*
> *Or like a transient, frail and gaudy flower,*
> *Pluck'd from its stalk, and wither'd in an hour?*
> *No— While fond memory holds her wonted seat,*
> *While virtuous actions their reward shall meet,*
> *When kings and princes shall forgotten lie —*
> *Thy name, O, CROWNINSHIELD! shall never die!*

But in Salem, where the congressman's remains were landed on May 18 in an elegant coffin leaded in Baltimore, there were those who did not share Albert-Horatio's sentiments. Among them was Jacob's brother-in-law Gardner, who claimed the exclusive privilege of writing his obituary. The piece was so vicious it could not be printed.

Worse followed. At Bentley's funeral oration the nephew of Jacob's old enemy Timothy Pickering bulled his way into East Church and loudly vilified all Crowninshields, living and dead. One feels that John Randolph's "Yazoo" would have thoroughly enjoyed the whole thing.

A half century later, in the midst of the Civil War, Edward Everett Hale wrote a story, one "with a national moral." In it a young army officer, Philip Nolan, says, "Damn the United States! I wish I may never hear of the United States again!" He never did: the Secretary of the Navy directed that poor Nolan be confined aboard cruising warships for life "to make it certain that he never saw or heard of the country." In Mr. Hale's story, the Secretary of the Navy was "the first Crowninshield." Of course, there never was a "man without a country" nor was Jacob ever Secretary of the Navy. But had they been, one feels Nolan's fate would have been less protracted. Although commingled with self-interest, Crowninshield's love of country was fierce; he would have hanged Philip Nolan. As a child he had written, "New England is My Station"; his station remained New England.

In 1809 a voyage was made that would have infuriated Jacob. Napoleon regarded American vessels, however slightly tainted by British contact, as subject to confiscation. At the same time the British insisted that any American vessel intending to trade with the Continent first check into a British port and pay a tariff. Into these tentacles, the Crowninshield *Margaret*, with a hodgepodge cargo of sugar, pepper, codfish and rum, sailed early in the year.

Her master, Captain Fairfield, had received every admonition to keep clear of the two great European antagonists; he was to proceed to neutral Tunis. But once in the Mediterranean, Fairfield called at Sardinia (at the moment British) for water and for news. Scrupulously faithful to orders, he made it explicit to the authorities that he had no wish to trade at the island. Proceeding to Tunis, *Margaret* was pounced upon by what appeared to be a British man-of-war. Within gunshot she ran up another set of colors; she was the French privateer *Le Constant*, and *Margaret*, sullied by the innocent pause at Sardinia, was her prize.

While his ship awaited condemnation in Italy, John Crowninshield in Salem anguished over a slip of paper on which he toted up the options and odds. Calculating the value of *Margaret* and her cargo at $70,000, his insurance would pay only $13,500. What were the chances of condemnation for so trifling a violation of Napoleon's edict? Was it a violation at all? But John knew the Emperor needed cash; the Emperor always did. The risk was too great.

Crowninshield also knew that the officers of *Le Constant*, although they adored their emperor, little liked to share their spoils with one of his prize courts. A deal was made: *Margaret*'s cargo was sold and the proceeds divided between the privateers and John. In this painful way he got to keep his ship. Months were consumed by these negotiations and it was not until April 1810 that *Margaret* sailed for Salem.

Having survived, after a fashion, the toils of Europe, the vessel wallowed home through heavy seas in a rainstorm, when suddenly, in Fairfield's words, "the wind shifted in an instant from ESE to SW and although the helm was hard to weather," he "could not get the ship before the wind, but was instantly hove on her beam ends." *Margaret* had capsized in mid-Atlantic, badly damaging her small boats. Only the longboat was sound, and Fairfield and a few of his men took to it. Forty-six men, however, remained on the hulk, which appeared likely to sink at any moment, and whenever the hovering longboat came close, they hurled themselves toward it.

Fearful that the longboat, which was secured by a line to the wreck, would be swamped, Fairfield shouted a warning; he would cast off and abandon them. Nightfall brought a deadly game of tug of war. "The people on board the ship," wrote Fairfield, "being exceedingly anxious to get into the boat (which had they affected we should all have inevitably lost) kept hauling the boat towards them; we then bent on another rope, and veered out as they hauled; but finding they were determined to sink the boat by getting into her, we were obliged (after stating repeatedly to them our situation) to tell them that provided they persisted in getting into the boat, we should be obliged, tho' very reluctantly, to cut the rope and leave them; after which they disisted from hauling the boat towards the ship."

Dawn found *Margaret* awash, her exhausted and terrified sailors piteously clamoring to join Fairfield, who by noon had managed to collect from the debris a drowned pig, a goat, a bag of bread and a jug of brandy. For hours the two groups faced one another over the swells. When Fairfield fashioned a sail and raised it, those on the wreck were convinced they were to be abandoned. Several leaped into the sea and swam toward him; once more he moved further off.

Next they baited a trap. Aware that the longboat was without compass, sextant and water, they shouted that he could have these if only he would come closer. But Fairfield, "seeing they were all determined to pursue the same plan," sailed away.

Within a day or so those left behind ran out of fresh water and when one died of thirst, they fell to drinking brandy in the appalling sun. By evening fifteen were dead. A couple of the living set about repairing a tiny yawl previously thought hopelessly smashed. Into it five men clambered and after three weeks of indescribable hardship during which two died, they were rescued by a passing ship. The bottom of the yawl had been scraped paper-thin by constant bailing; the men had stayed alive by making nets of their handkerchiefs in which they caught tiny fish.

Captain Fairfield's group had also been rescued, and in Salem the survivors faced one another and exchanged terrible accusations. Fairfield had deserted them, the charge went, and those whom they had left on the hulk; Fairfield should have stood by; he was a coward. Shortly the charges and countercharges assumed the political overtones dominating the town. Who was to blame for the loss of *Margaret* and twenty-eight of her men? Some blamed Crowninshield, others Fairfield; all blamed the French. For twenty-seven years after John's ship slid beneath the sea, litigation raged; no settlement of consequence was ever made.

The dead Jacob would have blamed the British for the disaster. He would have said that the vessel should not have gone to Europe at all. For most of his thirty-eight years, Jacob had looked to the East Indies for riches.

But he was wrong. The fullness of the family fortune would not be found beyond the Cape of Good Hope, nor would its acquisition be troubled by the thirteenth clause of John Jay's treaty.

On September 7, 1812, old George watched his *America IV* claw out of Salem Harbor as no Crowninshield ship had before. A mass of white sail, she looked like some great bird rather than a ship. In July and August her upper deck had been removed and her tonnage greatly reduced.

What George feared and Jacob had wished had come about: war with Great Britain. *America IV*, laden with long nines, carronades, muskets, blunderbusses, pistols, axes, tomahawks and boarding pikes, and a crew of about a hundred and fifty men, including marines, sailed as a private armed ship — a privateer.

Her captain had been instructed to "cruise against and capture the vessels goods & effects of his B. Majesty & his dependances" in such a manner as to make it most profitable to George Crowninshield and Co. Prizes were to be sent to the nearest port "according to the wind," and there would be no objection to relieving vessels other than British of their cargoes should "circumstances" arise. If any capture was not worth bringing home, it was to be burned.

In an earlier time, long before Dr. Johannes Kaspar Richter von Kronenscheldt set foot in the New World, there arose among nations a custom of authorizing wronged individuals to take reprisal against a foreign prince or power. Thus sanctioned, one could seize the goods and person of any subject of the offending state. On the sea the right of reprisal became known as a "letter of marque." Without such a letter a private armed ship was simply a pirate and its occupants, if caught, were promptly hanged.

In the summer of 1812, no man felt more wronged than old George Crowninshield and none turned privateer with a greater will than he. As usual the United States Navy was nothing compared to that of His Majesty, and Madison was quick to authorize the use of private armed ships against British commerce. Naturally, because such ventures were at the owner's risk, the government contributing only a piece of paper, any prize became the personal property of the privateers.

No one could build and sail ships as could the Crowninshields, and they had never been strangers to cannon. None of the terrible red tape that had plagued the building of the *Essex* in 1799 ever attended any ship constructed by George Crowninshield. Nor did he have the difficulties of one Ebenezer Fox, who wrote woefully of his efforts to obtain men for the United States Navy's *Protector*, twenty guns: "The recruiting business went on slowly, however, but at length upwards of three hundred men were carried, dragged and driven aboard; of all ages, kinds and descriptions; in all the various stages of intoxication from that of sober tipsiness to beastly drunkenness; with the uproar and clamor that may be more easily imagined than described. Such a motley group has never been since Falstaff's regiment paraded in the streets of Coventry." Shunning official naval service, young and able men flocked to the Crowninshield privateers. Of these only the most audacious were selected; one of *America IV*'s captains, its most successful, James Cheever, Jr., was only twenty-two years old.

The incentives were potent indeed. He who first spotted a rich prize could in that instant realize more money than he could earn in a lifetime; the first to board an enemy ship could earn nearly as much. Those incapacitated in action were compensated on a scale far more generous than that applying to the United States Navy. Typically, a privateersman received $50 for the loss of an "eye or a joint" (the hand or foot), and a leg or arm was worth $300. In cases of cowardice, the penalty was forfeiture of one's share of the profits, a fate worse than the yardarm or the cat-o'-nine-tails to Crowninshield crews.

For old George on that September day, what thoughts and memories there must have been. The British had almost strangled his father, John, and they had nearly done the same to him and his sons. It had always been so. He had fought clear of and beaten his despised Derby in-laws; he had destroyed the old order; he had become rich and would have been richer yet, had not the long shadow of Great Britain fallen upon him in the Indian Ocean. His *America IV* sailed for the North Atlantic, for that streak of silver sea the British called their lake (how the thought fed his soul), impelled by the rancor of a lifetime as much as by the wind.

Adeona, Aeolus, Alexander, Ann, two *Apollos, Arrow, Benjamin, Black Joe, Blonde, Britannia, Brothers, Busy, Ceres, Cod Hook, Curfew, Dart, Diamond, Diana, Duchess of Bedford, Edwin, Eliza, Elizabeth, Enterprise, Euphemis,* two *Friends, Falcon, George, Grenada Packet, Harmony, Henry, Home,* three *Hopes* (whose names availed them not), *Hunt, Industry, Invincible Napoleon, James and Charlotte, Jane, Joachim, Jubilee, Leicester, Leopard, Levant, Lion, Lively, Lord Ponsonby, Lucy, Lynn, Margaret, Maria, Martha, Mary and Joseph, Moore, Neptune, Nymph, Paragon, Phoebe, Plutos, Polly, Pomona, Prince of Asturias, Princess Elizabeth, Prometheus, Providence, Ralph Nickerson, Ramacetta, Rapid, Recovery, Sally, Sovereign, Sprightly, St. Francis de Assisi, St. Lawrence, Swift, Tercilla, Theophilus, Thistle, Traveller, Union, William, Winter, Zelpha.*

So named were the vessels captured by the Crowninshields in the War of 1812: some taken as prizes, some released to carry their crews to British ports, some broken up for firewood, and some sent to the bottom. Altogether, a half-dozen Crowninshield privateers had captured or destroyed some eighty enemy ships in the course of the war; old George had unloosed hawks into a dovecote. One privateer, *Jefferson*, was so tiny and so crowded with men that it reminded a Maine woman of "so many goslings on a tray." Nonetheless, with her carronade and single six-pounder, she had taken the second prize of the war.

The most successful, *America IV*, had never really been in much danger. Little wonder: she could make thirteen knots, and there were times when she averaged more than ten knots for twelve consecutive hours. So terrible was her reputation that H.M.S. *Dublin* is said to have been especially fitted out by the Royal Navy to destroy her. One day at dusk *Dublin* had her quarry almost within gunshot, but by dawn the Yankee privateer was only a speck on the horizon.

On the evening of April 7, 1815, *America IV* fired a forty-gun salute and dropped anchor for the last time. The war was over. Among her crew there were few casualties. Discipline had been taut, and in all her months at sea only one of the crew had been punished. Something of the spirit of these men may be seen in the poetic manner in which the legal proceedings were recorded:

> *This Court's composed of men of knowledge*
> *And genius; though not bred at College, —*
> *Chever, Widger, Hugget, and Brown,*
> *Whose firm integrity is now well-known.*
> *Their minds being well on justice bent,*
> *Aft on the lee-poop they were sent,*
> *Where they debate upon the cause,*
> *Governed by their Country's laws.*
> *They try the culprit; find him guilty*
> *Of theft, a crime both mean and filthy.*

*   *   *   *

The Boats'n pipes all hands to muster.
No time for whining, plea or bluster!
The judge announces the just sentence,
And many stripes produce repentance.

*   *   *   *

For the low cur, who'd meanly cozen
A poor marine, must take his "dozen."

All through the war and for months after the Treaty of Ghent, the prizes of *America IV* and other Crowninshield privateers flowed to American ports, where they were condemned and auctioned off with an alacrity old George could have only learned from the British themselves.

Cargoes varied. One of the more exotic attracted the inquisitive Reverend Bentley to Marblehead on August 19, 1814, "to see the . . . Hyene & the Jackalls" which "had been on very short allowance & were now recovering. . . . We only inspected but did not examine these animals, which were tame & feeble in extreme from their short fare on the Voyage. The Hyene was the striped Hyena. It impressed me more as a Fox than a dog from his wide front, & sharpening at the muzzle. Its fore legs were much stouter than the hinder, but to the eye not much longer, but it had all the ferocity of its native state. Persons in the Vessel could go freely to it, but still it would bite upon the least irritation. It stood patiently tied, till the strangers passed between decks; it then kept in continual motion the length of its rope in & out. It often bites off its rope, but is not feared by the Crew. The Jackalls chuse not to come in sight, but when the seamen are below show no hostility, till attempts are made to seize them."

For the Parson, the hyena had been a happier experience than that provided by the officious Professor Jenks of Bath, Maine, some weeks earlier. In a letter the professor had invited Bentley's attention to *Falcon*, a Crowninshield prize at Bath which contained, among other things, "books shipped by the British & Foreign Bible Society consisting of 400 English Bibles, 300 Testaments & 500 Dutch Bibles" originally destined for South Africa and now for the auction block.

Professor Jenks had implored Bentley to persuade the "Messieurs Crowninshields" to release them for the edification of the inhabitants of the Cape of Good Hope.

Now the stout Unitarian had very little use for English or Dutch Bibles and even less for Professor Jenks. Yet he was on the spot. As a man of God, must he not advance the Lord's work among the heathen? The situation was further aggravated by Bentley's certain knowledge that old George Crowninshield cared not a whit that Bentley might be on the horns of a dilemma. For some weeks the minister of the East Church maneuvered among Professor Jenks, God, the Devil and the Crowninshields, and as always he brought about sweet reason. Some of the Bibles found their way to Africa; most were auctioned off in Maine.

Certain captures were of special interest to the Crowninshield ladies, as is seen in the delighted letter of Benjamin's wife on May 19, 1815: "I am . . . much gratified. I wish I could tell you what I have seen. In the first place the most elegant ladies' clothing — perhaps two dozen gowns trimmed in the most superb style mostly muslin with brussels lace — perhaps ten pounds per yard — some crepes, silk, etc. in the box with I suppose the married ladies' dresses as they were much larger. There were most elegant infant clothes worked in the handsomest manner and likewise trimmed with lace and a dozen suits . . . trousers and gowns of the most delicate muslins and cambric trimmed with lace and wrought bonnets, caps, turbans, all of the first cut, shoes, etc. etc. Some of the books most elegantly bound and some very common. One elegant looking-glass but not very large, just the size for our sitting room. Elegant pictures — landscapes in colours and Bonny [Napoleon] in different situations, said to be very fine, but these we did not see, in the back of the store and it was too stormy to have the light admitted. Very beautiful table linen and linens, cottons, cambrics and muslins all of the first quality, and it appeared to me there were as many goods or more than at Bath. . . . The plated baskets were beautiful and some of the jewelry very handsome. There were six pearl pins, very plain, no colored stone with the pearls."

On April 6, 1815, another prize had caught Mary's fancy: "We have not seen the invoice, but . . . there are many pretty things — some jewelry, ladies' dresses, bonnets, etc. etc. [Benjamin] sent me a letter this morning he found on board from a gentleman in London . . . saying he sent the veil in a box with Mrs. J. bonnets and six shades worked agreeable to patterns sent, hoped the binding of the books would suit, and the pin set in the newest style. How disappointed the lady must be. It is thought the cargo will bring $40,000." After a supper of roast leg of lamb, Mary was shown the invoice, "everything pretty and jewelry — must be handsome from the cost . . . buckles for shoes, blue stone, cost very high, bracelets, elegant pins, ornamented combs, elegant silver baskets a dozen pair, handsome candlesticks, books elegantly bound and valuable works — children's books and trinkets so we can all be gratified with pretty things."

Mary wondered whether the baubles had not been a part of the cargo of *St. Lawrence*, which had been captured earlier by *America IV* and which proved to be worth $500,000, the most valuable of the Crowninshield prizes. In addition to bringing in a good deal of cash, *St. Lawrence* brought a kind of literary immortality to "our family" when, many years later, Washington Irving wrote *Tales of a Traveler*. In one of the tales, Irving's bumpkin, Tom Walker, sells his soul to the Devil. Negotiations commence in a gloomy, swampy grove of trees into which are carved the names of great malefactors who presumably have preceded Tom Walker in satanic pacts. One such tree was marked "Crowninshield," and Tom recalls "a mighty rich man of that name, who made a vulgar display of wealth, which it was whispered he had acquired by buccaneering."

St. Lawrence had been an American vessel under British license engaged in illegal contraband trade, a kind of smuggler, fair game for "our family" and the property of the Irvings of New York.

One of the new owners of *St. Lawrence* was the Secretary of the Navy. In the bland, rounded features of Benjamin Williams Crowninshield there was none of the predatory angularity of his dead brother Jacob. (His middle name, Williams, had been added to distinguish him from his cousin "Sailor Ben" and from "Sailor Ben's" son, "Philosopher Ben," for both embarrassed him.)

America **IV** *in Pursuit of* Princess Elizabeth. *Painting by George Ropes, 1815. Courtesy of the Peabody Museum of Salem*

Benjamin Williams Crowninshield. Courtesy of the Peabody Museum of Salem

The fourth of George's sons, Benjamin, had suffered badly from childhood diseases and all his life he was to be terribly afflicted with asthma. At a precocious age he determined to prolong his life by exercising extreme abstemiousness. He was assisted in this resolve by the enormous Mary Boardman, whom he married in 1804 and who, at six feet, dwarfed him.

From the beginning, Mary had enjoined Benjamin never to exert himself and there is every evidence that he fully complied with her wishes. He fretted over putting on a couple of pounds and over his growing baldness, which attracted flies. About him there was an inertia, a colorless circumspection not shared by his brothers. The political correspondence of his Washington years is characterized by the volte-face of the politician, the abiding wish not to offend. And Benjamin seemed always sleepy, almost comatose. But sleepy or no, he was a Crowninshield.

Samuel Eliot Morison has described an earlier voyage of *America IV* commanded by another Crowninshield: "On July 2, 1804, she left Salem with very positive and emphatic orders to proceed to Sumatra for pepper, and nowhere else. . . . 'Obey orders if you break owners,' was a maxim of the old merchant marine. Yet this independent master received at Mauritius such favorable news of the coffee market that once more he determined to disobey. On November 30, the 'America' passed 'through the straits of Babelmandel,' and at Aden and Macalla Roads she took in coffee, gum arabic, hides, goatskins, and senna, and cleared for Salem.

"Now by June, 1805, when the 'America' was sighted from Salem town, pepper had fallen and coffee risen to such an extent that the owners were praying that [the master] had broken orders! Unable to restrain their impatience until she docked, the Crowninshield brothers put off in a small boat. Approaching her to leeward, they began sniffing the air. One was sure he smelled the desired bean; but another suggested it might be merely a pot of coffee on the galley stove. Finally, disregarding all marine etiquette, Benjamin W. Crowninshield shouted, 'What's your cargo?' — 'Pe-pe-per!' answered the Captain, who was enjoying the situation hugely. 'You lie! I smell coffee!' roared the future Secretary of the Navy through his speaking-trumpet." He had indeed smelled coffee — a fortune in the stuff.

Benjamin was forty-two and in the fullness of abstention when President James Madison decided to reward the Crowninshield Republican enclave in the North:

> Washington, December 15, 1814.
>
> BENJAMIN W. CROWNINSHIELD
>   Salem, Mass.
>
> SIR: —
>
> Mr. Jones having retired from the Secretaryship of the Navy, my thoughts have been turned to you as a desirable successor, and I have this day sent in your name to the Senate for appointment. I hope you will excuse my doing it without your consent, which would have been asked if the business of that Department had less urged an avoidance of delay. The same consideration will apologize for my hoping that it will not be inconsistent with your views to aid your country in that station, nor with your convenience to repair to it as soon as you may receive notice that the Senate have given effect to the nomination.
>
> Accept, Sir, assurances of my esteem and of my friendly respects —
>
> JAMES MADISON.

Hurrying toward Washington to assume his new station, Benjamin paused at the United States Navy Yard in Boston long enough to divert eighteen new long nine-pounders to *America IV*. (His self-abnegation never extended to the making of money.)

One turns, with a sinking heart, from the bales of patronage letters which have survived Secretary Crowninshield, hoping for relief among his personal correspondence. But one does not find it. We learn only from the neat, clerkly hand that he hated Washington as a "barren void" and that his children were never free of agues, chills, headaches and the malady called St. Anthony's Fire. Over the years Mary's letters become more and more those of a parent to a delicate child. One wishes Benjamin would cast aside his blandness, even Mary, take to drink perhaps, maybe even take some sultry mistress, or at least move someone like John Randolph of Virginia to vituperation. But he never did. Among the more remarkable of his letters from Washington is one recording his astonishment at the number of pickpockets in the capital when Monroe was inaugurated. The distress of the privateer whose vessels had been the scourge of the Atlantic had increased when he learned that some were "white folk."

Yet this slow, unimaginative and dutiful man was the only one of his brothers and sisters to increase and transmit his share of the Crowninshield wealth to his present-day heirs, and apart from the deep incursions of successive tax levies, it has remained intact.

In old age, he was a great collector of clocks, and when their numbers became intolerable, Mary would, in his absence, send a batch off to auction. Now Benjamin loved auctions, especially those of clocks, and frequently he would buy his clocks back again, admiring some little feature or other without knowing they had once been his. When a grandchild spoke of going to church, she was chided, "You don't go to church, child, you go to meeting," and was given a gold piece.

Toward the end, he lived on tea and crackers; flies tormented his pate and he had a wig made to keep them off, which Mary would not let him wear indoors. Bewigged, he took to the streets in search of drunks, whom he lectured on the evils of intemperance in his asthmatic wheeze. Some could scarcely stand; yet something in the gentle little old man's presence held them fast. At his death in 1851, he had indeed lived longer than his brothers, puzzling the physicians who examined the corpse: clearly, heart disease should have killed him long ago.

Benjamin Williams Crowninshield left a son and grandson in whose debt all Harvard men must remain. The former, of the Class of 1829, found himself "rusticated" after dumping a bucket of water over the head of one of his professors — surely the stuff of dreams to many a Cantabrigian before and since. Thirty years later, when it was decided that the Harvard crew could be better identified if they wrapped colored handkerchiefs around their heads, his namesake purchased some for the purpose. Today, on a fall afternoon when the band urges on the men of Harvard and the crimson banner flaps above Soldiers' Field, few know they owe its color to six red handkerchiefs picked up at Hovey's store one muggy June day in 1858.

"The War has Ended most gloriously For the Nation and our Selves," exulted George Jr. in the spring of 1815. Mary Crowninshield was determined to "gratify" herself "with . . . dresses . . . to shine out in Washington next winter. Who can buy them better than I can? . . . Who has done better?"

No one had done better. The indices to the value of money have changed greatly since *America IV* fired her forty-gun salute in Salem Harbor in 1815. On balance it seems reasonable to say that in today's currency the value of the Crowninshield prizes in the War of 1812 was $15,000,000, perhaps $20,000,000.

What mattered more to old George, the damage to Great Britain was and is incalculable. Although worthless, the most valuable capture to him found her way into the logbook of *America IV* on February 7, 1815: "At half past 4 P.M. saw a sail on our weather bow." For four hours the privateer chased H.M.S. *Princess Elizabeth* in cloudy, breezy weather. When the English vessel was overhauled by the much faster *America IV*, she ran up American colors and "gave us a broadside." The action became general for a few minutes and *Princess Elizabeth* was nearly blown out of the water by Crowninshield cannon.

Unlike the other prizes, which were merchantmen, *Princess Elizabeth* had been a ship of war. Again and again old Crowninshield pressed Captain Cheever for more details. How many holes had been shot in the Briton? How big had they been? Was Cheever sure there had not been more?

It was a time for "Crowninshield Punch," the more savory because it was brewed from captured English stores:

The Juice of 18 Lemons, no seed or Peel Allowed
Three Quarts of Cold Tea (Young Hyson)
One and one half 1½ lbs of Loaf Sugar
Mix, Have the Sugar thoroughly dissolved before adding
One Quart of Red Rum, Pine Apple Jamaica, or St. Croix.
One Pint of Brandy Rochelle Preferred
One Pint of Hollands Gin
One Quart of Red Wine of France (Claret or Vin Ordinaire)

But those who raised their glasses did so without dreaming that the ascendancy so desperately gained by the little German doctor's descendants in struggles on land and sea would be swept away in a single night fifteen years later. "Our family" was to abandon the scene of its conquests even more ignominiously than had the heirs of "King" Derby, and none was ever to return.

Family differences were now almost internecine. To old George it seemed that not much had changed since that long-ago breakfast when he had mixed his children's various wants together in a bowl and pleased none of them. George Jr. and John had long hated one another: George Jr. felt that John owed his father too much money and John thought George Jr. a fool. Benjamin and his wife would not speak to John, who thought Benjamin "heartless and high faluting." In his turn, Benjamin considered John a visionary and a boaster. Sally Crowninshield never spoke to George Jr., nor he to her. All snubbed Richard's Irish wife, and old George often wondered aloud why Richard had married the whore. And he worried about young George — too easily swayed by Richard, the old man thought, and why would young George never marry?

It seemed to him also that the astonishing successes of the War had deepened these animosities, and so they had. In 1809, the firm had been reorganized and had continued without Richard and John, who had gone out on their own. At the time, George had distributed among his sons the old firm's assets, something less than a million dollars, advising:

NOW SONS
I think You will Possess Ample Fortune Enough to Make you all Happy if . . . Pease & Union amongst you all is Cultivated, As I think it is not too Late to Attempt & which is My Earnest wish to See Established Before I Bid you a Lasting Farewell. Your Father
GEORGE CROWNINSHIELD

The successful privateering had been done by ships belonging to the partnership of old George, young George and Benjamin. John had borrowed heavily from them to outfit *Diomede* and had allowed himself to be captured by the British after a spectacular but short-lived success. Richard had not gone to war at all and Benjamin and George Jr. were determined that neither John nor Richard should share in the spoils. Just how were "Pease & Union" to be cultivated?

How, really, could he attempt anything when his "cold turns" could no longer be relieved with gin? A male nurse became necessary, and on first seeing him old George had cried out, "You will get nothing by it." When Richard brought his wife for a visit, the old man had snarled, "How come you to bring down that damned woman?"

Surrounded by heirs who mostly loathed one another, old George struggled with his will, the several versions of which brought loud disagreement. "How do you feel?" a son asked. "Three quarters over the bridge," came the reply, and then he sent for a pigeon for lunch. He drowsed and awoke to excoriate the United States government. He had loaned it over a million dollars and it was sure to fail. Forgetful — or mindful — that the prizes still in Salem Harbor must be shared with his privateer crews, he urged his sons to loot them as best they could before they were auctioned off.

Wearing an old green velvet cap, he sat facing seaward, having refused to die abed. His left eye bulged horribly, and one by one his senses took leave of him. Why, God Damn all Doctors and Chyrugeons too. How was it he was always surrounded by fools? He would sail for India, for the pepper gardens of Sumatra. A privateering against the English, God Damn them. No prizes — by God, burn them to the waterline. How against the French? What difference did it make anyway? The God Damned French . . . Was there not yet a score to settle? He would pay them off. Ships and Cannon he had aplenty. What else was he to do with them anyway? They would not Idle at his Wharf.

The United States government? He owned more Vessels than they. Had it not always been so? There were times they had come a-begging and they were Damned for it. Once he had even had to pay its miserable bills to the wretched Bey of Tunis. Yes, it was all so clear; his mind was made up. Three or four Sail off Bordeaux. Long nines and Swivels. What could be more obvious? "King" Derby would understand. And where *was* "King" Derby all this while?

Never allow the crew to drink Rum below decks after Sundown for it led to Mutiny. Display the Cat for all to see. Nail it to the Masthead. Be an Anchor lost, they must Fish for it. Did they imagine he was made of Money? How the delay in his Voige? What? Who were they anyway? He knew; he had always known. Cowards, Crasey Fools to boot.

Water. He wanted water. The doctors insisted on brandy; he spat it out. "Why, God Damn you, give me cold water." A glass was brought and he drank it off. He glared about him. Once more the old Anglophobia surged, but the oath his lips formed was unspoken.

Two

A Voyage of Pleasure

George Crowninshield, Jr.
(1766–1817)

From along the banks of clear streams falling to the sea, the leaves of the pandanus had been gathered for days. Great piles of the stuff were woven into thousands of yards of rope and then twelve ropes into cables as thick as a man's arm and this in a country of muscular men. Only the strongest from all over the island were wanted on the beach that day in the name of Kamehameha II, King of Hawaii.

When at last the cables were stretched along the sand toward the mountains, powerful swimmers carried them through the surf to the wreck that lay on her side in ten feet of water, masts pointing seaward. The throngs summoned took their places along the cables and a wrinkled but still authoritative chieftain solemnly enjoined the massed ranks to silence. They were to grasp the cables firmly, rise together at the signal, and facing the mountains, to pull with all their might — never should they look back toward the sea — and so instructed, they sat quietly in the sand until a priest intoned:

> *Hearken by night, and hear by day, O Lono*
> *Come for the tree, and take to the sea-side . . .*

The plea to the most ancient and efficacious of Hawaiian gods had for centuries been sung to marshal human effort when a large tree for a canoe had to be dragged down to the sea. But on this April day in 1824, it was no log they sought to drag down a mountainside, but a brigantine of nearly two hundred tons burthen, the King's personal yacht, and they were to wrest it from an unwilling sea over a reef and onto the shore.

77

A Boston missionary, Hiram Bingham, who witnessed the scene, wrote: "The multitude quietly listening some six or eight minutes, at a particular turn or passage in the song indicating the order to march, rose together, and as the song continued with increasing volubility and force, slowly moved forward in silence; and all leaning from the shore, strained their huge ropes, tugging together to heave up the vessel. The brig felt their power — rolled up slowly towards the shore, upon her keel, till her side came firmly against the rock, and there instantly stopped; but the immense team moved on unchecked; and the main-mast broke and fell with its shrouds, being taken off by the cables drawn by unaided muscular strength. The hull instantly rolled back to her former place, and was considered irrecoverable. The interest of the scene was much heightened by the fact that a large man by the name of Kiu, who had ascended the standing shrouds, being near the main-top when the hull began to move, was descending when the mast broke, and was seen to come down suddenly and simultaneously with it in its fall. Strong apprehensions were felt on shore that he was killed amidst the ruins. Numbers hastened from the shore to the wreck, to see the effects of their pull and to look after Kiu. He was found amusing himself swimming about."

King Kamehameha II would not have been at all amused to learn of the loss of his most prized possession, the swift and beautiful brig he called *Haaheo o Hawaii* (*Pride of Hawaii*). But then Kamehameha would never know. He had been away visiting George IV in England (whom he regarded simply as a distant, if somewhat more affluent, brother); and in the royal absence some of his retainers had gone for a sail. Off the windward side of Kauai everyone on board, including the captain, had gotten thoroughly drunk on a local favorite, New England rum, and the vessel had gone aground.

King Kamehameha had first seen the yacht four years before in Lahaina Roads, Maui, and from the beginning he had adored her. She had been brought there by Captain John Suter of Boston for the express purpose of unloading her at the highest price to Kamehameha, who was, in the view of Samuel Eliot Morison, "a weak-minded and dissolute prince," who "cheerfully stripped his royal domain in order to gratify tastes which the Boston traders stimulated. They sold him on credit rum and brandy, gin and champagne, carriages and harnesses, clothes and furniture, boats and vessels, until he had tonnage and liquor enough for an old-time yacht club cruise." But in truth the champagne and gaudy trappings signaled the terrible, mute desperation of an exotic insect hopelessly transfixed between pin and mounting board: the island King was caught squarely between the English and the Americans.

In any event, while Kamehameha had indeed wanted the brig at any price, at the moment he had no money. This problem was deferred by a credit arrangement whereby the King promised to pay for the ship in future and exorbitant deliveries of sandalwood, an aromatic much in demand in China. The Yankee had been pleased and the King, delirious with joy, had hurriedly put to sea among the islands of his domain.

The maiden voyage of *Pride of Hawaii* was also recorded by Hiram Bingham: "Unexpectedly arriving at Honolulu, the firing of the guns at night in Waikiki Bay, announced the King's approach, and our village was soon in an uproar. The loud roar of the cannon . . . from the fort, and Punch-bowl Hill — the successive flashing of their blaze on the dark curtain of the night, and the reverberating echoes from the hills and valleys of their report — the shouting of the noisy natives, and the voice of the crier demanding hogs, dogs, poi, etc. to be gathered for the reception of his majesty (who was in his cups), formed a combination of the sublime and the ridiculous not soon to be forgotten by the missionaries. The King landed Sabbath morning, amid the continued noise, which was now increased by the yelping and crying dogs, tied on poles, and brought in for slaughter."

Pronouncing the shakedown cruise a great success, King Kamehameha shortly resolved to put his vessel to a more practical purpose. In July 1821, with five wives in tow, the tipsy monarch set sail for Kauai, one of the more westerly of the Hawaiian Islands. There, after weeks of merrymaking, he kidnapped his host, the even more drunken Kaumalii, and swept him off in the royal yacht to exile in Honolulu.

But above all, *Pride of Hawaii* had allowed the royal ruler to confound such Christian missionaries as Hiram Bingham, who arrived in numbers during the first quarter of the nineteenth century and whom the King found increasingly tiresome. When their importunities, laden with fire and brimstone imported from Boston, became unbearable, he simply put to sea for a while with his wives and plenty of champagne. And now his yacht, at once so beautiful and useful, was gone forever.

Nor had Kamehameha's trip to England been a success. To start with, niggardly English advisors in Hawaii had insisted that he be accompanied by only one wife. Annoyed, but also wishing to make the best impression on George IV, he had selected the most imposing, Kamamalu, who was six and a half feet tall. With $25,000 in a strongbox and Kamamalu, the King sailed for England late in 1823. En route, he stopped at Rio de Janeiro and had been pleasantly enough entertained by Dom Pedro, but upon arriving in London, he discovered he had been robbed of most of his cash.

Worse followed, for Kamehameha and his queen found English weather cold and England cold in other ways. He wanted the British to protect him from the Americans and could not understand the easy, bland equivocations of King George's ministers. Nor was the atmosphere improved when the English ruler casually referred to Kamehameha's domains as "our Royal Sandwich Islands," or when he alluded, not very privately, to Kamehameha and his weighty spouse as "a pair of cannibals." Again and again the royal audience was postponed, and it looked as though George IV was in a fair way to administer a snub. Killing time, the pair visited Westminster Abbey, where Kamamalu bolted her pew and made for the door at the boom of the organ. Kamehameha, unmoved, had stared at the ornate ceiling, wondering what held it up. In England the only happy moment had been when his entourage found a grey mullet in a London fish market. Delighted, they carried the delicacy to their hotel and consumed it raw along with twenty bottles of wine. And that was the end of happiness. Kamehameha and his queen contracted measles; they lacked resistance to the disease; and in England, without ever meeting George IV, they died.

80

THEIR MAJESTIES
KING RHEO RHIO, QUEEN KAMEHAMEHA; MADAME POKI,

The Hawaiian royal family in England, 1823–1824. Courtesy of the Peabody Museum of Salem

George Crowninshield, Jr. Courtesy of the Peabody Museum of Salem

The dead King's ship, washed by the surf off Hanalei, had been for a while a packet ship between Boston and Charleston, South Carolina. But in the beginning she was *Cleopatra's Barge* of Salem.

An oil portrait in the Peabody Museum of Salem shows a seated, thickset figure gazing at some presumably marine vista. He clasps a telescope in his lap. Below the plump face there is scarcely a chin; above, the eyes are large and blue. The features are arranged in a kind of self-imposed severity their owner evidently thought commanding and therefore fitting. Clearly the subject has composed himself for a role, and the compressed lips and sideward glance of the eyes suggest that it would be unwise to interfere with it. In the background, framed by drapery that never was, a handsome brig under full sail battles the deep. The ship is *Cleopatra's Barge*, the first American vessel built solely as a seagoing pleasure yacht, and the man is her owner, George Crowninshield, Jr.

Born in 1766, he was the eldest son of Mary Derby and George Crowninshield. By 1815, as has been seen, the family fortunes had been made, and with their consolidation, enthusiasm to augment them waned. Henceforth it was to be a matter of preserving wealth through investments less precarious than the sea that had given it. The place of George Jr. in the family partnership had not been that of master of vessel or merchant. Rather, his talents had been absorbed in the minutiae of outfitting ships. His childhood schooling had been neglected or perhaps, because he was uneducable, omitted. In any case, all his life he could scarcely read or write and loathed to do both. Unlike his brothers, he spent most of his time at home in Salem. As may happen among sons too long with their mothers, George Jr. never acquired a wife. He had, however, a certain reputation.

First and foremost he was enchanted by the excitement of fire fighting, the shiny, clattering machinery rushing about, and by the possibility that latent within the confusion some heroic role awaited him. Another and more dependable source of pleasure was his splendid curricle (a light two-wheeled carriage drawn by two horses abreast) of canary yellow, always certain to attract attention as it raced along the narrow streets of Salem to no particular purpose. No one else had anything like it; nor could its driver be mistaken for any other Salemite: George was always clad as colorfully as his curricle. His coats were expensively, if oddly, cut to specifications of his own design, and more striking still were his waistcoats appliquéd with such eye-catching patterns and devices as caught a restless fancy. He favored high Hessian boots of glittering black from which tassels of red and gold swirled madly. George Crowninshield, Jr., crowned his heavily powdered pigtail with an enormous, shaggy beaverskin hat somewhat akin to the busbies of the Coldstream Guards. While there were those in Salem who were struck dumb with admiration, others, perhaps more numerous, were not.

The rescue of persons in danger at sea was another consuming passion. More than once, we are told, George boldly jumped overboard to save people from drowning, and after one such occasion in 1801 he was awarded the Gold Medal of the Massachusetts Humane Society. Nevertheless, some mariners were inclined to think that when they were endangered at sea, the true peril was likely to arise when George Crowninshield exuberantly arrived on the scene. He treasured the Society's award, carried it with him always, and was fond of displaying it to puzzled strangers at the moment of introduction. Yet his accomplishments were attended by strangely patterned extremes of gaiety and gloom — the dappled sunlight harshly bright, the shade too somber. He was not a happy man.

It seems likely that George Jr. would have remained an irritating but harmless village spectacle had it not been for the sensational events of June 1, 1813. That day, off Marblehead, the United States warship *Chesapeake*, commanded by a Captain Lawrence, whose crew was as cowardly and mutinous as Lawrence was brave, was trapped by H.M.S. *Shannon* after having refused a challenge from the British man-of-war earlier that day. Professionalism carried the battle in exactly eleven minutes. Although Captain Lawrence, mortally wounded, uttered the words later transmuted by a nation starved of success into the resonance of "Don't give up the ship," immediately it was given up. With *Chesapeake* and her dead, who included, besides Captain Lawrence, a Lieutenant Ludlow, the triumphant British sailed for Halifax, Nova Scotia. For the Americans nothing was to be salvaged from the debacle except the exasperations of Lawrence — but the episode was to have a curious effect on George Crowninshield.

Some weeks later, a Salem sea captain named Joseph White suggested the propriety of an American party's going to Halifax to bring home the bodies of Lawrence and Ludlow, which had been buried there with full naval honors by the victors. The expenses would be shared by several Salem men of substance. George leaped at the idea. A Crowninshield ship, *Henry*, sailed to Halifax, where George was received by the enemy with the greatest cordiality. Lawrence and Ludlow were returned home. A Salem historian, James Duncan Phillips, has described the subsequent events: "On August 24, the bodies which had remained on the 'Henry,' which was draped in black, were removed on barges by sailors in uniform rowing minute strokes, while the 'Henry' and the United States brig, 'Rattlesnake,' fired minute guns, and landed on India (now Phillip's) Wharf. All the vessels in the harbor wore their flags at half-mast. Then a procession was formed at one o'clock under Major John Saunders. The two hearses, preceded by the Salem Light Infantry and accompanied by the pallbearers — Captains Hull, Bainbridge, Creighton, Stewart, and Blakely, and Lieutenants Bullard and Wilkinson of the United States Navy — and followed by the town officers, the Marine Societies, and other distinguished citizens of Salem, Boston, and the vicinity, proceeded through densely crowded streets to the Branch Church on Howard Street while the Salem Artillery fired minute guns on the Common. The windows of the line of march and even the housetops were crowded with spectators, while the bells on most of the churches tolled."

Very much present was George, ecstatic with pleasure. He had given it out that the idea had been his, as had been the expenses. Overnight, although he had never heard a shot fired in anger except from afar, he became as great a hero as Lawrence. For a trifling investment and a couple of fibs, he was now the subject of the most expansive accolades. Adulatory broadsides were printed, the newspapers praised him lavishly, and George's parched soul drank deeply of the heady stuff.

Inevitably there were detractors, notably in Philadelphia, who averred that "Crowninshield had gone to Halifax under the pretense of bringing home the dead bodies of our naval heroes, but really in the hope of making a fortune by the purchase of American prizes" (a much frowned-upon kind of profiteering in the War of 1812). But the Philadelphia spoilsports were wrong. To bask in the glory and drama of Lawrence was all George had wanted. And if he could cause that glory to be refracted the more brightly, so much the better for him and for that matter Lawrence, who of course had nothing further to say anyway.

The recipient of the Humane Society's gold medal had discovered that heroic scenes of great moment, like rescues at sea, need not be fortuitous: they could be staged. The thirst raised by the Lawrence episode had always been there and it would never again be slaked, much less by the fire engines of Salem or his yellow curricle.

Two years later, in 1815, George found himself forty-nine years old with a fortune and nothing really to do. For some months he toured the Mississippi, and one day in Kentucky he marveled at the "Dear Running Wild in the Woods" and at the "2 Bears" which "past Us one Day & would Not run for us altho we made all the Noys we Could." But such splendid occasions were few and the restless man returned to Salem, where he amused himself with small-scale philanthropy (it was noticed that if these activities failed to attract the widest notice, the Crowninshield beneficence would suddenly abate and the donor fall into dark and disagreeable moods). He drank little and was indifferent to what he drank — so indifferent, in fact, that he frequently mistook wine for brandy. He rarely found pleasure in the company of women and then only in those of the lowest sort. Ignorant, painted whores were most to his taste, but it was not their sexual favors he purchased. He prized a far more valuable commodity — an unqualified admiration for him and all his works.

The truth was that he loved himself above all — a love the chunky little man in the tasseled Hessian boots and shaggy busby found best gratified in pageantry. The tableau might be blurred, contrived, even specious, the illumination strange and confusing; yet if the scene had color and drama, was peopled with great figures and included himself prominently, then no man was more genial than George Crowninshield, Jr.

But in Salem, then as now, the elements of such a scene were sadly lacking. In fact they could not be found anywhere in the country, for the great of America were colorless and drab to George. Perhaps he knew them too well: Madison, Monroe and Jefferson were close family friends. Jefferson in particular, with his shabby breeches of red corduroy and his even more revolting habit of tying his own horse in front of the White House to save the expense of a servant, was easily the most regrettable of the lot.

Now Europe was another thing. There, great families moved amid endless pomp and circumstance. George particularly admired Charlotte, the conspicuous Princess of Wales and heiress apparent to the English throne. Young and beautiful, she was the toast of Europe, admired wherever she went, glittering with resplendent gems and always surrounded by great personages. If only he could be in her presence, some of the splendor would be his. But for some reason Salem, Massachusetts, had not been included in the magnificent peregrinations of the Princess of Wales.

If Charlotte was George's storybook princess, Napoleon Bonaparte was greater yet; he was everything a man could be and George's admiration for him was boundless. In fact there were times (while chasing a fire in his yellow curricle) when he imagined that he shared many of Napoleon's attributes, a fancy his whores, after a round or two of drinks, were ready enough to confirm. But the Emperor of the French now languished on St. Helena, an extinct volcano, where his stomach was slowly being consumed by cancer and he was reduced to quibbling with his English keepers over such imperial matters as this or that day's wine allowance. No, it did not look as though the Emperor would ever visit George in Salem. Still there was Lucien, Prince of Canino, and what could be wrong with the Prince of Canino if he was the brother of Napoleon?

But how to be among such great personages? The answer was simple — if they would not come to him, he would go to them, and to assure the most favorable reception, he would go magnificently, as no American had gone before. He would build a beautiful and luxurious vessel. They would not be able to resist it or him. There would be lavish entertainments aboard in every port of Europe, and what a figure he would cut, the talk of two continents! It would be a voyage of pleasure without precedent or parallel. A memory arose of the elephant his brother Jacob had brought from India in 1797 and the stir Jacob had created. George would go his brother one better: he would return from his voyage with some greater trophy to display.

Ships in early nineteenth century America, as before, were designed and built for strictly utilitarian purposes. Whaler and warship alike might have certain frills, provided they in no way whatever detracted from any essential function — and provided the frills were inexpensive. And in early nineteenth century America, as before, pleasure was not regarded as the essential function of anything. It should not be thought that this attitude stemmed altogether from the so-called Protestant Ethic. The men like George's father who amassed trading and privateering fortunes of a vastness not seen before in America felt no inherent revulsion towards hedonism. Yet it was impossible for them to forget that they had become rich, not by brilliant, bold strokes, but by painstaking attention to detail and the assumption of carefully calculated risks all too frequently attended by fearful losses. To the extent pleasure interfered with profit it became a sin not against God but against the ledger books, a class of literature less forgiving than Holy Writ.

We shall never know what thoughts passed through the sober, sixty-three-year-old brain of Retire Becket on the spring day in 1816 when George Crowninshield called to reveal his plans. "Tyrey" Becket was descended from a family who had been building ships in Salem since 1655. Each Becket generation built better than the last, and many of their ships were regarded as masterpieces; but Tyrey, with all his accumulated experience and expertise, had never dreamed of the sort of thing George had in mind. The dour artisan could think of no precedent, but his thoughts finally turned to the swift and successful privateer *America IV*, which he had built for the Crowninshields in 1803. Although *America IV* had been intended as a merchant ship of six hundred tons, Becket had converted her into a privateer of twenty guns in 1812 by cutting her down — "razeeing," as the process was called — and greatly increasing her sail area and speed. So modified, the ship had never been outsailed; she would be Becket's model for George's ship.

The vessel that took shape in the mind and shipyard of Retire Becket resembled nothing in appearance so much as a small man-of-war — a hermaphrodite brigantine (rigged square on the foremast and fore-and-aft on the mainmast) of 192 $41/95$ tons, 83 feet on the waterline, 22 feet 11½ inches on the beam, and 11 feet 5½ inches of draught. Within six months she was completed and no expense was spared. While still on the stocks, her spars were on end, her yards crossed and her rigging set up so that apart from cabin furnishings she was almost ready for the sea when she was launched on October 16, 1816.

The vessel did not resemble a man-of-war in other ways. She was gaily painted in a variety of bright colors; to starboard she was a series of contrasting horizontal bands, while to port an elaborate her-ringbone pattern of gilt and enamel glowed above the translucent waters of Salem Harbor. Every facet of the hull susceptible to gilding had been covered with gold leaf, and in addition to the splendid figure-head adorning her bow, a large and brightly painted wooden Indian in war paint and with feathers and arrows served as pendant to the capstan.

But it was the interior of the vessel that was most surprising. Dr. Bentley, one of the first to inspect her, wrote on December 6, 1816: "By invitation I visited the Hermaph. Brig. . . . lately built by Capt. G. Crowninshield, and now fitted for sea in a manner never before observed in this Town. Her model is excellent and her naval Architecture the best. The rigging is in the highest improvement as to its form and complete & of the best materials and workmanship. The best patent

Cleopatra's Barge. *View of the port side. Painting by George Ropes, 1818. Courtesy of the Peabody Museum of Salem*

Cleopatra's Barge. *Reconstruction of the main cabin on display at the Peabody Museum. Courtesy of the Peabody Museum of Salem*

horizontal windlass with two stations just aft of the foremast. A rudder fixed to move with great ease and safety upon a new patent. The belaying pins of the Mast of brass. Below is the berth for the officers. Next is the dining-room finished of the best materials & furnished with the best carpets, elegant settees with velvet cushions, chairs with descriptive paintings, mirrors, buffets loaded with plate of every name, and the best glass and porcelain. Adjoining are the berths for the owner and passengers with apartments having all the articles for the ship assigned to their own particular vessels and beyond about midship the kitchen with all the necessary furniture for its purposes. In the forepart of the vessel are the berths of the seamen. The expence must have been very great but the aid to improvement and enquiry is great and extensive."

Dr. Bentley added: "Nothing has been suffered to enter not in the highest style of excellence. I should have been very glad to have had an inventory of the contents of this vessel."

Perhaps Miss Mary Williams, writing to a young friend, came closer to the inventory Dr. Bentley lacked: "The sleeping room is very pretty, the hangings of the bed a rich variegated yellow patch, full curtains and handsome fringe. We found a yellow cat lying on the bed; the captain said she came on board of her own accord, and had chosen her position, and he intended to take her with him for good luck. His 'hall,' as he styles it, is large and lighted from the top; in the centre hangs a superb lamp that cost $150. The beams of the ceiling are edged with a gilt beading, and two ropes covered with red silk velvet twisted with gold cord are passed along, to take hold of when the vessel rolls. There are two elegant sofas, about the length of four chairs each, the seats of similar velvet; a border of gold lace on the edge and a deep red fringe. The design on the back is four harps [lyres], the strings of large brass wire, and the wood mahogany and burnt maple. Cost $400. A Brussels carpet, orange color and brown with a mixture of green; two square mirrors at opposite ends, with gilt frames; a lamp each side, with a gilt eagle standing by. The finish of the room, maple and mahogany varnished; columns with gilt capitals alternated with cupboards, through the glazed door of which we saw the china and glass. . . . The plate is very rich; a superb tea-urn, twelve or fifteen inches high, with a lamp underneath, sugar dish and cream pitcher corresponding, and two dozen tumblers. Captain George unfolded the table linen and showed us his kitchen. Beside all these rooms . . . is another in the stern, which serves as a drawing-room to the 'hall.' In the foreward part are the sailors' rooms, where we did not go; staterooms with curtains. The sailors are dressed uniformly. The capstan I admire, but must tell you about that when we meet. It is matched by the figure of an Indian, with his arrows on his back, to stand on deck. Among all these beauties I have neglected an important one. Under the mirrors at each end of the room is a large golden cornucopia, and around the walls as a cornice is a row of gilt hat-pins, perhaps for the King of Naples to hang his hat on, as I hear the captain says the royal guest is to sit on that sofa."

The yellow cat Mary Williams saw lying on the bed was Pompey. Pompey had not wandered on board as George said, but had been brought from the Crowninshield farm in Danvers and was an example of George's quickness to distort even small matters. The tabby was named after a British ship that had been captured by Salem privateers in the Revolutionary War and renamed *America*, becoming the first of four Crowninshield vessels of that name. The golden cornucopia Miss Williams feared to neglect was in keeping with the brig's name, *Car of Concordia*. But suddenly, for unknown reasons, George changed it to *Cleopatra's Barge*, provoking ridicule from certain members of the family, who thought it "foolish" and that it would "be laughed at." There was, however, some hazard in mocking the hero of the Massachusetts Humane Society, and on December 16, 1816, George settled the score: "If I should die on my voyage, it's my wish and desire that Sally Crowninshield my sister and John Crowninshield my brother should have only one ten dollar bill apiece."

After a private showing, the yacht was thrown open to the public, and on January 14, 1817, the Salem *Gazette*, which had given over in its struggle with "our family," enthused: "The elegant equipment of this vessel, by Mr. Crowninshield, for a voyage of pleasure, as it is an entire novelty in this country, has excited universal curiosity and admiration. Whilst she was lying at the wharf in Salem, we have heard she attracted company from various surrounding places to view so

perfect a specimen of nautical architecture and sumptuous accommo-
dation. Eighteen hundred ladies, it is asserted, visited her in the course
of one day. 'Cleopatra's Barge' measures about 200 tons, and is
modeled after one of the swiftest sailing ships which was ever driven
by the wind. Being introduced on board, you descend into a magnificent saloon, about 20 feet long and 19 broad, finished on all sides with
polished mahogany, inlaid with other ornamental wood. . . . The after
cabin contains sleeping accommodations for the under officers of the
vessel. The owner's and captain's staterooms are very commodious.
The conveniences for the kitchen and steward's apartments may be
considered models in their way. There are aqueducts in all parts of the
vessel which require them. The intention of Mr. Crowninshield, we
understand, is to proceed in the first instance to the Western Islands,
thence thro' the Straits of Gibraltar, and following the windings of
the left coast of the Mediterranean, will touch at every principal city
on the route, which will be around the Island of Sicily, up the Gulf of
Venice to Trieste, along the coast of Albania and the Morea, through
the Grecian Archipelago to the Dardanelles; if permitted by the Turk-
ish authorities he will proceed through the Sea of Marmora to Con-
stantinople; thence coasting along the ports of the Black Sea, to the
Sea of Asov, he will return by the way of the Isle of Cyrus, upon the
south side of the Mediterranean; stopping at Acre, Jerusalem and
Alexandria, on his way, and sailing by the Coast of the Desert to that
of the Barbary States. Emerging from the Straits he will proceed
through the British Channel and North sea, up the Baltic to Peters-
burgh, thence along the Coast of Norway to the North Cape, and perhaps into the White Sea.

"From this point," allowed the *Gazette*, "he may go to Spitzbergen
and Iceland, and thence crossing an immense ocean to the coast of
South America touching at various parts he will complete the tour of
his destination, and arrive at Salem."

George, who some thought would be gone as long as three years,
had wanted to embark before Christmas but the continous swarm of
visitors who came aboard was irresistible. On December 29, 1816, he
delightedly wrote his brother Benjamin, the Secretary of the Navy:
"You would be astonished to see the multitudes that visit my brig —

or yacht — as they call her. I have had 1900 women and 700 men in one day, and an average of over 900 per day for the past two weeks." It was far better than the Lawrence–Ludlow affair; there were no dead naval heroes lying about to detract attention from George.

Meanwhile the Secretary had procured more than three hundred letters of introduction for his brother's convenience wherever he might drop anchor. Among them are the following:

Boston, 20th December, 1816.

My Dear Sir

The bearer is George Crowninshield Esq. brother to the Hon Secretary of the Navy, visits Europe on a voyage of pleasure in his elegant "Cleopatra's Barge" which will exhibit honor to his country by her style of Architecture, and the elegant taste displayed in her equipment.

I have much pleasure in introducing Mr. Crowninshield to your acquaintance; and when I inform you that he is the gentleman who brought the Corpses of our gallant and lamented Officers — "Laurence [sic] and Ludlow" from an hostile land to their native shore, I am confident I need not add to the fact of so philanthropic a deed to insure to him your most friendly attention.

Your sincere friend
Wm Bainbridge

Commodore Isaac Chauncey
Commanding the U.S. Squadron in the Mediterranean

Washington, Nov. 27th, 1816.

Sir

Mr. Crowninshield a brother of our Secretary of the Navy intending to visit Europe, I take the liberty to introduce him to your acquaintance and kind attention. Independent, in his fortune, he travels for information and amusement only, and to the innocent and honorable nature of his pursuits he unites in his personal character every fair claim to the protection and good offices of our ministers in foreign countries.

With great respect and esteem I take the honor to be your very obedient servant.

Jas. Monroe

Honorable
John Q. Adams
Envoy Extra. & Minister Plenoʳ
of the United States At London

By the end of 1816, the proposed voyage of *Cleopatra's Barge* had attracted the attention of all who followed carefully the course of U.S. maritime affairs. George was happily besieged by people who wanted to go with him as naturalists, draftsmen and historians, and by others who simply wanted to seek pleasure at his expense. All were rejected. George chose as captain a first cousin, Benjamin Crowninshield, who, to avoid confusion with George's brother, then Secretary of the Navy, was called Sailor Ben. Also invited to go on the cruise was the Sailor's son, who was known as Philosopher Ben.

Although a female relative wrote off Sailor Ben as a "good natured, rattling, unprincipled man," he was something more than that. Then almost sixty, with a long nose, large pendulous ears and pale eyes, he was the finest type of New Englander. At the outbreak of the Revolutionary War he had been serving as midshipman on board a British man-of-war then stationed off the American coast. Immediately he had gone to the vessel's commander and asked to leave the ship. Permission was granted and, there being no American navy, the eighteen-year-old sailor offered his services to the Massachusetts militia and had been savagely wounded at the battle later known as Bunker Hill. In time he had become a merchant captain, an audacious privateer, and three times a prisoner of war of those whose navy he had joined as a child. A surprisingly gentle man, his letter of advice written in old age to a young man about to become a naval officer is something more than worldly. Spelled out in the spidery but unhesitant hand is a fundamental decency natural to the best Americans of his time and now largely vanished.

Philosopher Ben, the Sailor's son, was thirty-five, balding, a petulant individual of wide interests, and so called because of a distinct cast of mind. Should, for example, a man fall overboard, a more pedestrian intellect would think of rescue. The Sailor's son was more likely to wonder how it was that fish swam better than men, and the question would engender a series of loosely linked speculations on the nature of the universe rarely of benefit to a drowning man or to Philosopher Ben. He was dedicated to poetry, history (he was persuaded that Cheops bankrupted himself with the pyramids), astronomy, economics, medi-

"Philosopher Ben" Crownin-shield. Watercolor portrait, 1804. Courtesy of the Peabody Museum of Salem

"Sailor Ben" Crowninshield, master of Cleopatra's Barge. *Courtesy of the Peabody Museum of Salem*

cine, botany, weather statistics, Hebrew and, less academically, homosexuality. In old age (he lived until 1864), he amused himself by abstracting from Plymouth Colony records such items of interest as:

> Plym. Oct. 1660
> The wife of William Holmes being accused for being a witch, Dinah Sylvester testified 'that she saw a beare about a stone's throw from the path,' (which she took to be Holmes' wife) but being examined and asked what manor of tayle the beare had, she said she could not tell for his head was towards her. Holmes wife was released — At the next Court Dinah Sylvester was ordered to be whipped for slandering Holmes' wife — or to make a publick recantation and pay the costs of court. (she chose the latter) [sic]

And the misfortune of Richard Turtall, whose fate Philosopher Ben failed to record:

> 1655 Plymouth — We the grand jury present Richard Turtall for lascivious carriage toward Anne Hudson, the wife of John Hudson, in taking hold of her coat and enticing her by words, as also by taking out his Instrument of nature, that he might prevail to lye with her in her own house.

Homosexual peccadilloes had terminated his education, first in Cambridge, Massachusetts, and later at the College of William and Mary in Virginia. The precise cause of the Cambridge expulsion is obscured by illegible Latin, but the difficulty in Virginia is clear enough: in the view of the authorities there had been too many boys in one bed. Philosopher Ben was keen to continue his studies in Europe, having nothing else to do anyway.

The first mate would be Joseph Strout, experienced on many a Crowninshield vessel. Almost as experienced was William Dean, the quiet and efficient second mate. An old and prized sycophant of George's, Samuel Curwin Ward, was appointed clerk. Some years earlier, according to the Reverend Bentley, Samuel Ward, having "been much abroad from his family, often at the public Taverns, & very negligent of his affairs," had been "distrained upon by his Creditors" and "obliged to shut his doors." Sandy-haired and hooknosed, he would also be secretary to the owner, whose aversion to the written word was profound. Given to bluster and drink in more or less equal measure, Ward drew up the sailing documents for the *Barge*, which afford an example of the vivid epistolary style that so endeared him to George: "To one or more ports, places, cities, islands, townes, boroughs, villages, bays, harbours, basins, rivers, creeks, lakes, inlets, outlets, situated in the known world, between the latitude of the Cape of Good Hope, and the artic Circle, once or more times. . . ."

Of the crew the most remarkable were Hanson Posey, the "blackman steward," and William Chapman, the "blackman cook." Born a slave in Washington, Hanson Posey's manumission had been purchased by George's brother Jacob, and when his liberator died in 1808, Posey found his way to Salem. Wily and a tireless liar, he was as devoted to George as George was to him.

Chapman, the popular cook, had had a more singular history. As a boy he had sailed with Captain Cook on the early voyages of discovery. A few years after Cook was massacred in Hawaii, Chapman returned there and married a native girl. Living nearby was a man who confided to Chapman that in 1779 he was wandering in the woods near the spot where Cook had been killed. There he found some entrails which he ate, thinking them to be those of a pig. Subsequently he learned that they were those of the great explorer.

A trial run to Cape Ann was held on January 14, 1817. Everyone in town came on board and had a high time including a Captain Beach, who "was so badly off" he had to be put to bed and next morning found himself in Salem Harbor. By February, the *Barge* was icebound and George, powdered and dressed in a fur coat, traveled to and from his yacht in a horse-drawn sleigh, which caused his sister-in-law to remark that he appeared as "happy and satisfied with himself, as our boys are with their new sled."

March came. The harbor was free of ice. Yet George dallied. Was not another set of fish knives needed for the salon? Always, the *Barge* required more paint and gilt. When refurbishing was done in high winds, buckets of paint and gold leaf splashed overboard. Liveries of

99

green and gold (the Napoleonic colors) were procured for Hanson, the black steward, and for three of the youngest of the crew.

Finally at nine o'clock on the morning of March 30, 1817, to the cheers of "a great concourse of spectators" on India Wharf, the beautiful craft glided out of Salem Harbor carrying "Caesar and his fortunes," fourteen men, the three hundred letters of introduction, and Pompey, the yellow cat. Behind them *America IV* lay at anchor, where she would rot away and her cannon, muzzles down, would become fence posts. The voyage of pleasure and transatlantic lion hunt was under way.

In a letter to her husband on April 2, 1817, Mary Boardman Crowninshield struck an ominous chord: "I wrote you George sailed on Sunday. He even took young Ben as well as Old. Much is said about his choice of companions — and I am sorry — but they may appear better abroad than at home."

Cleopatra's Barge was swift and the trip to the Azores uneventful, except for certain peculiarities of her owner which officers and crew found puzzling. One of these was George's penchant for being guided by dreams, of which he had a great many. Should he, for example, dream of wild horses, a storm was imminent and the vessel had accordingly to be prepared for foul weather on even the most benign of days. This could be troublesome, for George very frequently dreamed of wild horses. Samuel Ward, the clerk, was given the job of properly logging the dizzying stuff of George's dreams lest they be forgotten and ignored, and when these portents were alcoholically transcribed by the hand of Ward, bizarre reading followed.

More dismaying to Sailor Ben was the owner's bent for sudden nautical innovation. One day in mid-Atlantic George concluded, after some reflection and a dream or two, that if all the ship's hatches were thrown open, the inward flow of air would lighten the hull and so increase the speed. It was no matter that rain might be falling on the Atlantic in solid sheets; the hatches remained open. But more mystifying yet was his occult manner of giving orders. Hardly ever was there a direct command; instead, there would be a series of carefully guarded

100

hints dropped over a period of time. Sometimes this was done by placing objects here or there, or by taking them away, and if their import (which of course had to be construed in the light of recent dreams as recorded by Ward) was not immediately grasped by all, George would fall into a sullen rage.

The landfall under the steep cliffs of Flores in the Azores on April 14, 1817, was inauspicious. Assuming the exotic vessel to be a Carthaginian pirate and her equally strange and colorful owner to be a pirate chieftain, the inhabitants refused to let George land. Nor was the ship's company favorably impressed when finally the fuss abated and they were allowed to come ashore. "Of all the nations, kindred and tongues," growled old Sailor Ben, "I never met with such a miserable set of beings as here offered themselves to our view, filthy, ragged and uncouth." Also piqued was Philosopher Ben, for his bald pate had been taken for that of a friar, in his view "one of the most disgusting sights . . . his head shaven and bare, a coarse woolen habit covering him, from the neck down to the heels, and tied round the waist with a cord. His fat paunch and rosy gills, with lumps of fat hanging about his jowls; and in this connection with the beastly life of lust and laziness he leads, eating the substance of the poor and industrious." Worse yet, he added, "They smell as strong as pole cats."

As the *Barge* sailed on, things began to look up. The American consul in Madeira threw a splendid ball in George's honor. In his turn George held a public reception on board, an event recorded morosely by Philosopher Ben in his diary: "Our vessel was filled with these characters, intermixed with hes and shes, puking on the stairs, on the carpet, and about the decks, rolling from side to side, drinking wine and running to and fro from the after cabin to the cook's room, presenting a scene of confusion that I am altogether unable to give an adequate description of. The space from our vessel to the shore was covered with boats, and alongside never less than fourteen, and sometimes more, fighting and running one another down to get alongside first. Such was the confusion that none on Board could get dinner regularly."

At Madeira, a dozen ducks were acquired and penned on deck.

These George intended for the table when the Princess of Wales joined him for dinner; no one was to touch them. At four o'clock on May 2, they stood off with a light breeze for Tangier, where George made further preparations for the reception of the Princess, and where Philosopher Ben inspected the Arab boys who hung about the quay. For five days the brig was painted and gilded.

At seven o'clock on the morning of May 14, in fine weather, *Barge* lay off the Rock of Gibraltar, which Philosopher Ben compared unfavorably with the Maine seacoast and the Mississippi River. A cabin was readied for the Princess of Wales. And to the anger of Philosopher Ben the pickles were locked up lest they be eaten by other than royalty. Oddly, George's eager inquiries after the Princess of Wales drew little response from the English authorities of the fortress. The Princess, they said, was not at Gibraltar, and wherever she was, they were careful to add, she was not "circumstanced" to receive George. He swallowed his disappointment; after all, Europe was full of princesses, many more beautiful than the English one, and probably richer too.

When the *Barge* left Gibraltar behind for Málaga, some small but vexing problems arose that were never to be solved. The fop of Salem had brought with him to Europe only three shirts and two pairs of pantaloons, and he adamantly refused to buy more. As a consequence, Hanson, the black servant, had to spend a great deal of time washing and ironing. And because he was also the steward, chaos erupted in the kitchen and dining room, especially when there might be, as in every port where the brig dropped anchor, a throng of visitors requiring the preparation of as many as four breakfasts in a morning.

Also trying was the fact that George had brought only one cheap razor. When it was spent, he borrowed, in turn, the razor of every man on board, and would return it only for as long as it took the owner to shave himself (George would stand there, hovering, until the shaving was done). But far more resented was his habit of refusing to tell anyone except Sailor Ben, who was enjoined to silence, what the next port of call would be. On the voyage of pleasure no one was ever to know where he was going.

After stops at Málaga and Cartagena, where the brig was painted and gilded again, she sailed on May 25 for Majorca, where the United

States naval squadron in the Mediterranean lay and where there occurred a serious incident. The officers of the American fleet extended every honor to George and his vessel. Elaborate dinners were exchanged; night after night the bands of the various warships serenaded *Cleopatra's Barge*. No entertainment was spared in honor of the brother of the Secretary of the Navy. But one bright Majorcan morning, George instructed Mr. Strout, the first mate, to visit the American warships and ask for anything he could get. Shamefacedly the mate made his rounds, begging for supplies, none of which were needed but which the puzzled naval officers tactfully gave. After one such foray, Strout returned with a small keg of copper nails and George, "as tickled as a child," sat fingering them in his gilt and velvet saloon. Next day at breakfast, Sailor Ben, who had been informed by Strout, gently reminded George that his wealth and position as a brother of the Secretary of the Navy made his behavior unseemly. It was of course the wrong thing to say to a man whose head was a cabochon of the finest water, whose very urine gleamed with incalculable portent, and who had been decorated by the Massachusetts Humane Society. George went white with anger. The matter, he swore, "touched his honor." Never again would he see the American fleet. Giving orders to sail at once for Barcelona, he locked himself in his cabin. And he was as good as his word. Never again would he entertain or be entertained by the United States Navy.

In six days at the Spanish port he wined and dined upwards of twenty thousand people. Philosopher Ben described a typical day: "Entertaining company by invitation at a troublesome breakfast, dinner, and supper; and in the meantime thronged with a crowd of canaille attracted by the wonders of the Cleopatra's Barge.

"They must see the saloon; examine the buffet; hear a dissertation on bird's eye maple; know the price of each article in America; take some wine; and then sit down till another crowd, eager to enjoy the same privilege, presses into the room; and what with seasickness among the ladies, the strong and offensive odour of friars, beggars, and garlic, the company below is obliged to undergo a regular inquisition.

"And now a more arduous task commences, for the saloon only has been seen. The owner's stateroom must be looked into, the after cabin for the officers must be investigated, and then the whole current must be concentrated in the narrow passageway in order to examine the kitchen. Unfortunately this current from the saloon (towards the kitchen) is met in its course by a more curious company from deck, descending the stairs and rushing like a sluice of 'Fleet Ditch' upon the counter. Here is jamming, and squeezing, and turbulence. Friars with thick hoods and fat bellies, generals, colonels, etc., etc., dressed for the occasion, priests in black robes, and hats of three feet in diameter, and ladies, aye of every sort, colour, and size, under heaven.

"Never was there such a group, never such a crowd, and smell, since the days of Noah's Ark. Charybdis was not more dangerous to ancient navigators. Here the two currents separate: one enters the saloon, the other presses on. On the right hand, they are shown the steward's room, filled with glasses, empty bottles, tinware, tiers of kegs, containing liquors, wine casks, pickle pots, etc., etc., presenting a picture of confusion not much unlike the crowd itself. From the steward's room on the right hand, they come to the 'necessary,' and then to the store-room, and lastly to the kitchen. Here Rumford himself would have had a task. For who can explain in Spanish, French, Italian, Latin, etc., the mysteries of boiling, roasting, baking, steaming, frying, etc.; and this must be done, for out of such a crowd, especially of ladies, there will be found some exceedingly curious person. From the kitchen they return through the narrow passage to the stairs, and, by constant perseverance, they arrive on deck, in the midst of a crowd that fills every point of space between the taffrel and the bowsprit. All passes off very well in a quiet sea, but when the vessel rolls, it is no uncommon sight to see 15 or 20 ladies and gentlemen, in a most miserable plight, reclining over the rail or stretched out on deck. Here is a scene which displeases every delicacy."

Barcelona was easily the most spectacular showing of the yacht since she had entered the Mediterranean. On June 7, a Saturday, "a lady far advanced in pregnancy on passing through the Cabin was so crowded that she was overtaken by the pains of labour and had to be carried on shore," and the evening was enlivened by a drunken Spanish army officer who forced his way on board with a pistol. Although George "turned away from 1800 to 2000 of the ragamuffin class" and "admitted none but genteel and well dressed people," curiously enough no princesses were among them. George's only Spanish notable was a fat, angry and perspiring general who asked to be put ashore as soon as possible.

Clearing Spain, the *Barge* entered Marseilles Harbor on June 11, where George chose to have part of her interior extensively remodeled for the reception of important but as yet unidentified guests who evidently would be living aboard for some time.

"The after cabin," an exasperated Philosopher Ben complained, "is covered with fresh paint. The kitchen is all in disorder, the sides of the vessel are painted, and a great number of touches and daubs make it impossible to move without smooching one's clothes. In every port we have entered, something or other of this kind has been going on. We have been here fifteen days, and have done nothing but alter and re-alter, change the colour of this part, retouch another; a black streak is made white, and a red one yellow, cream colour is made blue, and mahogany colour green; tassels of gold cord are taken down and others of silk substituted. Green velvet, gold tassels, silk, gold leaf, paper hangings, cushions, curtains, flower pots, clocks, musical seats, porcelain, painters, gilders, tinkers, blacksmiths, joiners, trimmers, upholsterers, ladies, gentlemen, whores, ragamuffins, etc., etc., are all on board continually; such are the materials of combination. Such is our amusement in Europe. We begin at daylight and go to bed in the middle of the night."

To the maddening din was added that of the several minstrels and guitarists on board, who strummed night and day, and the quacking of the ducks on deck, as yet spared a royal table. Pompey, the cat, hid as best she could below. The paint, never allowed to dry, ruined the Napoleonic liveries of green and gold and a good many of the guests' coats and gowns. Some seamen threatened to quit rather than go over the side in rough water and engage in the tricky business of applying gold leaf. But though one almost drowned, the gilding proceeded as before.

105

By the time the *Barge* reached Marseilles, her public entertainments assumed a certain formality. After George had spent the better part of the morning arranging his plate to the best advantage, Samuel Ward would open the saloon door and cry "*Cochon là*" to get visitors to remove their hats before entering the cabin. George would then give a kind of lecture (interpreted by Ward) on the boat and its furnishings. He was particularly anxious to represent every article on board as American in origin — although, in fact, a great many were of European manufacture. With perfect equanimity he would point to a French clock and say to a puzzled French visitor, "Manufacturez in America." In French ports he preferred to speak extremely bad Italian (and in Italian ports, worse French). The more eloquent Ward did most of the talking, as in this conversation with a Marseillaise about Napoleon's future: "No vietur — do you tink, he will reste in Saint Helena, or vene here? A present he reste a demi distance la New York." The response, if any there was, is unrecorded.

English visitors, especially, would ask George about the differences between the Federalists and Republicans in America, and he would explain that the Federalists were bad because they hated Napoleon. If pressed for more, George would turn on his heel. He disliked speaking with those who spoke his own language, avoided them, and frequently he angrily ran them off the yacht.

Visitors naturally wanted to know what the vessel had cost. The ship itself had cost $50,000 to build, and although there is no figure for the furnishings, it is not improbable that very nearly that sum was spent on them. The $50,000 figure George was fond of inflating; Ward fell in with the game and the sum was gleefully pushed upward at every port. Yet surprisingly, no French princess availed herself of these attractions.

If the crew had been greatly amused in Marseilles by a near-sighted Frenchman who mistook the painted Indian for the captain, doffed his hat and tried to introduce himself to it, there was little else to take pleasure in. The ship was fast becoming an unhappy one. George was convinced that people were stealing from him, as indeed they were in every port where he stopped. Quantities of plate, china, and practically everything movable had been stolen by the mob. He, however, was convinced that the loss lay with his officers and crew. At Marseilles cigars and all liquors except bad rum, brandy and some sour beer were locked up and the key tendered to Hanson. George also saw fit to entrust him with the ship's supply of cash, although Hanson could neither count to a hundred nor tell the truth. Hanson was also assuming duties of a different kind: George instructed him to spy on everyone on board, including Sailor Ben, and report their doings. This Hanson did for the remainder of the voyage, and nightly when he went to tuck George in bed, he had a stock of small stories frequently invented and invariably malicious. In such ways did the former slave find his way into the heart of the dreamer of wild horses. In July he commenced to sleep on top of the ship's money chest in George's room, and no man on board could expect to eat or drink without currying his favor.

Before long, George appropriated the entire afterpart of the vessel for his exclusive use; the officers and Philosopher Ben found themselves crammed into a small, uncomfortable cabin, together with Ward, two musicians, a cabin boy and the cook. The officers, including Sailor Ben, found that Hanson's services were reserved exclusively for George and fended for themselves as best they could. About this time, the first mate, Strout, reported to George that the supply of hams hanging below was rotting. George's response was something like this: "You like ham, don't you, Mr. Strout?" "Yes," replied Strout. "Very well," said George, "let them rot."

On July 2, 1817, the *Barge*, under way with a light air from the northwest, was making all sail for Toulon, for George had heard that the American fleet would soon be arriving in Marseilles. In spite of his having missed the channel and gone aground, things took a turn for the better at Toulon. The French authorities came on board for George's Fourth of July party and there was, according to Philosopher Ben, "every opportunity to learn the sentiments of the French officers respecting Napoleon. They whisper his name in the most expressive manner; they look at the eagles which ornament our cabin, put their hands upon them with the greatest affection, turn their eyes up to

107

Heaven, and oftentimes breathe a sigh which melts the heart. At the sound of his name they start into enthusiasm; and if you reciprocate their assertions, they seize your hands, clap you on the shoulder, and even embrace you. At the name of Louis no gesture expressive of contempt is omitted. At sight of the portraits of Blücher, Wellington, etc., they stamp, curse, and lose all patience, and this too, undisguisedly before us. In Toulon we find soldiers, heroes, and men of honour; in Marseilles, the meaner class of mercantile citizen, men whose politics and conduct depend upon commerce." But no princess accompanied them.

From Toulon the *Barge* sailed on to Genoa, where Philosopher Ben experienced "considerable inconvenience from swarms of fleas which are left on board by our visitors. But they are not so large nor so numerous as in Spain." Yet for George, Genoa was one of the more pleasant ports. First of all, the Baron de Zach, director of an observatory in Saxony, came on board and was lavish in his praise. "I will now relate what once I witnessed on board an American vessel, the Cleopatra's Barge, which arrived in the month of July, 1817, at the port of Genoa from Salem, one of the handsomest towns in the State of Massachusetts, U.S.A. Lat. 42 35 20 N., Long. 73 9 30 W. All the city crowded to see this magnificent palace of Neptune; more than 20,000 persons had visited this superb floating palace, and were astonished at its beauty, luxury, and magnificence. I went among the others. The owner was on board; he is a gentleman of fortune of Salem, who had amassed great riches during the late War with Great Britain. He was brother to the Secretary of the Navy of the United States. This elegant vessel was built for his own amusement, after his own ideas, upon a plan and model new in very many respects, and was considered the swiftest sailor in America. He had travelled or sailed for his pleasure in this costly jewel that appeared more the model of a cabinet of curiosities than a real vessel. He had left America in this charming shell for the purpose of visiting Europe and making the tour of the Mediterranean & had already touched at the ports of Spain. . . . What instruction! What order! What correctness! What magnificence! was to be observed in this Barge! I could relate many more interesting particulars concerning this true barque of Cleopatra!"

So, for that matter, could have the aged and nearly blind Lord Carrington, who came aboard for breakfast on July 13. George always reveled in titles, and on the voyage of pleasure certain deckhands augmented their pay by addressing him as "Most Illustrious Commander"; it was worth five dollars on the spot. When the Englishman addressed his host as "My Lord," George, suffused with pleasure, leaped from the table and ran about the deck delightedly telling everyone that a real English Lord had taken him for the same. Before returning to the breakfast table, he filled a flowerpot with eggs and enthusiastically toasted the perplexed and now silent Lord Carrington.

There were other delights ashore, one of them a battered hand organ he purchased for fifty dollars from a dumfounded street musician. That evening some Italian ladies came aboard to sing. Their delicate arias were accompanied by flutists and by George's discordant hand organ, the strange sounds drifting over the waters of Genoa Harbor. Thereafter, no entertainment on the *Barge* was complete without the organ, which was ground to pieces within weeks. When George tired of cranking it, someone else was given the job. The music went on.

Truly Genoa had been charming: the effusive Baron de Zach, the even more delightful Lord Carrington, and at times as many as forty boats alongside, full of visitors clamoring to see his ship. Assiduously avoiding the cruising American flotilla, George made for Leghorn on July 15, whence he would travel inland to Florence, where no doubt a princess awaited the stateroom so splendidly redecorated in Marseilles. Genoese royalty, it was true, had been scarce, yet he was in fine form and, when passing vessels were spoken, he leaned red-facedly far out over the taffrail to shout, "We are going to Italy for a princess!"

The Florentine princess in the fissured mind of the dreamer of wild horses was Empress Marie Louise, wife of Napoleon. She was, in 1817, blond, blue-eyed, with a slack Hapsburg jaw and an unquenchable libidinousness. She wore out her lovers and resented the two sentinels posted at her bedroom door because she could not conveniently bed them both. The Empress had also a tendency to eat enormous amounts of cream pastry, which made her sick, and when her

109

gold tongue scraper failed her, she would complain to the numerous and querulous physicians who flocked about her that she was pregnant and that she disliked children. At the age of twenty-seven she became the mother of Napoleon's son, the King of Rome (who to avoid any tedious, possibly hazardous, apprenticeship as heir apparent had been crowned at birth), and her once-remarkable figure was gone forever. When Napoleon was first exiled, Metternich, for political reasons, had not wanted her to go along. Nor had her father, Francis, the Emperor of Austria, who had a highly developed instinct for survival. After some thought, it was agreed to assign a career diplomat, Count Adam Adalbert von Neipperg, to keep her happy. He had done so. Shortly she was known as Mme. Neipperg and Napoleon governed in Elba without an empress.

His escape in 1815 had inconvenienced her and she had denounced him; within weeks the Battle of Waterloo settled the matter forever. In 1817 Napoleon was in exile again, this time on St. Helena, a very long way away. Marie Louise was rich, comfortably ensconced in Rome, and gave birth to the first in a series of indifferently concealed Neipperg bastards. She had absolutely no wish to have anything further to do with the former Emperor of the French except, of course, the title of Empress.

In Florence, George waited for days to entertain Marie Louise, and although he daily bombarded her with letters of introduction, he was brutally snubbed. The Empress would not even see him, and when he sent messages asking her to visit his beautiful ship, there had been that most mortifying of responses, none at all. Crushed and unhappy, he had to content himself with Napoleonic bric-a-brac purchased in the streets of Florence: some newly minted coins, some alabaster busts of the great man such as had for years been manufactured by the thousands for tourists.

Florence had been a disaster. Was it possible that the *Barge* was to have no Cleopatra? Storming back to Leghorn, George ordered that the yacht sail at three o'clock in the morning. He was heartily sick of Europe; he was going home to Salem. And then suddenly, without explanation, he canceled the order and made for the island of Elba. He did not speak for an entire day and George's disappointment must be shared by all, for the thought of the Empress Marie Louise and the hero of the Lawrence-Ludlow affair cruising about the Mediterranean on *Cleopatra's Barge* fevers the imagination.

On the yacht Hanson had become impossible. He insulted everyone with impunity; no one except George could get anything to eat or drink. One day Hanson found an empty bottle in Sailor Ben's cabin and insinuated that it had been stolen from the rum store. Hanson also liked to "creep up the stairway, slink over in the forechains and crawl along the main chains in order to eavesdrop." There he would stay for an hour "on pretense of disordered bowels" in order to provide his master with trifling shipboard gossip. In a way Hanson had replaced Ward as George's principal associate and confidant, for Ward was commonly so drunk he could not move from his bed and it was all he could do to roll over and foul on the splendid carpeting.

Indeed, Hanson had come very close to being in charge of the vessel and took pleasure in whipping a twelve-year-old cabin boy named Hodgdon for no reason at all; George stood by impassively, and no one dared interfere. Now George was fond of children and they of him, and in these beatings one senses uncomfortably: "As pedants out of the schoolboys breeches do claw and curry their own itches." After Florence, the owner took his meals alone, and one by one the ducks on the deck, reserved for royalty since Madeira, disappeared.

At Elba the harbor "was perfectly smooth and the gentlest breeze scarcely moved our vessel over the expanse" and "all was tranquility and peace." The words of Philosopher Ben turned out to be premature, for the moment George went ashore he hired a band to play the "Marseillaise" for the locals, much to the distress of the Bourbon authorities, who loathed the French Revolution, Napoleon, and all both stood for. The indiscretion somehow smoothed over, George toured the island and Philosopher Ben gathered and pressed Elban wildflowers. George acquired a piece of carpet from the room where Napoleon had usually slept, two tile fragments from the great man's bathroom, a bunch of grapes from the vines in front of the house, and a few apples. The fruit George intended to preserve.

And in Elba on the last day of July, George dictated to his clerk what is probably as insightful a document as any he has left behind: "At 1 P.M. set out on horseback accompanied by five gentlemen to visit a hermitage. On arriving there found a small building of two stories, built of stone and mortar, situated on a rock 350 feet high. This building was erected 310 years ago, at which time the Spanish had possession of this island.

"The hermit, who now occupies this place, is named Andrew Rose. He is 44 years old and has resided here 26 years. He haş no other companion than a large dog. This man told me that Napoleon had visited him twice, and that each time he refused refreshment. He said Napoleon joked with him very familiarly about living a single life, recommending him to marry.

"We tarried here one and a half hours, during which time we partook of two bottles of excellent muscat wine, which was very refreshing. The furniture of this house consists of one jug, a pitcher, a tumbler, and an iron hook bended for a gridiron. This hermit promised to lock up his dwelling and visit my brig, expressing his admiration at a view of her from the mountain. By this visit I have received great pleasure."

Napoleon had found the island a very agreeable refuge when his empire collapsed, and here, George, battered by the catastrophe of Florence, renewed his strength and resolved upon further campaigns in Italy. Once again all hands were employed in painting and gilding, although by now the surface of the *Barge* was almost entirely gold leaf. George's spirits had vastly improved when one day at Elba he bought a pair of Napoleon's boots that the Emperor had left behind because, it was said, they were too small for him. Hurrying on board George tried to put them on. But they were too small. No matter — had he not always known that his feet were the same size as the Emperor's? He had enjoyed his visit with Andrew Rose, the hermit; he had Napoleon's boots; and he was ready for his new Italian venture. He would go to Rome where, if there was no Marie Louise, there were plenty of Bonapartes.

But the Crowninshield elation might have been dampened had he

112

Napoleonic relics collected by George Crowninshield, Jr., during his "voyage of pleasure." Courtesy of the Peabody Museum of Salem

Cleopatra's Barge. *The master stateroom. Courtesy of the Peabody Museum of Salem.*

not been oblivious to what everyone else on the yacht, and not a few in Rome, had been aware of for some time. *Cleopatra's Barge* with her fantastically variegated hues, her herringbone-patterned port hull, her painted Indian, and her bizarre and buffoonlike owner had become known as the "Harlequin of the Mediterranean."

Among the Bonapartes in Rome awaiting the not very stealthy approach of the Hessian-booted lion hunter from Salem was Lucien, Prince of Canino and brother of Napoleon. The Prince was forty-two years of age in 1817, and the distrust he had had for his brother from childhood had given way to dislike when Napoleon, in need of money, had sold Louisiana to the United States. At one fell swoop, Lucien had been deprived of his principal income: the sale of land, offices, and trade concessions in the New World. In addition to extravagant display of an Italianate sort, the Prince liked to give classical names to his friends (reserving Brutus for himself), and was also given to indiscriminate fornication. He was not stupid. In Imperial days, when Pope Pius VII had been short of cash, Lucien had purchased the estates of Canino from him, a good investment because the Emperor's fall in no way disturbed either Lucien's Italian possessions or his title. In fact, one feels that the fall meant very little to him at all. In Rome he lived quietly — or at least as quietly as any Bonaparte ever did — and well.

Once a Corsican beauty, Pauline, one of Napoleon's sisters, was vain, stupid, and for some reason extraordinarily fond of displaying her feet (she gave receptions for the purpose). It is said she liked to warm them in the breasts of her female attendants, who stretched out on the floor for the warming. A nymphomaniac, she was frequently exhausted and had to be carted about Rome in a kind of portable bed.

And there was Napoleon's uncle, Cardinal Fesch, who had grown rich purveying arms and supplies of equal inferiority to Napoleonic armies in Italy. In 1817 he was fifty-six years of age, a glutton, very wise, and the possessor of the most spectacular collection of French, Dutch and Italian primitives in Europe, some of which, it was whispered, he had even paid for.

114

The Cardinal's sister (and Napoleon's mother), Madame Mère, was unaffected and very difficult to fool. At the time of her son's first exile, Madame Mère had simply removed to Italy, unaffectedly taking with her something like fifteen million francs.

In Rome, this clamorous, heavy-lidded clan connived endlessly against everyone and of course against each other; and they all displayed a Corsican wiliness in exploiting Napoleonic exile as they had the days of Imperial power. They were consummate stage managers and the tableaux were irresistible to many.

And they were delighted to see George. Immediately and dramatically he announced his intention of "rescuing" Madame Mère and escorting her to the New World. But although George pursued the theme for a week, unaccountably the mother of Napoleon still did not seem to understand. The Cardinal showed George his art collection and asked him how he had gotten his money. Lucien, Prince of Canino, was charming but somehow not anxious to go to America. After nine days of this, it was the gracious Pauline who came to the rescue of the would-be saviour of Madame Mère. She produced Napoleon's adopted son, who indeed wanted to go to America with George, a sentiment solemnly echoed by all the Bonapartes and Cardinal Fesch.

For Crowninshield, while it was not quite the same thing as bringing the Princess of Wales to Salem or Empress Marie Louise or even Prince Lucien to Salem, an adopted son of the Emperor who had been recommended by a princess was better than nothing and would fill a stateroom. George would, Pauline was sure, understand that while the young man was penniless at the moment, a very great fortune, an empire perhaps, would someday be his. The understanding George, with an armload of Napoleonic trinkets (including a lock of hair Pauline had grandly clipped off for him) and the very silent adopted son of the Great Man, sped for Civitavecchia, where the yacht lay at anchor. On reaching port the new passenger confused his host by picking up four of his friends who would be going to America with him. It was, he explained, a package deal. Had not Pauline told George?

On August 18, 1817, the yacht set sail for Salem, and somewhere in the Tyrrhenian Sea the terrible truth broke. Napoleon's "adopted" son was not that at all; he and his companions were simply impoverished fops who had been hanging around Pauline and whom she had wished to be rid of. They, in their turn, having found the Roman pickings slim, were agreeable to going elsewhere, anywhere. The Bonapartes had taken the measure of George Crowninshield, Jr.: the lion hunter had been bagged by the lions.

Wretched, George did the only thing he could: he pretended his guests did not exist. After pausing at Gibraltar on September 2, the "Harlequin of the Mediterranean" sailed at four o'clock with a fair wind and was soon out of sight with her French prizes. Philosopher Ben, sated with the voyage of pleasure and determined to see Europe without a paintbrush, remained behind in Gibraltar, where he vented his spleen on George: "He is the greatest lump of deception in the whole world of man. . . . his conduct is so extraordinary, and is so contradictory and absurd, that no man, under an acquaintance of two or three months would be able to unravel it."

By October 3, 1817, the *Barge* was once again moored along Crowninshield Wharf and the Frenchmen had filed off silently into obscurity. The Reverend Bentley, in the columns of the Salem *Register*, editorialized: "The celebrated BARGE OF CLEOPATRA has returned to our port. She has displayed in Europe the first example of a visit to European ports, in a vessel which had no other object than a view of the commercial cities which Europe contains. The visit is in the style of our American researches." Probably the Reverend Bentley was right. There *was* something very American about the voyage.

At any rate, George seemed in good spirits again (he had been rather glum until the Frenchmen had melted away). Yet in spite of his robust appearance, to a settled paranoia had been added the searing pains of angina pectoris. He had no house in Salem, disliked living with relatives, and lodged with an old girl friend at a seedy inn a few miles to the south of the town. As much as he liked the place, he found it impossible to get a good night's sleep. He was troubled by strange knockings, eerie groanings and voices that spoke to him of the hereafter. His paramour seemed oblivious to these sounds and when he complained to the innkeeper, the response was a dumfounded stare. George quit the inn and went to live on board the yacht in Salem Harbor with Hanson and other servants.

Now his thoughts turned to another voyage of pleasure, this time to England, the North Sea and the Baltic. Never again would he go to the Mediterranean. He disliked Spaniards, the French were no better, and the Italians worse. Surely in Sweden, or better yet Russia (did not St. Petersburg abound with notables?), he would be given a reception to his taste. Of course the *Barge* would have to be refurbished, but why not? There was nothing to keep him in Salem, and the yacht would be more magnificent than ever. Once more he ordered her gilded.

An old friend, John Dodge, came aboard for supper on November 9, and afterwards they sat before a fire of coals in the galley. George's florid face glistened with pleasure as he described a new and more spectacular cruise. Yet as he talked he huddled still more closely to the fire — behavior Dodge thought strange in a man long impervious to cold and much else. Dodge suggested that a brass chimney would carry the smoke off and be a handsome ornament. George readily agreed, and Dodge left his host in good humor.

But brass chimney or no, there was to be no other voyage of pleasure. About nine that evening George called Hanson, saying "I feel dreadfully," and asked for a glass of gin. Hanson turned to comply and his master pitched forward dead. The harlequinade was over.

Almost immediately, the Reverend Bentley was sent for. "I arose & went down to him," Bentley wrote. "The body was then prepared for the grave & lodged for the night in the elegant apartment of the Cleopatra. What an awful contrast when I sat with a shimmering taper by the body of my friend in the place which once gave him so much pleasure and now had become his tomb! What a contradiction between the gayest apartment I ever beheld & death!"

George Crowninshield, Jr., was only fifty-one and was thought to have been in good health. There were those who could not believe he was dead. Before long, Bentley assumed a different tone: "The death of Mr. G. C. so suddenly gave an opportunity to display the most wretched state of superstition, wealth absorbing the heart, our female friends wretchedly educated & worse associated. We were the slaves of the most miserable fears. Knowing nothing of nature, a man who died suddenly, tho with all the marks of dissolution, was in a trance."

Days passed. Only when George, always obese in life, became badly bloated could he be adjudged truly dead and the body interred. Even so, doubt remained: "after burial and with the dead, a watch was placed to know whether he wished to come out again." George gave no sign he wished to come out again.

Although the Mediterranean excursion was neither a voyage of pleasure nor a successful lion hunt, George Crowninshield's singular obsessions were not entirely in vain. *Cleopatra's Barge* had been regal unto herself. Nothing like her had been seen before, and nothing like her has been seen since; all along he had had a queen, not from any throne of Hanover or Savoy, but from the oaken ways of Retire Becket's shipyard. True, she had been a trifle overrouged, but that has always been a royal prerogative, and it might have pleased George to know that in the end she shook off the bar sinister of commerce and found her way to royalty in the person of the King of Hawaii. Kamehameha II was not of course the kind of royalty George had ever had in mind, but he was, after all, a legitimate monarch, and in some ways rather like George. Kinder than the Massachusetts Humane Society and Captain Lawrence, *Cleopatra's Barge* has preserved the dreamer of wild horses from oblivion, a fate he would not have liked. George Crowninshield, Jr., goes down in history as the owner of the first American pleasure yacht.

Pompey, the yellow cat, had been lost at sea.

THREE

---◆◉◆---

Dick and the Godlike One

---◆•►---

Richard Crowninshield (1804–1830)

No one knows where Captain Joseph White of Salem passed the early evening of April 6, 1830. Perhaps he was a guest in the spacious rooms of the East India Marine Society, which he had never bothered to join. Over a bowl or two of rum punch, the Captain would listen attentively enough to the younger members. But there were times when he might as well have dozed. True, they were all ship captains and had sailed, as membership required, off Cape Horn or the Cape of Good Hope. But what of that? What really did they know of life? He, Captain White, had outlived their grandfathers and fathers through the last French war, the Revolution, the ruinous embargo, and the War of 1812. Soldier, trader, privateer — he had been all of these. And now he was an aging merchant prince worth over a million dollars, whose wharf reached into Salem Harbor for the riches of the Indies alongside the wharves of the Derbys and the Crowninshields.

As for the pirates of Borneo, the West Indies and Algeria, he knew all about them; in fact more than once he had been little better than a pirate himself. As to smuggling, who among the great families had not smuggled? Gossipy Reverend William Bentley had muttered darkly at the not inconsiderable years Captain White had dedicated to slaving, but neither had the Captain been alone in that. Besides, what was below decks was the business of the master. And who had Bentley been anyway if not the captive preacher of the Crowninshields?

At eighty-two the Captain was still hale and hearty, with few regrets. As he was perhaps excessively fond of remarking, he wished to "go off like a flash" — the prospect of a lingering death revolted him.

121

Though it pained him that his long-dead wife had left him no heir, he took comfort in his nephew, Stephen, who had done well enough both on the quarterdeck and in the Senate. Thank God for Stephen, since the White family females seemed to bear more watching than most. Years ago the miserable Mr. Eulen had married a White girl against the Captain's every exertion. Eulen had then promptly left her, taking everything he could get his hands on, embezzling more, and finally writing her "that he was but an old man and that if she was uneasy at his long absence, she could easily call in her neighbors." Eulen subsequently vanished forever.

More recently the Captain's beautiful grandniece and favorite, Mary, had wanted to marry young Joseph Knapp. The smooth-faced, snub-nosed boy had captained some of White's ships and, while White had no complaint on that score, he did not want him as an in-law. Amid furious arguments, Mary had defied him; she vowed she would marry Joe Knapp no matter what the old man thought. In his turn, Captain White vowed to disinherit her. Both did as they had vowed.

But lately — and it was just as well — there had been a kind of reconciliation between them. Mary's mother, Mrs. Beckford, was the Captain's niece and housekeeper, and he would do nothing to separate them. So it was that Mary and her husband, Joe Knapp, were frequent guests at the stately brick mansion on Essex Street only a few yards from the East India Marine Society.

The house and its gardens were the Captain's pride and that of Salem. Superbly conceived by Samuel McIntire, the mansion had delicately carved mantels and friezes that displayed restraint, great wealth in repose. Chinese lanterns cast a benign glow over Irish crystal, Hepplewhite sofas and chairs, services of Canton and Nanking, carved sideboards by McIntire, and panels of French wallpaper, each representing a different month of the year. The whole offered mute and splendid testimony that ships carrying the blue-bordered White flag had run before the winds of every sea on earth.

For that matter all Salem was staid and prosperous. The tall masts of Indiamen rose above the harbor and the smell of new canvas and

Captain Joseph White. Oil portrait by James Frothingham, 1824. Courtesy of the Essex Institute, Salem

The Gardner-Pingree House in Salem, originally built for merchant John Gardner in 1804. It was in this house that Captain Joseph White was murdered. The house was subsequently sold to the Pingree family, and it exemplifies the fully developed Federal style of the architect Samuel McIntyre. Courtesy of the Essex Institute, Salem

Stockholm tar filled the onshore breeze. It was a quiet time. The Salem *Gazette* had to content its readership with prim approval of the Governor General of India, who had somewhat unenthusiastically promised to discourage the practice of burning Hindu widows. And it noted without much interest that the English Parliament proposed to remove, to what extent no one knew exactly, the civil liabilities of Jews. In Alabama the mistreatment of Cherokees gnawed fitfully at a New England conscience conveniently forgetful of what the men of Essex had done to the Pequod Nation in an earlier time, and in keeping with this high moral tone, the *Gazette* regretted that Thomas Jefferson had not, among other things, been "regulated by a purer religion." And who among the *Gazette*'s readers could fail to be charmed by an account of Captain Delano of the brig *Eagle* off Savannah, who discharged his musket at a seventy-foot sea serpent with the head of an alligator? When the angry creature responded by rapping the ship's stern sharply with its tail, the good captain — who had a history of such experiences — flung away his weapon and jumped into a bale of cotton.

But always the *Gazette* sought to edify and improve its readers. Hence the popular, fictitious "confessions" it ran of drunkards solemnly beseeching the reader to shun *mania a potu;* and the more spectacular accounts of young maidens losing their chastity in careless moments and being condemned to a remorseless, pitiable future. Like the drunkards, these unfortunates invariably wound up in a grimy workhouse with a venal, implacable workhouse master; no other end seemed possible or even proper.

But most of all, Salemites delighted in the *Gazette*'s fanciful accounts of crimes of stealth. If the criminal was of good family, tall and darkly handsome, and had incidentally seduced a young lady or two (preferably, but not necessarily, also of good family), then the moralizing grew truly rhapsodic. Readers were happily and inexpensively transported to that most delectable of nineteenth-century worlds, where at the same time one could purse one's lips in disapproval, squirm with pleasure and, by way of a dividend, be improved.

As was his custom Captain White, who cared nothing for such matters, retired early on this moonlit night of April 6. No matter that Mrs. Beckford would be away visiting Mary and Joe Knapp, his servants would look after his needs. But in the morning the old man did not arise at his usual early hour; an anxious manservant found him in bed, his skull crushed and thirteen stab wounds in the region of his heart. Captain White had indeed "gone off like a flash."

There was no sign of a struggle and the Captain's assailant had left nothing behind in the house. Robbery had not been the motive: apparently nothing had been taken from the mansion; silver plate of enormous value remained untouched, and the Captain's iron strongbox near his bed still contained the "roubleau of doubloons" which the dead man was known to keep there. All the most thorough search disclosed was a plank stretching from the garden the Captain so loved to a window on the ground floor. Murder for the sake of murder seemed to be the only motive.

The frenzies excited in Salem and Boston in 1830 by the murder of Captain White are best likened to a presidential assassination in our time. As surprising as it may seem to our sanguinary age, murder in early nineteenth century America was an extremely rare crime. Immediately a very solemn convocation of medical men determined the cause of death — a savage blow to the temple probably with a "bungdriver, a loaded cane or a bludgeon." The stab wounds were ancillary, the physicians thoughtfully explained, and the absence of bruises caused by the guard hilt of a knife or dagger was due (at least in part) to a "considerable thickness of fat on the Captain's ribs." Stephen White offered $1,000 reward for the killer or killers of his uncle. Other substantial sums were offered by the selectmen of Salem and by the Commonwealth of Massachusetts. The town watch was doubled, and on the floor of the Town Hall, after a fulminating address by the Reverend Mr. Henry Coleman, a man of "great piety and learning," a committee of vigilance was empowered to search every building, interrogate any person.

Salem was then a town of about fourteen thousand, where everyone seems to have known everyone else. As rumor flew, Salemites in-

The murder of Captain White, as conceived by a contemporary artist. Woodcut copied from Knapp's Second Trial, Conviction, and Sentence. *Courtesy of the Essex Institute, Salem*

evitably began to distrust one another and old personal grudges became easily converted into suspicions of murder. Who could be safe any longer? Merchants sold out — then had to replenish — their stocks of pistols, muskets, cane guns and whatever else was likely to keep an assassin at bay. Locks, bolts and good watchdogs were at a premium, and in daylight the streets echoed with the nailing of shutters. These same narrow lanes, mostly unpaved, were deserted at night except for the agitated and sleepless members of the Committee of Vigilance, spurred on by the indefatigable Reverend Coleman. Behind bolted doors frugal Yankees burned whale oil all night as they never had before. Strangers in town were shunned. Perhaps not since the witch-hunts had tension been so palpable.

Once again the Devil was afoot in Salem, from which fear emanated in waves. In Cambridge a young Harvard student, Oliver Wendell

Holmes, wrote his friend Phineas Barnes: "Nothing is going on but murder and robbery; we have to look in our closets and under our beds, and strut about with sword canes and pistols. Poor old Mr. White was stabbed in the dark, and since then the very air has been redolent of assassination."

In solemn procession Captain White was borne to the New Burying Ground in a hearse followed by grieving kin, who included Stephen White and Joseph Knapp in tall hats and black frockcoats. The night before, Knapp had kept the deathwatch in the house on Essex Street where, surrounded by candles, Captain White had lain for the last time. By his will, the Captain left the bulk of his estate to Stephen.

Weeks passed. Pressure grew on the Committee of Vigilance, which had been meeting nightly and had, after the manner of committees everywhere, appointed subcommittees. Yet nothing really came from these efforts. Was it possible that even the further exhortations of the Reverend Mr. Coleman were to no avail?

In fact matters seemed to be getting worse. On April 27 Joe Knapp and his younger brother Frank were attacked at night near Wenham Pond by three disguised desperadoes and barely escaped with their lives. Tension in Salem swelled anew. It looked very much as though there were a conspiracy to do away with the entire White family.

Then a few days later, on May 2, two young men-about-town, Dick and George Crowninshield, were arrested for the murder of Captain White.

The father of the two prisoners, who were languishing within the gray granite mass of Salem Gaol, was not much disturbed. He seemed, a sister-in-law wrote, "insensible of the consequences" and she thought him "hardened to such things." Nothing ever went right for him anyway. Short, fiercely erect, cross-eyed and bad-tempered, yet considered a "good conversationalist," Richard Crowninshield, Sr., fatefully mingled great ambition with extraordinarily bad judgment. Born in 1774, he had, like his more famous brothers, gone to sea when scarcely more than a boy. Later maritime adventures were prescient and unqualified disasters. He lost his schooner, *Charming Sally*, off

Guadeloupe to the British in 1793 and a spanking new brig was con-
fiscated at Naples on her maiden voyage. Worse yet, his cargoes did
not sell well; he was forever in the market at the wrong time.

Bent over a writing table in Salem his father, old George Crowninshield, had scrawled letter after affectionate letter of advice and encouragement. He would, he promised, make Richard "as rich as any
of the others," if only Richard would listen. The trembling hand
touched on every aspect of sea commerce: what and where to buy;
when to sell; who to have as endorsers on bills of exchange; and, more
importantly, whom to trust and whom not. Although he complained
it was difficult to write because "thier is Somthing Coming over my
right Ey that sems like Cobwebb," the shrewd and garrulous George
Crowninshield never ceased to counsel Richard as long as he lived.
Again and again he stressed, "It is easy to Get Money but Hard to
keep it." And there were times when, at a fresh stupidity of Richard's,
the old man's temper flared across the now scarcely legible pages:
"You will find Greater obstacles than Me in your way." But Richard
seems never to have listened.

In 1800, to the despair of his family, Richard had impregnated and
married a fiery, illiterate Irish chambermaid he had met in a New
York hotel. The girl was ignorant of even the names of her parents,
but she was to exercise a curious hold over him all of his life. Repelled
by an unrewarding sea, Richard built a woolen mill in New York,
which he vowed would "bring the riches of the Indies" to him. Almost
instantly it failed and Richard was bankrupt.

Like most Crowninshields Richard was litigious, though more liti-
gated against than litigating. His twenty years of success in evading
his creditors by removing to another state and jurisdiction prompted,
in no little measure, the federal regulation of bankruptcy, to which
Richard was a kind of unwitting and horrified midwife. The particularly trying year of 1817 led him to seek the counsel of a young lawyer
named Daniel Webster. Negotiations were, however, suspended when
Richard balked at the size of Webster's fee. Neither dreamed that
Webster would, after all, participate in Crowninshield legal problems
and that again his fee would be questioned.

Richard was no privateer. Yet the death of his father made him

*A view from Buxton Hill: "South Danvers, Mass." Lithograph
by J. B. Bachelder, 1856. Courtesy of the Essex Institute, Salem*

rich in 1815. His brother George Jr. might very well dedicate himself to pleasure and *Cleopatra's Barge*, but not Richard. Richard would become even richer, richer than any of them. He removed to Connecticut and built another woolen mill at great expense, which burned to the ground when scarcely completed.

Not at all discouraged, Richard returned to Salem and in nearby Danvers frantically set about building yet another woolen mill at Buxton Hill. Here at last would be attracted the riches of the Indies. And if they were not? Well, then he would sell it to the Baptists for use as a meetinghouse. How could he go wrong?

One might think that Richard would have started by erecting the mill itself. But no. His house must be built first — a suitable mansion of brick and slate imported from England. It was to have three stories, a two-story ell for servants, and tunnels that would connect it with the factory. The mansion took a very long time to build. Its long driveway was lined with great trees and on all sides were upland meadows, woods, pastures and orchards of apple and walnut. A clear rippling brook flowed into a willow-lined pond that Richard had dammed to power his new mill. From England came three hundred Merino sheep, and the bucolic scene with its promise of industry moved the Reverend Bentley to enthusiasm.

But somehow the mill could not be put into operation. Unaccountably there were delays in getting suitable machinery and then, Richard complained, he "could get no proper workmen." Not until skilled laborers were imported from Ireland could operation begin. Then, after an elaborate ceremony presided over by Richard, the factory, crammed with wool, was set in motion. It seemed to work well. But the next day it, like its predecessors, burned to the ground. All was lost. No Baptist buyer ever viewed the rubble where a few "wild Irishmen" squatted.

Immediately Richard's weavers, his hatters, and his sheepherders moved into his greenhouse and thence took up residence in the mansion house under circumstances the Reverend Bentley found "indescribable." They liked life with Mr. and Mrs. Crowninshield, if only he would build another factory. Anxiously, the cross-eyed man cornered his brother George, lately returned from a voyage of pleasure. Would he finance a new mill? George was sympathetic; he rather liked Richard. But on an ebb tide two days later the "harlequin" of the Mediterranean lay dead in Salem Harbor.

Hatless and perspiring, Richard made off with his brother's spectacular yellow curricle. Threatened with arrest, he gave up the carriage and beat a splenetic retreat to Buxton Hill, only to return to Crowninshield Wharf and buy the *Barge*, now stripped of its splendid furnishings, for $20,000. Salem was agog to see what would happen next. It did not have long to wait.

Richard's creditors were once more closing in; he attempted to defraud them by disposing of the yacht in Boston, but they got wind of the scheme and he lost both his purchase price and the yacht. On April 8, 1819, the Reverend Bentley was moved to comment: "Little did G[eorge] C[rowninshield] expect that his C. Barge would so soon come to such a market, & little pity is shewn to R. C., setting aside the dishonest purpose of the conveyance, for exposing a property of such extraordinary name & in such suspicious circumstances at such a place. There is the greatest complexity of ignorance, impudence, vile purpose & exposure in this fraud ever known. The fame of the C. Barge carries it everywhere & admits no concealment of anything belonging to it."

On the next day Bentley, whose tireless pen was soon to be stilled forever, recorded his final exasperation against the Crowninshields of Buxton Hill: "R. C. who lost the Cleopatra's barge by fraudulent conveyance lately & who sent a gang of Irishmen to the list of State paupers debased by the ———— in his own house, has suffered from the elopement of one of his daughters with two Irishmen. The tales of this family exhibit something yet unknown in this part of the country for want of domestic economy, education of children, management of affairs & conduct among their servants and neighbours."

Not much later, hobbling by, old Dr. Nichols was astonished to see Mrs. Crowninshield beating her husband with a broom. When she spotted the old man, she cried out with her ready Irish wit, "Oh, Doctor, sure I have found a corn broom is the best thing to clean a gentleman's coat with!"

133

Indeed, family life at Buxton Hill was less than ideal. One son, Edward, was a raving madman given to making peculiar utterances at mealtimes, which so enraged his father that Richard frequently flattened him on the spot. Edward's brothers, Dick and George, who were a year apart, attended a public grammar school in Danvers, where Dick, having been expelled as "an unruly and mischievous boy," formed a plot to burn the schoolhouse down. But one of the other conspirators took fright and disclosed the plan to the authorities. The pattern of betrayal is worth noting: it was to recur with grim and fatal consequences.

Their next school was a private one in New Hampshire, after which, their father hoped, they would attend Harvard College. Late one night they lodged a cow in the headmaster's library and the confused, bawling, incontinent beast almost destroyed the place. The Crowninshield boys and their associates were closely questioned but all stood fast. Dick and George went undetected. Somewhat later, the headmaster, concluding that dress was being carried to the "most ridiculous excess," proposed an essay competition in damnation of foppery, the winner to receive a silver medal worth five dollars. Dick, a consummate fop (a reputation he was to enjoy the remainder of his life), managed, with George's assistance, to persuade the more literary contestants to submit indifferent papers in exchange for the pleasing irony of Dick's getting the prize. On the day of the award, the gratified headmaster, after a florid speech in honor of Dick, reached for the silver piece negligently kept in his desk for the occasion and found nothing; Dick had mixed irony with larceny. Once again students were interrogated, and when one of the conspirators told all, Dick was expelled. For some months he hung about the school playing practical jokes on the local farmers — pranks increasingly tinged with malice and sometimes, as when he cut off horses' tails, with sadism.

In 1824 Richard Sr. paused in his pursuit of ruin long enough to conclude that Dick and George needed a taste of military discipline. His choice fell upon an academy in Norwich, Vermont, run by an ex-army officer named Partridge, who had formerly been the Superintendent of West Point. Here, felt Richard, his two sons would be prepared for better things. An unadmiring South Carolinian classmate of the Crowninshield brothers remarked in his memoirs that Commandant Partridge was called "Old Pewt," not from the buttons adorning the blue uniforms worn alike by students and faculty, but because the word resembled his signature which he scrawled indecipherably in order to make its forgery as difficult as possible for the cadets. It turned out that "Old Pewt," who had been cashiered from the United States Army, was somewhat unmilitary himself. Tall, ungainly, and with his arms sticking out awkwardly from his sides, he marched clumsily about, sometimes favoring the jeering students, over whom he had not the slightest control, with a fixed and ghastly smile.

Unsurprisingly, such rules as he might promulgate were either easily transgressed or entirely ignored. Entire classes might disappear for days on end and when they returned, "Old Pewt," glad that they had returned at all, never punished anyone. Worse yet, for reasons we shall never know, he was fond of telling the boys, on the rare occasions when he was able to assemble them, of his "disgrace" at West Point. In this atmosphere the Crowninshield boys flourished. George was especially popular among the faction noted for a low moral tone. Dick, thought his southern classmate, "was little better than a fool." At any rate, prepared for better things or not, they soon left and when they did the last site of their formal education was found robbed of several hundred dollars.

For the next few years we catch only fleeting glimpses of the two brothers. Dick, who had an uncommon flair for organization, directed a short-lived band of jewel thieves specializing in the finer hotels of New York City. When it was broken up by the police, Dick demonstrated another flair: abusing the family influence so laboriously accrued by his grandfather to avoid prosecution.

At twenty-two, the unsuccessful jewel thief was unusually tall, and his lithograph portrait of the time is that of a handsome man — the face is aquiline and alert dark eyes brood over a prominent, slightly underslung jaw; the black hair is elaborately curled and, as always, he is fashionably dressed. No such image of George, who did not become as famous, survives. In 1827 he wandered picaresquely through

Georgia in the company of an agreeable and determinedly petty crook named John Palmer in what was to become a fateful relationship. Palmer later recalled, in what must be one of the strangest memoirs ever written, that George, although heavily burdened with gambling paraphernalia (they were on foot), managed as well to carry a "Kent bugle." Its blare echoed loudly, pointlessly, across the savannahs as they swindled their way northward.

Dick also went south, a sojourn occasioned by a particularly nasty spate of grave robbing in the Salem area uncomfortably aggravated by the statutory rape of a neighbor's daughter. In Charleston, South Carolina, the young and handsome northerner whose uncle had been Secretary of the Navy under both Madison and Monroe was readily lionized by a hospitable society.

Dick had a great deal of charm; his manners were excellent and for some months he was the toast of the town. More and more frequently he was to be seen with a young lady of one of the old Charleston families. He proposed marriage; the belle blissfully accepted and her parents announced themselves pleased with the very eligible young suitor from Salem. Yet with singular prescience her father made inquiries of friends in the North. So utterly appalling were the replies he received that Dick quit both his beloved and Charleston, but not before seducing the young lady who, we are told, shortly died of shame and a broken heart.

In Salem once more, Dick set up a small machine shop. His father was pleased; no doubt his son shared his own mechanical genius. Although Dick preferred to spend his time with another, more congenial, enterprise — a gambling house (guised as a "reading room") in South Fields where young Harvard swells from Cambridge were gulled — his mechanical tinkerings were in the end to result in a unique product. His brother, George, having put aside his Kent bugle, turned his lesser talents to the establishment of a small whorehouse conveniently near Dick's "reading room." But both reserved the more esoteric activity for a large cave in Wenham Woods where, with their girls and suitable associates, they gathered for days and from which emanated dark tales of robbery and worse. In 1829, George's old friend Palmer, who by now had served a term in the Maine State Penitentiary, was a frequent visitor to these haunts and lived with the brothers at their father's mansion on Buxton Hill.

To the distress of the Committee of Vigilance and the Reverend Mr. Coleman, the two bad Crowninshields in Salem Gaol were indicted only on the basis of a rumor, the source of which was as disreputable as they were. Hard evidence was lacking; the real reason for their presence there was their reputation.

Public feeling about them is perhaps best seen in a letter of their young cousin Sally, who feared when she heard of the murder that Dick and George would be found "to have a hand in it." But Dick could prove he was at home with his family; George could demonstrate that he had spent the night of the murder with two of his favorite tarts, Mary Bassett and Mary Jane Weller. Faced with the Crowninshields' vehement expressions of innocence, it looked as though they could not be convicted.

Then on May 14, Captain Joseph Knapp, Sr., a Salem sea captain and the father of Joe Knapp and his brother Frank, received a mysterious letter from Belfast, Maine:

> Belfast, May 12, 1830
>
> Dear Sir, — I have taken the pen at this time to address an utter stranger, and strange as it may seem to you, it is for the purpose of requesting a loan of three hundred and fifty dollars, for which I can give you no other security but my word, and in this case consider this to be sufficient. My call for money at this time is pressing, or I would not trouble you. . . . It is useless for me to enter into a discussion of facts which must inevitably harrow up your soul — no — I will merely tell you that I am acquainted with your brother Franklin [Frank], and also the business that he was transacting for you on the 2nd of April last; and that I think you was very extravagant in giving one thousand dollars to the person that would execute the business for you — but you know best about that — you will see such things will leak out. . . . Direct yours to Charles Grant, Jun., of Prospect, Maine.

Captain Knapp was greatly confused by the letter, and assuming

John C. R. Palmer, Jr. From a drawing. Courtesy of the Essex Institute, Salem

Richard Crowninshield, Jr. Pencil sketch from a drawing in the Essex Institute. Courtesy of the Essex Institute, Salem

that it was intended for his son of the same first name, took it to him. Young Joe and Frank were equally puzzled; they knew of no Charles Grant or of what he wrote. It was all "devilish trash" to Frank, who nonchalantly suggested that the letter be sent to the Committee of Vigilance: the Reverend Coleman might make of it what he would.

A day or two later, Grant took pen in hand once more, this time to the Committee of Vigilance:

> . . . I think it time to inform you that Stephen White came to me one night and told me that if I would remove the old gentleman he would give me $5000; he said he was afraid he would alter his will if he lived any longer. I told him I would do it, but I was afraid to go into the house, so he said he'd go with me, that he would try and get into the house in the evening and open the window, would then go home and go to bed and meet me again about 11. I found him and we both went into his chamber. I struck him on the head and then stabbed him with a dirk; he made the finishing stroke with another. He promised to send me the money next evening, and has not sent it yet, which is the reason that I mention this.
>
> Yours, &c.   GRANT

It now appeared that both the Knapp family and Stephen White were perhaps linked to the crime. The committee reacted by sending to Belfast a letter, some money with the promise of more to come, and a committeeman to watch the post office and arrest whoever called for the letter. Grant, who "came on in the mail" in irons, was a "good looking chap" and "doubtless quite a pleasant traveling companion," thought a Salem observer. And so George Crowninshield had found him three years before: "Grant's" real name was John Palmer.

Under inquiry Palmer informed the committee that on April 2 at the Crowninshield house on Buxton Hill, George Crowninshield told him that Frank and Joe Knapp had offered Dick and George $1,000 to murder Captain White.

Within hours the Knapp brothers joined the Crowninshields in jail.

April had indeed been the cruelest month but now the dogwood and crab apple trees flowered everywhere and the maple buds reddened and swelled along Essex Street. The time of apprehension, of naked fear, was gone; that of vengeance had arrived. A confident prosecution prepared its case: Dick would be tried as principal, the Knapp brothers and George as accessories. The penalty for both crimes would be death by hanging.

In his cell Dick passed these bland spring days in the writing of poetry, especially to his sister Sarah, as on May 15, the occasion being his approaching twenty-sixth birthday:

Unhappy day! You'll find me in a gloomy cell,
And thoughts of keen sensation in my bosom swell;
In my infant years I was happy; then by friends caressed
I'm now misfortune's deadly aim and by the world oppressed.
There is one consolation buoyant on the wings of time
That my soul is pure from guilt, and this most horrid crime.

And he unpoetically concluded with a slap at Palmer: "The perjured State Prison convict that they intend to bring as evidence against us will be none to their credit; what prompts him to this perjured confession? Is it in anticipation of getting pardoned? Or is it wealth? I leave it to an impartial jury to decide. I will write to you again. Adieu tonight."

Equally concerned with the credibility of Palmer was the Committee of Vigilance. After all, Palmer was a demonstrated thief, forger and counterfeiter. Although Salem raged for blood, Palmer's word was not good enough. Additional evidence was needed.

The Reverend Mr. Henry Coleman felt himself equal to the challenge. Joe and Mary Knapp were members of his church, the Independent Congregational; indeed he had married them, and he strongly suspected the guilt of his parishioner. He was, he told Joe in Salem Gaol, "sorry to see him there," a sentiment readily echoed by Joe. He had always been a "friend to your dear wife whom I look upon as a child," and for hours on end he used every form of persuasion to extract a confession: he cajoled; he wheedled, threatened and promised.

140

As well as spiritual advisor to a strayed member of his flock, Coleman was now detective, lawyer, and prosecutor. (One feels he would have liked to be jury and hangman as well — something he ultimately became.)

When the man of God, presumably representing the Governor, offered a "pardon" in exchange for a full confession, Joe wavered, feeling that Frank, who was likely to hang in consequence of the arrangement, should agree. Coleman, trembling with excitement, rushed to the latter's cell.

The proposition struck Frank as a little "hard," but after considerable browbeating by Coleman he agreed that Joe could confess if he pleased. It then occurred to the delighted minister that he had no authority to offer anyone a pardon. Besides what he really meant was immunity from prosecution — did not everyone understand this? — and were not his motives of the highest order? Coleman hurried off to the Attorney General, rousted him out of bed after midnight, and obtained immunity for Joe.

By Joe Knapp's account, Joe and his brother had thought that Captain White had made a will in favor of Stephen and they reasoned that if the Captain were made to die without a will, then under the Massachusetts laws of intestacy, Mrs. Beckford, Joe's mother-in-law, would receive one half the estate and this they would turn to their advantage. For weeks they had pondered just how and where Captain White's intestacy could be effected, but somehow they lacked the nerve.

At last they put the matter in the hands of Dick Crowninshield, who for $1,000 agreed to do the job. Shortly before the murder Joe arranged for his mother-in-law to visit him and Mary; then he unlocked a lower window from the inside of the Captain's house and took from his strongbox a will (it turned out to be the wrong one). The scene was set for Dick, who early on the evening of April 6, pleading an upset stomach, retired early at Buxton Hill, sneaked out and rode the few miles to Salem, entered Captain White's house through the unlocked window, and crushed the sleeping man's skull with a lead-weighted club turned out in his machine shop. To make sure, he had plunged his ivory-handled dirk (his "nursemaid" as he called it) repeatedly into the heart and then as calmly as an attending physician felt the old man's pulse until it was no more.

Within an hour, back at Buxton Hill, he came down from his bedroom to complain again of indigestion.

The story had complications. Palmer had readily enough admitted his blackmailing letter to Joe Knapp but denied writing another signed "Grant" to the committee accusing Stephen White of the crime. What, asked the Reverend Coleman, did Joe know about this? It had been a hoax, said Joe. He had written it to shift suspicion from him and his brother. The attack on the Knapp brothers at Wenham Pond, which had further alarmed Salem, had also been fabricated.

With Joe's confession, the noose tightened around Dick Crowninshield's neck. But it was not to be the Commonwealth's rope. On May 22, the tall, dark and indifferent poet of Salem Gaol composed for Sarah a theme in response to a rose she had sent:

In fervor to God I sincerely pray,
That I may keep in the virtuous way.
That when with this wicked world I part,
He may receive me with a gracious heart.

From Sarah, Dick requested a copy of Hutton's *Mathematics* together with his favorite book of music, Moore's Irish melodies. This done, he complained about capital punishment, which not even "the savages of the Western wilds, who never saw a Christian, would inflict upon their greatest enemy."

At the same time, Crowninshield turned his pen in another direction. He was convinced that if, somehow, he could get in touch with Palmer, he would be able to persuade him to alter his testimony. Surely Palmer was in the cell below him. Drilling a hole in the floor he lowered on a string the following note:

IS YOUR NAME PALMER?

But Palmer was not in the cell below, and on June 5, 1830, Dick wrote the last of his literary efforts. The work was shaky, the letters clumsily formed, the grammar bad; the game was up.

Salem Gaol

DEAR FATHER,

These are the last lines from your undutiful son, that has disregarded your chaste moral precepts. That has always bestowed on the unfortunate being, that ere long you receive this cease to exist. My last request is, that you will have my body decently burried and have it protected from that deceting knife and may God's blessings rest upon you is the last wish of your son.

Farewell Father. Richard Crowninshield Jun.

In the early afternoon of June 5, Nehemiah Brown, the master of Salem Gaol, found Dick hanging from the bars of his cell. He had knotted two silk handkerchiefs together, one around his neck, the other around the bars. The cell had a low ceiling and the bars were not high enough for Dick to give himself a drop; he had had to crouch with his knees not more than a foot from the floor and force his own strangulation in a deliberate, audacious act.

But then Dick Crowninshield had never lacked audacity.

Salem was now defrauded of a public execution; the most urgent attempts at resuscitation were made by hastily summoned physicians. When a "galvanic battery" was applied to the still warm corpse without effect, the neck veins were opened but the disappointed surgeons found the blood quiescent, and before their eyes it ceased to flow. Dick was gone.

The public's desire to view the body of the celebrated Salem murderer was intense and a few of the privileged were allowed to do so before a hearse bore it to Buxton Hill for burial. Dick's last wish was granted; he was spared the "deceting knife." In his cell neatly arranged were his clothes and his books, all he owned in the world. Only an hour before his death he had cheerfully borrowed a razor from Nehemiah Brown and carefully shaved.

143

Also neatly arranged was Dick Crowninshield's legacy to the Commonwealth of Massachusetts. In the days preceding his suicide, Dick had spent several hours with his lawyer, Franklin Dexter of Boston, who had thoroughly explained that under the Massachusetts law of conspiracy, no accessory could be tried unless a principal had been first convicted. Again and again Dick had asked Dexter if he was really sure of his ground and Dexter assured him there was no doubt in his mind. No one knew better than Dick that he was the principal, and with Joe's confession he was as good as dead. His suicide would avert the ignominy of a public hanging and it would enable him to confound the authorities once again.

Salemites, already embittered at missing a very satisfactory hanging, were further disappointed to discover that the Knapps and George Crowninshield were now very likely to go free. Was it possible? Indeed it was, gloomily admitted Rufus Choate, one of the lawyers for the prosecution. An angry Massachusetts legislature met hurriedly to change the law, but unfortunately to do so would take time and, besides, there was a question whether it could be made retroactive. Somehow the guilty ones must be convicted within the framework of the present law. But how?

If it was to be done at all, thought Stephen White, it would take singular legal ability, more than that possessed by the aging Attorney General and his luminaries. Stephen's brother-in-law, Justice Story, who was a good friend of the famous Daniel Webster, thought Webster's services might be enlisted. But would the great man accept? After all, the triumphs of the Dartmouth College case, the Plymouth Oration and his devastating Reply to Hayne had made Senator Webster presidential timber. Would he agree to assist a puzzled prosecution in a sordid trial? Besides Webster knew next to nothing of criminal law.

In *Retrospect of Western Travel*, published in 1838, Harriet Martineau recorded Webster's reaction to Stephen White's invitation to participate in the prosecution: "A citizen of Salem," she wrote, "a friend of mine, was deputed to carry the request. . . . Mr. Webster was at his farm by the seashore. Thither, in tremendous weather, my friend followed him. Mr. Webster was playing checkers. . . . My friend was first dried and refreshed, and then lost no time in mentioning business. Mr. Webster writhed at the word, saying that he came hither to get out of the hearing of it. He next declared that his undertaking anything more was entirely out of the question, and pointed, in evidence, to his swollen bag of briefs lying in a corner. However, upon a little further explanation and meditation, he agreed to the request with the same good grace with which he afterward went to the task. He made himself master of all that my friend could communicate, and before daybreak was off through the woods, in the unabated storm, no doubt meditating his speech by the way. He needed all the assistance that could be given him, of course; and my friend constituted himself as Mr. Webster's fetcher and carrier of facts. . . . At the appointed hour Mr. Webster was completely ready."

En route, Daniel Webster may have reflected on other things as well. By 1830 the rickety boy with an overlarge head and staring cavernous eyes had indeed come a long way from the hardscrabble farm in Salisbury, New Hampshire. But there had been difficulties. By this time, the "Godlike one," the "Cicero of America," had become a confirmed spendthrift and a drunkard. Time and time again his admirers, and they were many, raised funds to alleviate his chaotic financial condition. All in vain. A neurotic passion for land, perhaps a result of the pitiful Salisbury acres, had led Webster to buy eighteen hundred acres in Marshfield, Massachusetts, and twenty thousand more in Indiana, Illinois, Ohio, Michigan and Wisconsin in reckless speculation. His promissory notes were nearly worthless; and he depended more and more on cash gifts from wealthy constituents. He also loved to entertain on the grand scale — perhaps this too was in memory of the penurious table in the Salisbury of his childhood. Neither of his two wives seemed to be able to restrain him. The "Godlike one" drove through Harriet Martineau's "unabated storm" to Salem because Stephen White had promised him a fee of $1,000. Webster needed the money and he needed it badly.

The trials began on August 3 in sweltering heat. No matter. They

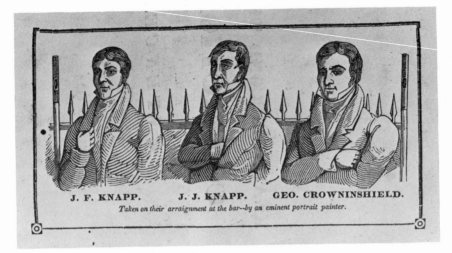

Woodcut of the conspirators, copied from Knapp's Second Trial, Conviction, and Sentence. *Courtesy of the Essex Institute, Salem*

packed the courthouse and those who could not gain access gathered around outside. Particularly eager was the throng of lady observers, who threatened to crowd the gentlemen of the press from their assigned places. The lawyers, darkly gowned and with their green bags before them, sweated in the close air: for the defense, Franklin Dexter and William H. Gardiner of Boston, assisted by Robert Rantoul of Salem — all capable men. In the dock stood the debonair, "genteely dressed," and composed Frank and Joe Knapp. They were flanked by a casual, almost gaily unconcerned George Crowninshield, who not long before had sobbed away his nights in jail.

The three presented legal problems that would have dismayed a lesser man than Webster. To begin with, Webster would have to convince the jury that although Dick Crowninshield had killed White, Frank had been a principal, not merely an accessory, and that he had been present, aiding and abetting in the murder. Should he fail in this, then Joe and George would go free. To convict Frank, the prosecution relied almost entirely on the promised testimony of Joe Knapp, for which he had received immunity. To Webster's dismay, after Joe Knapp took the stand, he remarked nearly inaudibly, "It won't do,"

Daniel Webster. Drawing by Robert Ball Hughes. Courtesy of the Essex Institute, Salem

and refused to say anything further. Perhaps he felt he could not hang his brother after all.

Webster's dilemma was allayed by the Reverend Coleman's ferocious memory. In the greatest detail and often verbatim, Coleman related Joe's confessions to the jury. It seems not to have troubled him at all that the words which were to hang both brothers had been elicited by him from Joe Knapp in Joe's belief that they were privileged communications from penitent to pastor. Franklin Dexter might complain bitterly about the procedure but he was powerless to stop it. At that time the rights of criminal defendants were not zealously guarded. Besides, Dexter had already privately concluded that both Knapps were guilty. Their defense became mere ritual as the trial wore on.

Webster produced witnesses who saw Frank in the vicinity of Captain White's house on the night of the murder or at least they thought they saw him. But how had he been dressed? In a "Camblet cloak" or perhaps a "dark frock coat"? No one was sure. Before the case went to the jury Webster must establish that Dick was guilty of the actual murder, that there had been a conspiracy. In the steaming courtroom, advancing his left foot forward and extending his right arm, the stentorian voice evoked the ghost of Dick Crowninshield for all to see: "Gentlemen, it is a most extraordinary case. This bloody drama exhibited no suddenly excited, ungovernable rage. The actors in it were not surprised by any lion-like temptation springing upon their virtue, and overcoming it, before resistance could begin. Nor did they do the deed to glut savage vengeance, or satiate long settled and deadly hate. It was a cool, calculating, moneymaking murder. It was all hire and salary, not revenge. It was the weighing of money against life; the counting out of so many pieces of silver against so many ounces of blood.

"An aged man, without an enemy in the world, in his own house, and in his own bed, is made the victim of a butcherly murder, for mere pay. Truly, here is a new lesson for painters and poets. Whoever shall hereafter draw the portrait of murder, let him not give it in the grim visage of Moloch, the brow knitted by revenge, the face black with settled hate, and the blood-shot eye emitting livid fires of malice. Let him draw, rather, a decorous, smooth-faced, bloodless demon; a picture in repose, rather than in action; not so much an example of human nature in its depravity, and in its paroxysms of crime, as an infernal being, a fiend, in the ordinary display and development of his character.

"The deed was executed with a degree of self-possession and steadiness equal to the wickedness with which it was planned. The circumstances now clearly in evidence spread out the whole scene before us. Deep sleep had fallen on the destined victim, and on all beneath his roof. A healthful old man, to whom sleep was sweet, the first sound slumbers of the night held him in their soft but strong embrace. The assassin enters, through the window already prepared, into an unoccupied apartment. With noiseless foot he paces the lonely hall, half lighted by the moon; he winds up the ascent of the stairs, and reaches the door of the chamber. Of this, he moves the lock, by soft and continued pressure, till it turns on its hinges without noise; and he enters and beholds the victim before him.

"The room is uncommonly open to the admission of light. The face of the innocent sleeper is turned from the murderer, and the beams of the moon, resting on the gray locks of his aged temple, show him where to strike. The fatal blow is given! and the victim passes, without a struggle or a motion, from the repose of sleep to the repose of death! It is the assassin's purpose to make sure work; and he plies the dagger, though it is obvious that life has been destroyed by the bludgeon. He even raises the aged arm, that he may not fail in his aim at the heart, and replaces it again over the wounds of the poniard! To finish the picture, he explores the wrist for the pulse! He feels for it, and ascertains that it beats no longer! It is accomplished. The deed is done. He retreats, retraces his steps to the window, passes out through it as he came in, and escapes. He has done the murder. No eye has seen him, no ear has heard him. The secret is his own, and it is safe!

"Ah! Gentlemen, that was a dreadful mistake. Such a secret can be safe nowhere. The whole creation of God has neither nook nor corner where the guilty can bestow it, and say it is safe. The human heart was not made for the residence of such an inhabitant. It finds itself

149

preyed on by a torment, which it dares not acknowledge to God or man. A vulture is devouring it, and it can ask no sympathy or assistance, either from heaven or earth.

"The secret which the murderer possesses soon comes to possess him. He thinks the whole world sees it in his face, reads it in his eyes, and almost hears its workings in the very silence of his thoughts. It has become his master. It betrays his discretion, it breaks down his courage, it conquers his prudence. When suspicions from without begin to embarrass him, and the net of circumstances to entangle him, the fatal secret struggles with the still greater violence to burst forth. It must be confessed, it will be confessed; there is no refuge from confession but suicide, and suicide is confession."

Jurors and spectators alike were mesmerized; they even forgot to fan themselves. But while the speech convinced everyone that Dick was indeed guilty and that there had been a conspiracy, the jury could not find that Frank's presence on the night of the murder was aiding and abetting. After all, he had been spotted (and that questionably) on Brown Street a hundred yards from Captain White's house. How could he have really helped Dick from that distance? After twenty-four hours they could not decide and a new trial was necessary.

This time the memories of the witnesses on Brown Street had been remarkably improved; those once doubtful were now quite sure they had seen Frank "skulking" around. Gone were the quibbles over "Camblet cloaks." The second trial lasted five days and Frank was found guilty. As the judge intoned sentence of death by hanging, Frank Knapp stood like a "statue of adamant" and then produced a quid of tobacco which he calmly chewed.

On September 27, 1830, the two brothers met for the last time in Frank's cell. During the trial their father had twice tried to hang himself and Mary had tried once but both had been saved. Joe himself was wasted and feeble in body. Often drunk, he refused to eat, bathe or shave. Surprised at Frank's calm composure, he asked him if he was as well as he looked. Frank said, "Yes, I can sleep as sound now on the soft side of a plank as I ever could," and bade him farewell.

Outside in the streets, an expensive pamphlet gotten up by the friends of the condemned man was circulating. It questioned the legality of the trial: the prosecution had been venal, so had the Reverend Mr. Coleman. Shakespeare was cited:

> *The quality of mercy is not strain'd;*
> *It droppeth as the gentle rain from heaven* . . . .
> *And earthly power doth then show likest God's*
> *When mercy seasons justice.*

There followed "THE SUBSTANCE OF KNAPP'S DYING PROTEST," in which Frank allowed that he would, rather than be hanged, leave the country, "perhaps forever," and "commence a new career abroad."

But now he must perish: "My hours are fast drawing to a close. It is some consolation, however, not again to stand where I have twice stood, to go through the humbling solemnities which I have before undergone, to see the smile of scorn, and retort the frown of others, to wrestle with the anxiety of the heart, and to depend on the caprice of the excited nerves. It is something to feel one part of the drama of disgrace is over, and that I may wait unmolested in my cell until for one time only I am again the butt of the unthinking, and the monster of the crowd. I am resigned to my fate, but on the oath of one who has but a single step on the threshold of eternity, I now, for the last time, declare my entire innocence of the horrid crime of which I have been convicted."

But mercy did not drop as the gentle rain from heaven. Instead Frank Knapp dropped from the gallows.

Few have been as well dressed on the "threshold of eternity." He chose blue pantaloons, a gray vest, a jeweled stickpin for his cravat, and a black frock coat. With a firm step he mounted the gallows, inclined his neck, and did all he could to facilitate the hangman's work. At his request, a neatly folded white handkerchief was placed in his hand and this he clutched spasmodically as he choked to death. So agreeable a scene attracted between three and four thousand spectators, among them his brother Joe, who ran to kiss the lips of the corpse.

It is curious to pause and consider the consequences of Joe's refusal to testify against Frank. The move cost him his immunity and he was then tried for the murder himself. Nor did his refusal save Frank. Had he testified as he had promised, it would have been seen that Frank was not at all on Brown Street, for the truth was that before the murder Dick Crowninshield had told Frank to go home and Frank had done so. But Joe remained silent and there was no one else to testify to that effect. Should this seem odd, it must be borne in mind that in those days a criminal defendant could not be a witness in his own behalf. Had Joe testified, the probability is that Franklin Dexter could have demonstrated to the satisfaction of the jury that Frank could not have been a principal. If so, both Knapp boys would have gone free.

It was the last of Joe's mistakes. First, he had misconstrued the law of inheritance. Then he had taken the wrong will. Now, finally, he had failed to destroy Palmer's incriminating letter when he had the opportunity. Had he found a way to silence Palmer, it is likely that the murder of Captain White would have remained a mystery. Whatever one may think of the affair, it is impossible to avoid the conclusion that the "Godlike one" found the atmosphere one in which oratory was easily substituted for evidence.

Apart from some carping by the defense about the propriety of Daniel Webster's fee (what had really been objected to was his presence), the only issue at Joe Knapp's trial in November was the admissibility of his confession. Although given under a promise of immunity, the judge was persuaded of its voluntary character and it was all over with Joe. On December 31, 1830, he writhed on the scaffold for four minutes. Although Salem agreed that the murder had from the beginning been his idea, his execution was not well attended and many congratulated themselves for staying away: no ghouls, they.

George Crowninshield was tried last, for the case against him was weak. Undoubtedly he had been deeply involved in the conspiracy, but an overt act could not be shown. Nor does the prosecution seem to have pressed its case; Webster did not participate and it is even possible that Salem had had hangings enough.

The doxies, Mary and Mary Jane, stated that George had been

152

with them on the night of April 6 and the glib testimony went un-
controverted. Lolling in the dock, he from time to time indulged in
flippant observations, as if the proceedings were intended for his
amusement. Acquitted, he lived another fifty-nine years, and finally
died in Roxbury, Massachusetts, in 1889. In his last years the Crowninshield eccentricity grew upon him; he dabbled in odd inventions
until at last his mind gave way altogether. But to the end he insisted
that Stephen White had killed the old sea captain.

Surviving George were his daughter and granddaughter, both a
source of unease to the old rake of Essex County. His daughter, whom
he had raised in the grand manner, married a hatter. He disowned her
and to spite him she set up a candy and popcorn stand at his door.
Years later, his granddaughter further appalled the last of the Salem
conspirators by running off with a Boston horsecar drover.

For Daniel Webster, the "Godlike one," the whole thing ended very
happily. He was paid a handsome fee. He had made a speech that
would make generations of American schoolboys sit up sharply in
their seats. And there was something more. His son, Fletcher, had
courted Caroline White during the trial, and Daniel left Salem with
a rich daughter-in-law.

Shortly after Dick Crowninshield's suicide a nameless bard had
occasion to compose a broadside:

> *Had Crowninshield, in the bloody field,*
> *Died, like a warrior brave,*
> *Glory had been his portion then —*
> *He had slept in a soldier's grave.*

> *Now deep disgrace shall take the place*
> *Of honour and of fame —*
> *Yea, the mean and vile, with bitter smile,*
> *Shall triumph o'er thy shame!*

> *Be thy name forgot: who can tell thy lot*

Where departed spirits roam!
Haply, at last, all thy penance past,
Thy God will receive thee Home!

While perhaps not "forgot," Dick Crowninshield's memory is a dim thing today, only an irrelevant footnote the bored law student may stray upon. Oddly, there is still a cult of White murder buffs who sort and shift the yellowed files much as dogs maul old bones. But in the 1840's Dick was a popular figure, the subject of inaccurate and uniformly edifying penny biographies. Strangely enough he was put to political purposes by one Henry C. Wright, "a non-resistant and practical Christian," who got up a pamphlet in 1848 condemning the Mexican War in general and Zachary Taylor in particular. Poor Dick is resurrected and made to answer an unknown interlocutor as follows:

QUEST. "Will you murder the innocent for pay?"
ANS. "Gladly, you have only to ask."

And so on. The same questions are then put to General Taylor, who unfortunately gives the same answers, whereupon Mr. Wright, by now in a frenzy, concludes that "Old Rough and Ready" is far worse than Dick. Moreover, the blustery hero of Buena Vista amused himself by driving stakes through Mexican babies, a species of rascality not even Dick would stoop to.

Wax museum exhibits were intensely popular at the time; they traveled from town to town and were set up in any public place. One depicted Joseph Knapp on his way to the gallows bidding a tearful Mary farewell. And on Boston Common in the late 1840's a wandering exhibitor

showed in a tent, for the fee of ten cents, the ghastly form of Captain White, lying in bed, and weltering in his gore. Over him, with knife raised, and with menacing face held close to the dead man, leaned the sinister figure of "Crowninshield, the hired assassin." A gentleman who had paid his admission fell into conversation with the showman. The latter admitted that business was good.

"You see," said he, "lots of folks want to see the figgers, and some of them pays again and goes in twice."

"You have to find board and lodging, of course," suggested the visitor.

"Victuals, yes," said the proprietor. "But lodging — well, the nights are warm and pleasant now here on the Common, and I don't have to go nowheres. I lets Crowninshield stay where he stands, you see, and I just takes the Captain out of bed, and gets in, in his place."

Some seventy years later, in 1915, the editors of *Town Topics*, W. Alton Mann's notorious New York magazine, ran a series called "Genealogies of American Society," commencing with the "Crowninshields of New England." Dick, and for good measure all of Richard Sr.'s issue, are neatly lopped off the family tree and the trunk so carefully smoothed and daubed that none would ever know that once it bore a branch which even the great Daniel Webster found thorny indeed. One almost sees the genealogist hurriedly pack his pens and charts, the tree surgeon his saws, ropes and paintpots, between sidelong glances at the altered, more seemly appearance.

In the end it may not be too much to suggest that we are curiously in Dick's debt. For it was he who helped set the style and tone of many a stage villain to come: a figure somewhat lecherous, overdressed, darkly caped and at one with the night, sneeringly, implacably dedicated to the Evil One, and who of course comes to a bad end — but, if you please, not too speedily. Evil, like Good, is infinitely complicated, and the abiding merit of the stereotyped villains of melodrama is that they spare us from inquiring very closely into a problem that, in the end, is insuperable anyway.

Captain White's house on Essex Street has over the years been beautifully restored by the Essex Institute and now stands as one of the finest examples anywhere of the late Federal period. Ironically, this was chiefly accomplished through the beneficence of yet another Crowninshield, Louise du Pont, and in gratitude the trustees have named the bedroom next to that where Dick made his stealthy entry so long ago the "Crowninshield Room." Those who knew that formidable lady will not be surprised that in her lifetime the tour guides were forbidden to speak of the murder. And even now, fifteen years after her death, they tend to assume a pained expression when asked about it and divert your attention elsewhere, as though a dose of prudery is just the thing to sober the caprice of history. So it is that the ghost of Captain White is forbidden the run of his own house by that of Louise du Pont Crowninshield, the wife of a collateral descendant of his assassin. Should this seem, spectrally speaking, untraditional, even a little unfair, the explanation is that in supernatural matters as well as others, money talks. But for all this, Dick's credentials as a first-class family skeleton remain unimpeachable.

Salem jail, although built in 1813 and greatly altered, still houses prisoners who lounge behind the green-painted bars and who somehow contrive disinterest out of their slack, limp postures. Yet mostly they are a cheerful lot, perhaps owing to the master, a kindly-disposed fellow in his early forties who looks not unlike a taller, younger and more handsome W. C. Fields. From behind an enormous cigar, the master, more wonderingly than anything else, observes that his charges are far better treated in every way than he was as a soldier in the United States Army at the time of the Korean War. In his cramped office are files, heaps of evidence (many inmates await trial), the flags of the Commonwealth and the United States, and the assorted, dreary memorabilia of penology. Yellow paint peels from the old walls, which bear framed red, white and blue patriotic slogans and a photograph of his father, who was master before him. An exuberant, somewhat fluorescent oil on plywood of Phil Esposito surveys the room with evident approval.

Prisoners still manage to get drunk as Joe Knapp did (a favorite method is to hoard the fruit cocktail often served as dessert and let it ferment). Drugs are a more intricate problem. It is not uncommon for a visiting mother to kiss her inmate son goodbye and pass a goofball into his mouth. Particularly difficult for the master, who is a very vigilant man, are new prisoners who before admission have swallowed a condom full of narcotics, which they will later excrete and use. Although the most thorough search will not reveal its presence, the technique is disadvantageous: occasionally stomach acid eats through the prophylactic and death by overdose follows.

A few years ago a prisoner hanged himself from the bars of his cell; he wrote no poetry, was not a hired murderer, and suspended himself with his belt.

As in 1830 the prison still houses females, and upstairs there is an old cradle used when the inmates of Dick's time gave birth. The matron, a believer in extrasensory perception, says the younger women in her charge hear a baby crying on stormy nights, as indeed she has. Not long ago it was arranged for the girls to decorate their own cells; tastes, much approved at the time, ran strongly to stuffed toy animals, but many of these on arrival were found to contain heroin and other drugs, impelling the authorities toward a more judicious view of cell decor.

The jail overlooks a small cemetery. Northerly, it abuts the Parker Brothers factory of "Monopoly" fame. In an area once the richest in the world and now clearly depressed, one of the few concerns to prosper does so by the endless manufacture of worthless money. We have come a long way from the Chinaman's map. There are pine and oak and a few flowering shrubs in the cemetery, and here on summer days the adolescent females of Salem are likely to disrobe and lie upon the grass among weathered headstones to amuse and taunt the male prisoners. They shout their names and telephone numbers upward and one thinks of Mary Bassett and Mary Jane Weller, whose pat testimony so vexed the jurymen of Essex County and spared George Crowninshield the rope. Some are scarcely fifteen and they crowd laughingly about. Particularly evocative of their mirth is their discovery that you are walking in the cemetery for pleasure; they giggle seemingly uncontrollably but their eyes, shifting endlessly to and fro, querying whether this or for that matter anything can somehow be reduced to advantage, belie much levity. A few yards beyond, not far apart and long oblivious to any tumult, lie Captain White and the Knapp brothers.

Several miles away in what was once Danvers and is now Peabody, one walks with Mr. Murphy, a pleasant, retired employee of the A. C. Lawrence Leather Company, who points with a forlorn pride to the forsaken factory buildings lining the slopes of Buxton Hill. To him it is a ghost town. One crosses rusting, weed-choked railroad tracks and walks slowly, for Mr. Murphy is an old man. Few come nowadays for any reason to the desolation of Crowninshield Street.

The English slate roof of Richard's mansion still gleams dully in the autumn afternoon but the interior has been gutted and gutted again. For eighty years, until 1970, the two lower floors were used as washrooms for the factory hands and a flashlight picks out closely packed basins and urinals. For some reason the water has never been turned off and from broken fixtures it seeps everywhere. One's footsteps echo dankly and occasionally a rat rustles among the rags in an old locker.

In the gloom Mr. Murphy explains that tanning was a wet and dirty business; the wettest and dirtiest employees used the bottom floor and those less so the upper. There are tunnels in the cellar which he informs you were intended to conceal smuggled slaves and that it is a haunted place. You suggest that they were built only to ensure access to an adjacent and doomed woolen mill, and Mr. Murphy nods politely enough, but the old blue eyes, much magnified by glasses, prefer his own understanding.

Nearby is Richard's once willow-lined pond so much admired by the Reverend Bentley a century and a half ago. Its waters are limpid, still warm in late October, and in the silence they murmur along the spillway that was to bring the riches of the Indies to Buxton Hill.

FOUR

The "Dutiful Ward"

Clara Crowninshield (1810–1907)

Strange knockings and eerie groanings from the hereafter — these had mightily oppressed the repose of George Crowninshield, Jr., at Mr. Oakes's seedy inn and forced him to flee and spend his final hours aboard his yacht. No sooner had he entered the hereafter than his brother John scented "Roguery"; there were, he said, "a thousand stories in Salem."

William Bentley had eulogized George: "Few men were more generous & very few had [a more] agreeable share of confidence. No man knew the practice of his profession better & no one who knew him denies that he had great virtues." Who, he had asked from his pulpit, could fail to recall the yachtsman with affection?

Within days one who could was the Parson himself. "This eccentric man," he fumed, "by living with the lowest, had all the manners of the lowest." This thing, he promised, was "as humbling to family pride & the world's honor" as it was "contrary to good hopes." Immediately the matter was brought before the probate court administering the intestate assets of the richest man the Reverend Bentley had ever known. "Our family," flushed with many a victory, pitted its power and influence against "a woman of the town" and a miserable "yeoman" innkeeper. And it lost. For the Harlequin of the Mediterranean had left something besides a fortune and a beautiful ship behind. Her name was Clara.

Today it is scarcely possible to imagine the problems of a bastard in the first years of the nineteenth century in New England. An illegitimate shared in the estates of neither mother nor father, and suffered an almost total loss of status. Bastardy was — who could doubt it? — at least partly the bastard's fault. Family was of far greater importance in those days; it was at once shelter, the source of aid and comfort, a refuge and an arsenal. Within it lay all that was stable. Just as church-going was a family affair so was nearly every other social occasion. Without a family, life could be all so dismaying, even shattering. What future did one have? Illegitimacy was hard enough if one was male and nearly hopeless for a girl.

One who was often dismayed but never shattered was Clarissa (later called Clara) Crowninshield. Her mother was Elizabeth Rowell, "a single woman," and one of George Crowninshield's more permanent whores. At Clarissa's birth in 1810, Elizabeth had "sworn her" upon a young Salem tradesman named Joseph McComb. The putative father had not resisted, yet Crowninshield had continued to see a great deal of Elizabeth. Although "our family" had not known of it, George seems early to have recognized the child as his. Having spirited her away from Salem, he had brought her to Mr. Oakes's Malden inn and paid him a dollar or so a week to look after her and, above all, keep her there. Clara was then about four years old, "a very playful child," and as Oakes later testified, George had introduced Elizabeth as Mrs. Crowninshield or surely he "would never had taken them in." George's whore had wanted desperately to be Mrs. Crowninshield but he had always put her off. In February of 1817, Elizabeth had begged George to take her with him on his voyage of pleasure to Europe. "The girl," wrote his sister-in-law, "he has kept so long . . . has been marking up elegant clothes — but I don't believe he thinks of taking her." Elizabeth shopped in vain; a man who yearned for the Princess of Wales had no room aboard his yacht for the likes of Miss Rowell. But she was able to wring from him a kind of unwitnessed promissory note for $8,000 containing the proviso that should George "perform the Voyage on which he is now bound in the BRIG CLEOPATRA'S BARGE and he should return to Salem then this OBLIGATION shall be void."

Voided it was and Elizabeth, with the assistance of Mr. Oakes, set about extracting other promises from a difficult and stubborn man whose head was now filled with thoughts of another voyage of pleasure. The strange nocturnal sounds that had tormented George were not the fearsome fancies of paranoia but the work of mortal hands, those of Elizabeth and Mr. Oakes, who "made ghosts & goblins to knock upon the Floor and worked upon his mind."

On George's death, the documents so adduced were presented for adjudication. They were in the handwriting of Mr. Oakes and promised $16,000 to "My Daughter Clarissa." With all the legal talent great wealth commands, "our family" attacked these unwitnessed papers. The money was a trifling part of his estate, yet every effort was made to exclude Elizabeth and her daughter from so much as a penny. Fraud! cried John Crowninshield. The papers were forgeries; if not that, they had surely been written under duress. If the court honored these tricks, he was sure Elizabeth and Mr. Oakes would produce more. Besides, Clarissa was not George's daughter at all, but Joseph McComb's or even Mr. Oakes's — in spite of or because of Mrs. Oakes. In Richard Crowninshield's opinion — and he knew his brother very well — George would never have left her more than $8,000, even if she was his daughter. But finally a judge, to Crowninshield disgust, awarded the little girl slightly more than $15,000, in those days a very respectable sum. Perhaps the probate court felt "it a debt of justice," as did, according to the Reverend Bentley, "the virtuous part of the community." The Crowninshields thereupon turned their backs on the little girl forever.

This delighted Mr. and Mrs. Oakes, with whom Clarissa lived, for the child had no mean fortune now and her mother was easily manageable. Unfortunately for the Oakeses one Benjamin Nichols was appointed Clarissa's trustee and almost instantly he concluded that they were every bit as unfit as Elizabeth Rowell.

But the innkeeper and his wife did not give up without a fight:

Malden Augt. 31st 1819

Mr. Nicholes Sir

    after calm deliberation on your taking Clarissa from us at this time in a moment when Mr. Oakes' health is so impaired that taking from him a child that he is so much attached to is . . . like taking from him a limb when he mentioned to her of her going from him not to return again for some months she burst into tears and replyed she would not leave him every time it is mentioned befor her she bursts into tears solicits me to write you not to take he[r] away from us at present it is not from any pecunary advantages we expect to gain that we wish her to continue with us but from that affection that a parent has for a child. . . .

Ignoring this whetting of beaks, Nichols bundled the hysterical Clarissa and her tatterdemalion belongings off to Miss Cushing's school in Hingham, where the formidable headmistress aimed to inculcate "correct sentiments" and "a high tone of moral feeling" in the child. The bastard daughter of a prostitute of course presented a special challenge, but the good lady confessed herself equal to the task; tuition would be payable in advance.

Although her new pupil was a cheerful enough little girl, Miss Cushing was sorry to tell Nichols that Clara's (as she came to be called) "want of ready obedience" and "trifling pursuits" gave her teacher some uneasiness. He was assured, however, that if the girl remained in her charge, these traits would no longer be prominent; indeed, "ere long" they would "entirely disappear."

The Yankee lawyer had been greatly pleased to hear this; moreover, he admired Miss Cushing's technique, which was to advance "an erroneous opinion" for the purposes of contradiction by the children on their slates. As soon as she could write, Clara wrote letters to her guardian — she had no one else to write to anyway — a correspondence that was to continue for eighty-five years: with Nichols until he died and then with his son, who succeeded him. Early letters, signed "your Dutiful Ward," were accompanied by those of Miss Cushing regretting her pupil's many erasures and inferior penmanship. Later one sees year by year the changes in her English. "Shew" becomes "show" and more reluctantly, with many a hesitation, a "drefs" becomes a "dress" and in time this hand would send telegrams.

Miss Cushing profusely apologized to Nichols for overcharging in the matter of tuition, only to overcharge again. Tactfully, such set-tos were followed by reminders of Clara's deficiencies, which regrettably had not yet entirely disappeared. Miss Cushing did not want to lose a paying pupil. Clara was "not willing to tax her intellect for composition" and sometimes "would never produce a line."

That Mr. Nichols was more to Clara than trustee is clear in a letter of 1823, in which she includes this verse:

> *From a belle my dear father you have oft had a line,*
> *But not from a bell under water*
> *Just now I can only assure you I'm thine,*
> *Your dutiful, diving affectionate daughter.*

Although sometimes cruel and incomprehensible things were whispered about her, the little girl learned French and to play the pianoforte, and she liked to sew and knit her own stockings (sometimes getting no further than the heel) in the evening when the slates were put away. But dreaded were what her fellow students looked forward to most of all: vacations, for these meant home and family. As they drew near she sought to calm her panic by long melancholy walks by the Hingham shore.

Whenever possible she spent vacations with the Nichols family in Salem, but there she was in the very camp of those who despised her and wished her no existence — the Crowninshields. On visiting a schoolmate's family, she was so fearful of not being invited back again that she would offer to pay her room and board before she had set foot in the door.

When somewhat timidly his "Dutiful Ward" asked permission to write her mother, the trustee agreed, but only as often as her teacher thought proper. Miss Cushing rarely thought it proper.

Clara made "continuous progress in the acquisition of correct sentiments" and in the lace handkerchiefs she sewed, and after she had been six years at the school Miss Cushing no longer felt uneasy. At fifteen, Clara was a good student, who found it "very curious to read of the different conformation of the various animals and to see how exactly their organization is adopted to their several wants. . . . The smallest insects are furnished with so many powers to . . . add to their enjoyment." In July of 1825, the class went to hear an oration by

Daniel Webster: his "Address to Lafayette." She had been thrilled. Little did she know that Webster would before very long make another speech, one that would echo in her mind all her life.

If Mr. Nichols had been pleased with Clara, she had reason to be pleased with him. Upon taking up his duties, he had invested her inheritance ("our family" thought it blackmail) wisely and well; she would never really want for money. And he performed another duty. When she left school for short trips, her stays were carefully arranged by the trustee in cautiously probing letters that too frequently brought replies like this one: "It would," wrote one John Marston on January 20, 1825, "be too hazardous for Clara to sleep at Mrs. Greenleaf's, on account of the danger of taking cold to which she must necessarily be exposed in the winter and spring months." But by now Nichols was skilled at shielding his ward from such rebuffs and all went well enough.

In 1827 Nichols felt that Clara's horizons should be broadened; she was removed from Miss Cushing's tutelage and installed as a boarder at the home of his sister, whose husband was the Librarian of Harvard College. In this genteel and mannered environment she flourished, and by the time Clara was twenty, she had developed into a pretty, if not beautiful, young girl. She was a trifle plump, to be sure, shorter than she wished but with large blue eyes, all clearly the stamp of the Harlequin of the Mediterranean. She dressed carefully; she was a cultured young lady who had mastered the art of polite conversation. All her life the harlot's bastard took the greatest care that no one would ever find the slightest fault with her. Nichols, as prudent as he was with money, was careful always to furnish her with enough to be a young woman of fashion. By 1830 he, his sister and Miss Cushing might well have congratulated themselves. Clara was what they and she wanted her to be: respectable, with all that meant in early nineteenth century New England.

As for her father's family, she never mentioned them, nor they her.

Suddenly her all-too-fragile security was shattered. Terrible rumors swept over Boston from Salem, dark tales of bloody murder and hangings. In the mail came ominous, terrifying and unsigned threats promising her a ghastly fate. She trembled; the name of Crowninshield was everywhere and her father's family were scattering from Salem as though some monstrous plague or the devil himself was at their heels. To the fearsome letters was added something equally bewildering: many of her little circle of friends — so patiently and timorously cultivated and whose correspondence gave her such pleasure — no longer wrote. In the streets of Cambridge she was eyed by muttering strangers, some of whom stared aghast. Others laughed. She, whom "our family" had sought to deprive of her very name and who had borne it stoically, patiently as a bastard, must now endure its odium. It was crushing; gone were all her hopes. From Cambridge she fled to Hingham and a somewhat discomfited Miss Cushing. Where else could she go? But even there the fearful words of Daniel Webster reverberated from a Salem courtroom; there was no escape; she was damned.

To Nichols's sister she wrote in July of 1831: "Time seems only to strengthen my bad feelings and I begin now almost to despair of ever feeling otherwise. While they last there can be no pleasure in life — it is a mere exercise of patience to live. . . . The mind acts upon the body in the first place and that again reacts upon the mind. Every feeling is paralised and every faculty . . . annihilated. I am in a state of insensibility. . . . I sit alone in my chamber with my eyes fixed upon the ground like a statue. . . . I cannot go on any longer."

These agonies were hastily imparted to Nichols:

DEAR BROTHER — I feel something must be done for Clara immediately . . . go to Hingham today and bring her directly to our house. . . . I know her so well, that at times her friends must act for her. . . . I know no one else [to whom] she will freely communicate her feelings. . . .
Yrs in haste,
Elizabeth

In Cambridge, Clara emerged from her terrible depression into what she called a state of "heroic calmness." Slowly she took an interest in life once more; she ordered her affairs; she bought an elegantly

167

engraved edition of Byron and before long craved the company of "excellent and cultivated" ladies. Nichols had been greatly encouraged by her recovery but he could not answer when, again and again, she asked him where "a suitable place" could be found for her? Who were those "desirous" of having her? It puzzled her that Catholics deliberately inflicted "corporeal sufferings on themselves" when all hers came without the slightest effort. Particularly tormenting were the Cotillions in Boston, full of "perplexities" and "fatigues." They were also full of muted asides and averted glances, for few young men would dance with her and then only dutifully, politely, without further interest.

In the fall of 1833, the restless and unhappy girl turned to a riding school on Mason Street in Boston that offered "a course of Lessons to consist of Sixteen, and one hour is devoted to each Lesson, for which Ladies will pay $16 and Gentlemen $20, for the first course in advance." Clara's sixteen dollars came to naught, however, for now she had other plans. She had found those who appeared "desirous to have me" but her fur cape was not "fit to wear another winter." Nichols must buy her a new, more handsome one, and very soon. She knew she was short; a large one would "bury me up too much." With a sigh of relief more parental than fiduciary, the Yankee lawyer sped to the furriers.

Those desirous to have her were Henry and Mary Longfellow of Brunswick, Maine, where Henry was teaching at Bowdoin College. Mary Longfellow was one of Clara's few loyal friends and welcomed her at the Longfellow home. Clara helped Mary with household chores; she made herself agreeable and was, said Mary, an "excellent girl," almost like a sister. Clara was delighted and Henry's fanciful disquisitions with his colleagues fascinated her. So did Señor Cortés, a Spaniard overflowing with wit and gallantry, who called her a "cherubin." Brunswick evenings were full of delightful discussions of everything — literature, politics, even an occasional tussle with Swedenborgianism. It was a new world to which her visits became longer and longer; she could "only complain that the time is too short." How pleasant it all was! How very far away Salem was!

Clara Crowninshield at twenty-four. From the sketch by Maria Röhl, Stockholm, 1835. Courtesy of the U.S. Department of the Interior, Longfellow National Historical Site

Henry Wadsworth Longfellow at twenty-eight. From the sketch by Maria Röhl, Stockholm, 1835. Courtesy of the U.S. Department of the Interior, Longfellow National Historical Site

About this time to Henry Longfellow came "good fortune at last": his linguistic abilities had been recognized by Harvard College. President Josiah Quincy had nominated him Smith Professor of Modern Languages. But the President hoped — in polite injunction and fine disregard of Longfellow's shaky finances — his nominee would, before assuming his duties in Cambridge, spend some months abroad to perfect "ye German."

Borrowing money from his unenthusiastic father and selling some of his books would not quite swing it. Although he was determined to meet the condition of the Harvard offer, his studies abroad might well be impeded by the demands of a sickly wife. What if Mary were to have a female companion who might also be a kind of nurse should the occasion arise (and he was sure it would)? His thoughts turned to Señor Cortés's "cherubin," who would do well enough — and would even help defray his expenses. Happily there was also a Miss Goddard, who, according to a contemporary, had "a large Junolike figure with a beautiful face" and a complexion "as white as a slice of fresh, boiled ham." Somewhat more to the point, the young lady's father was a prosperous merchant who was willing to pay Longfellow for chaperoning her in Europe. Clearly Miss Goddard, like Clara, did not seem to have anything else to do. A bargain was struck; all were pleased. Immediately the once "Dutiful Ward" was asking, other than timidly, her trustee for money. He complied. Who could ever have so compelling an urge to be gone? To the young scholar the way to Europe and to Harvard was clear. "In such a goodly number," Longfellow wrote, "the ladies will amuse each other, without too much of my assistance." He was "all on tiptoe to be gone."

On April 10, 1835, the party sailed aboard the *Philadelphia*, and Clara little realized that she would soon find her place — forever. In London she admired a Leonardo da Vinci landscape in the National Gallery, saw William IV's queen clatter by, and met her first real admirer, a usually tipsy British army officer on half pay named James Frazer, who took to following her and Miss Goddard about on tours of the Whispering Gallery (they could not hear a thing; he pretended he could) and the Zoological Gardens. Although she felt sorry for him, before long Clara wished "he would have the resolution to go away . . . it would be better for him." But Frazer did not. He hung about, bought her the "most beautiful album," and Clara primly noted in her diary: "It was better that he spend his money so, than in dissipation." What James Frazer needed was to acquire a set of correct sentiments of the sort old Miss Cushing knew so much about and maybe she would give him Channing's works; these he could read aloud to her before she went away. But Frazer lacked interest and the following day led her on a shopping tour in a part of London where the streets had a "strange appearance." Laughingly Frazer told her they were headed for his rooms. Clara made him turn back, and that night, when she started to read aloud to him, he stalked out. But each morning he called at her rooms as usual, sometimes terribly hung over. Clara hoped "to induce him to forsake his old companions and habits." In vain.

On to Sweden via Germany, where Longfellow wanted to see the poet Karl August Nicander. Frazer went along as far as he could, promised to write her at Stockholm, and "floated off" on the pilot boat.

Germany, which she instantly hated, made Clara appreciate England: "It seems a perfect paradise — how I should love to live there!" Germany was hot, dusty and primitive. She saw women washing in yellow river water "with all sorts of trash swimming about in it"; the public baths were atrocious, the sidewalks no better to walk upon than the streets, the language and food coarse and confusing. Sometimes it was so hot she had "nothing thin eno' to put on." She went for a droshky ride with a Pole, a Swede and a certain Charles Lavy, a feisty little fortune hunter who traveled about in search of an American wife of substance. Lavy was much taken with Clara — and the substance he imagined she possessed — all of which amused her.

On the way to Lubeck the fate of all travelers befell her: "Mary and I got out at one place. . . . Henry . . . rightly conjectured that we did not desire his company. One of our attendants who could not speak English stood in the doorway. 'What shall I say?' cried Mary. 'Ask for some water,' said I, 'and perhaps we may find a woman inside.' Mary began to cry 'Wasser! Wasser!' and touched her finger to her lips, but our German was unintelligible to the man or else he had the penetration to see through our subterfuge, for he immediately retreated and left the field to us. We went thro' a narrow entry into a large room where there was no light but what came in through the passageway, and here and there a straggling beam shot through sundry cracks. A female figure was standing there. Mary made up to her and began to make the most significant signs and we thought she understood. She pointed to a door on one side of the passage we came in, with a look of prohibition, and gabbered away something which I interpreted to signify that there was a sick man there. She took a yoke and hung it over her shoulder, talking as fast as possible all the time as if she fully understood our meaning, but instead of showing us the way, she quitted us forthwith and went about her own business. Thus we were none the better for our encounter with her.

"The time was going and we were afraid Henry would be impatient. I was just about to make a desperate effort when my intention was frustrated by the sudden apparition of a man from the prohibited door. On the opposite side was a most miserable looking straw-bed in a box raised like a berth at sea. From this the damsel had probably herself arisen. In the large apartment which contained no window I was not surprised to see a dog chained nor a pig in his stye, for I had heard of places where the domestic animals share the same rooms with the family. I heard the mewing of a cow, too, and on turning my head I started, for behind us was a range of stalls for animals. By the twilight I could just perceive a cow's head thrust out behind me, and since we had discovered the nature of the apartment into which we had penetrated we were anxious to retreat without making further discoveries. It was a barn or stable full of filth into which we had entered with all the respect in the world.

"We were provoked, Mary particularly, to think we had exposed ourselves to Henry for nothing and I had all the blame to bear for not trying to speak to the woman in German. They laughed at me and scolded at me and would have no sympathy with 'my foolish modesty,' as they called it.

"There is nothing like stern necessity so I prepared my sentence and at the next stopping place I told Mary I would ask if she would go in with me. I felt foolishly diffident about it. I was as much agitated as if I had been going to address an assembly. I nerved myself for the task, marched straight up to the first girl I saw in the kitchen. Without waiting for her to finish blowing a coal for her lamp I began — 'Kann ich heraus gehan?' She understood me and I felt a sense of relief I cannot DESCRIBE. She said something which I did not understand, but that was no matter. She went to the door and pointed to the place. 'Da?' said I. 'Ja,' she replied."

Once she was sick: "Henry came to call us down to dinner. I hoped he would not come into me for I had told the girl I should take none before. They came down but he came in to see why I did not follow. I told him I did not want any, but when he began to urge me and tried to tempt me by mentioning over the dishes, my heart sank, and because I had not the power of answering him I had to rise and feign a compliance by beginning to arrange my things. I knew he was waiting in the next room . . . and with my back towards him I commanded myself eno'. . . . I did all in my power to cheer up."

In Denmark there was a little fountain on a pleasant road where the coach had paused and a little boy gave her a glass of water to drink; it was good to leave Germany behind. Although Henry "played off" his little Danish in restaurants, Copenhagen was dull; it had to her the look of a place large yet strangely deserted, a "city of the dead."

In Sweden she planned to take French lessons from a master who spoke no English, to sketch, and to have "a nice time." She was amused by the half-naked children who played among Swedish country houses "put together like children's cot-houses — long, round beams with notches cut out at the ends to make them fit closely, and the ends left sticking out, and they are usually painted red in the principal towns."

But far more interesting was a gentleman in a black velvet coat with "such a truly Swedish face with light hair and light moustache that I did not dream he even understood English." The party exchanged, first in undertones and then more loudly, various remarks on the gentleman's moustache. "Just then a beggar came along and began to solicit Mr. Longfellow in Swedish. He knew eno' to say 'I do not understand you,' but the beggar went on. Then the gentleman . . . looking at Henry, said in a very distinct, audible manner, 'He wants some money.' " Clara had been attracted to him but immediately the moustached gentleman rode off "with a segar in his mouth" forever.

She received no letters from America and the old depression returned: "How long! how very long I had been away, and had I left no one behind who cared eno' for me to write to me? . . . How little consequence I am to anybody in the world. There is no substitute, after all, for natural ties. . . . Where can be found a more solitary being than I am, and what is to become of me as I grow older and lose the little buoyancy I have now?"

Jolted along "shocking streets" and through miserable pine forests and fields of scanty grass by a "stupid stuttery" driver, she felt worn out, "no longer capable of receiving any new, permanent impressions." As she had once walked the Hingham shore, she walked the streets of Stockholm alone until Longfellow upbraided her, saying that "no respectable woman walked out alone in Stockholm." She gave up her only source of pleasure; she was a "prisoner" and paced her rooms until it made Miss Goddard nervous. "It is shocking to be in such thraldom," she wrote on July 9. If only she could be like her Cambridge friend, Lucy Ashmun, who was adventurous and bold and cared little for what others thought of her. Lucy would have been a good traveling companion; Lucy feared nothing.

One day she looked out the window to meet the eye of Charles Lavy, who always convulsed her with laughter. The obliging Lavy was anxious that Clara be amused in Stockholm. Perhaps she would like to visit an iron mine. She teased him; she mimicked his tones and gestures. It was wicked to make fun of such a little "tailor," yet she thought even "a saint could hardly resist it." But Lavy didn't mind and a day or two later the girls accepted his invitation to visit some churches. Although Lavy had brought a bag of sugarplums, Clara felt the day had not been spent as it should have been. She went with Lavy to watch a great building burn ("a glorious sight") but leaning on his arm "tended very much to destroy the sublimity" of her feelings.

174

In the Swedish capital, Clara had her portrait ("shockingly stupid") painted, met a baron who was "an easy, fat, sociable gentleman with nothing remarkable about him," and regretted the abundance of Scandinavian graffiti. Swedish boys were just like American boys, she thought, and even a bronze bust of Charles X had not been spared.

About this time Mary Longfellow concluded that Charles Lavy was something of a nuisance himself. He was insignificant and indifferent to her barbs — and was he not Jewish? Longfellow, on the other hand, liked to have him around, perhaps because Lavy served to keep the girls off his neck. Clara really didn't object to the cavalier, although when he had asked her for a lock of her hair, she gave him a lead pencil instead. However, one day at Goteborg, where he had followed them, she schemed to be rid of him. "First there was to be a letter lying on the table directed to me, which they were to say came from Frazer, and then if he expressed any surprise at my getting a letter from him, they were to say, 'Why, did not you know Miss Crowninshield was engaged to Mr. Frazer?' But then the girls were afraid they should not be able to answer all the queries he might ask about the letter. I could have directed it, for I can write like Frazer, but we could not put on to it any postmarks, and then we should have been obliged to say the letter came enclosed to Mr. Longfellow. Henry tho't this would be making rather a tangled net of it and that it would be better to have a letter on the table from me to Frazer, and then the girls could say I had just received a letter from him and a letter that had been written some time [ago], for it was only the day before that we had told him that Frazer had not written a line to us, tho' he promised to and knew our direction. This [had] inflated him with hope. 'I shall [go] with [you],' said he. So the only way was to pretend that it was an old letter. . . .

Lavy came tripping in. 'The ladies have been to ride, I think.' He sat quite mute till Mr. Wyck had gone. Then I retired to my room under pretence of taking off my things but really in order to give the girls a chance to ring on their play. It put me in mind of the maneuvers in a French play. There was a low conversation which I could not understand, and then tea or rather coffee was brought. I could not tell whether the 'eclaircissement' had been made or not, but I walked out and tried to look as un[self]conscious as possible. I thought I could perceive a cloud lowering over the brow and I supposed the discovery had been made. Henry was full of fun and coughed into his cup and had to run into the next room to recover himself. . . . Lavy seemed to be paralyzed. He sat in mute astonishment while Mary Goddard, gaining courage, let fly a volley of poisoned arrows. The fellow did not long endure it. He rose with a deep sigh, took his hat and bade good evening. Henry had his head out of the window smoking a segar, and in that attitude he hazarded an observation now and then to help along the joke."

Longfellow and his *Jugendfreunden* arrived once more the following week in Copenhagen. Here there really was a letter from Frazer, who was taking leave of an indifferent England in order to offer his services to the Spanish Pretender, Don Carlos. Clara scoffed: the foolish fellow; it was another joke; and she tore his letter to pieces.

And there was news from America. Mary Goddard's father was dead of apoplexy; Mary must return at once. Thus the little party became three.

One day Clara read Irving's *Abbotsford and Newstead Abbey*, responding to " 'the white lady,' a young girl who was deaf and dumb, without relations, and by her infirmities cut off from all intercourse with the living." How familiar it sounded to Clara when she reflected "upon what I have suffered from my earliest recollection. . . . I only wonder that my reason did not forsake me. . . . Why are the useful and the happy and the beloved taken away? And why is the useless, dark thread of my existence protracted?"

Suddenly there was "the gentlest knock imaginable" at her parlor door, "so faint I thought my ears might have deceived me." It was Lavy, apologizing, scraping his feet, and offering to be of service. His only problem was that his watch was "the hour too slow." But once more he was left behind and the party sailed for Kiel on an odious-smelling steamer.

In Amsterdam, Mary Longfellow had what was thought to be a fit of ague and a doctor had been called. He was, according to Clara, "a little one-sided, dwarfish object who announced himself in French as 'le médicin.' Mary did not chuse to be seen and had her curtains drawn, so 'Monsieur le médicin,' seeing no other female, supposed I was the one and turning his back to Mr. Longfellow he hitched up to me. I was very busy sewing at the moment and took no notice of his advances. He began to hesitate and modestly commenced, 'Excusez — madam.'" The doctor, who reminded her of Tom Thumb in *Mother Goose*, left Mary some medicines in a vial and took his leave.

Mary grew sicker and the next night, according to Longfellow, there was "the very deuce to pay, and all in the dark! . . . It was a long time before I could muster flint, steel and matches, and strike a light." When he did, he was aghast; his wife had miscarried.

Clara had another letter, the last from Frazer, who had returned wounded to England from the Pretender's wars. What was worse, he told her, he had lost his fortune by a bank failure. Clara pitied him; he now expected to go to the East Indies for at least ten years.

In Rotterdam Clara walked along canals lined with pleasant houses and flower beds and watched birds skimming over the surface as if attracted by their own images in the water. But everywhere yellow leaves lay upon damp pavements and she shivered at these symptoms of winter. One day she saw, in a passing funeral, five *aanspreckers* (literally, black crows), who were paid by the family of the deceased to spread the news of the death and who gamboled about with weird, macabre gestures.

There was worse to come.

Mary Longfellow was again hunched with pain; physicians were called but there was little hope. Clara read a hymn to her:

> *My God! I thank thee! May no thought*
> *E'er deem thy chastisements severe.*
> *But may this heart, by sorrow taught,*
> *Calm each wild wish, each idle fear.*

Gloomily, Henry and Clara tended Mary around the clock, but on

November 28 she thanked her "dear, good little Clara" and died. "Henry kissed her cold lips and drew the rings from her lifeless hand and placed them on his own." That night Clara prevailed upon him to lie down on her bed and the poet wept himself to sleep.

Clara and Henry left Rotterdam a day or so later for Heidelberg, which soon brought out the Bostonian in her guardian, Mr. Nichols: she was in "an embarrassing situation," he wrote; she should take the earliest opportunity to return to America; she must do it directly. But Clara was in no hurry. She liked the Rhine: "A little balcony juts out from our room which commands a view up and down the river. What a scene of romantic associations! The genius of Byron has shed a halo over one peak and that of Schiller over the other. We opened the glass door of the balcony and listened to the rushing [of] the Rhine where its waters are compressed by the island. The hills were clothed in a soft vapor and the scene was charming." Nowadays it is easy to see much of Longfellow's *Hyperion* in Clara's account of their trip: as when they looked out a window one night to admire a Gothic ruin (it turned out by daylight to be the chimney of a neighboring house). They met William Cullen Bryant — in Clara's words, "tall and thin with a pale, furrowed countenance, a forehead high and narrow, and no handsome feature except his eyes, which are blue and bright and thoughtful." Mrs. Bryant had "a very pure feminine countenance and a very peculiar eye."

Clara Crowninshield's earlier aversion to Germany was forgotten. Now she praised the cooking, the wines, and the servants. Christmas was delightful; Mr. Nichols, Frazer, Lavy and all Crowninshields were far away, Henry Longfellow nearby. She shuddered at the prospect of being "uprooted, to be dependent upon utter strangers for society, comfort, and happiness, and then to be set down in the strange city of New York by myself with no friend in the world ready to hasten to me and welcome me and take me home!" Her one and only true friend in America, the once-lively Lucy Ashmun, was dying of consumption. Perhaps she would remain forever in Europe. Why not? Together Clara and Henry planned a tour of the Swiss Alps.

But suddenly her hopes were dashed, perhaps by fear of what Mr.

Nichols or Josiah Quincy of Harvard might think or by some quarrel. At any rate, Henry went on to Switzerland alone and Clara wept in Heidelberg. Never had she felt so "desolate and severed from the world." She wrote and implored him to return but Longfellow ignored her pleas and when he reappeared after an absence of two months, he was clearly a different man.

Clara now wanted to leave Europe. And so she did. But not before a stop in Paris, where Mr. Lavy, "the same old good-hearted creature," appeared. She took leave of her admirer for the last time "with many pressures of the hand"; he wanted to go to America with her and confided that his fear of having to marry an English rather than an American woman was now grave indeed.

In America once more, Clara pursued German studies in Cambridge, purchased Audubon prints by the hundreds at four dollars each, did pretty much as her trustee expected, and seemed in a fair way to be an old maid. In New England in 1837 there were few serious suitors for the hand of such a Crowninshield as she. But there did appear an interesting German named Louis Thies, who seemed to care very little about bastardy and its consequences. Louis improved her German, now very good; he liked art and so did she. Once apprenticed to an apothecary, he had become an expert on German engravings and was later mourned as "a man of simple habits, warm domestic affections and spotless life." In Louis Thies Clara found someone to whose happiness she was indispensable. True, there were signs that Thies's "simple habits" included a marked dislike of work of any kind. But what did this matter when she was an heiress of sorts? They would travel abroad, maybe live in Europe, all of which struck Thies, who thought most American ways confusing and a little expensive, as a good idea. With the help of old Mr. Nichols, Clara and Louis drew up a marriage contract which in modern terms came closest to a kind of joint checking account, with Louis's drawing ability somewhat limited. After a while they were off to Europe, where Louis pursued his passion for engravings. As long as the drafts kept coming (by now Clara's demands for more money were a little imperious), all went well enough, and two children, Louis and Clara, were born of the marriage.

In 1848, Benjamin Nichols, who had dragged a screaming little girl with her ragged dolls from a Malden inn once rent by ghostly noises, died. Clara was sorry the old man was gone. She had been fond of him (although maybe he could have done a little better with her investments). It looked as though Nichols's son, also named Benjamin, would be her new trustee. But why did she need anyone at all? Why not just send the principal amount to Germany? Mr. Thies approved of this course of action. Young Mr. Nichols equivocated, posed legal barriers (it was a good account), and hung on to the money.

And it was just as well. Very soon Germany was wracked with revolution; "indeed the whole continent" was suddenly unsettled. Perhaps the Thies family should return to America. They did so in a kind of triumph in 1849, with a collection of art to be exhibited in several American cities. But after so long an absence she found Hingham so "fashionable" that it was impossible to get a washerwoman until after the Fourth of July. Louis took to traveling about Europe whence he badgered her for bank drafts.

By 1851, all Clara's paternal uncles were dead, unmourned by this bastard daughter to whom they had never spoken. Except for the prudent Benjamin, they had, before dying, been separated from their fortunes. The cross-eyed and erratic Richard, an unsuccessful manufacturer, died of typhoid fever and ruin in 1844. The bold and handsome John had never again duplicated his successes on the pepper coast of Sumatra; and privateering, which had so enriched Benjamin and Clara's father, was only the beginning of successive disasters for him. In February of 1814 he had built, in New York, *Diomede*, a finely modeled schooner, and in April went to sea with a doubtful crew. In five weeks *Diomede* took nine prizes, was betrayed, and was captured by a British man-of-war. John was sent as a prisoner to Dartmoor, Nova Scotia. Though Dartmoor, Nova Scotia, had not the infamies of Dartmoor Prison in England (a grim pile of rock upon a desolate moor where "King Dick," a black homosexual, clubbed his fellow prisoners into submission, monopolized the sale of beer, ran a boxing school, and kept two or three comely white lads), it was not much better. The Nova Scotia prisonkeeper was one Captain Cocket, an English officer known as the Scarecrow. When starving and sick American prisoners complained they would die, Cocket liked to remark, "Please do, His Majesty has acres enough in which to bury you." And, assisted by a set of particularly brutal Scottish physicians, bury them the Scarecrow did, by the hundreds.

Captain Cocket was well acquainted with the privateering exploits of the Crowninshields and his enmity toward his prisoner was bottomless. In the War of 1812, both sides customarily exchanged prisoners on their word of honor not to engage in further hostilities. The system was called "parole," and if a parolee broke his pledge there was a system of "retaliation," whereby a prisoner still in custody was punished for the parolee's breach of honor. John's trouble began in June 1814, when it was agreed that he be exchanged for a certain Captain Bass, a prisoner of the Americans in New Jersey. Bass, stipulated the Scarecrow (who was a friend of the Bass family in England), would have to be delivered to him before John could be released. Shortly, however, word reached the prison commandant that Bass had escaped his American captors. Now Captain Cocket was also a friend of certain Nova Scotian merchants who had suffered badly from Crowninshield privateering. He continued to insist on Bass's presence without telling his captive that Bass was no longer exchangeable.

Summer passed into fall and John wondered where Bass was and "for the first time in some time past," he was reduced to tears when the Scarecrow sent the other officers and crew of *Diomede* to Dartmoor, England, and the ministrations of "King Dick." The days grew short and gloomy, and although the United States President, under Crowninshield prodding, offered to exchange any one of several English prisoners for John, the Scarecrow balked. His prisoner wondered at "the particular likeness" the British had for him and harvested the potatoes he had planted in the spring.

One day in October there was a knock at the door of his prison hut and there stood Captain Bass, who apologized and forthwith sailed for England. At this, Crowninshield offered to kill Captain Cocket whenever he could find him after the war. In retaliation the Scarecrow clapped him in irons.

Sick and starving, the brave and sturdy man sank into deep despair. He recalled a French prisoner whom the English had kept in Nova Scotia for twenty-one years. As for him, he would rather die now and be buried in "His Majesty's acres" than be like "the Creature emerged from the Batile [Bastille] . . . every faculty all but gone." He was sure that if he should ever be released, his friends would "all be in heaven" but, characteristically, he still would have "no dishonorable or improper applycations . . . made for my release — that would wound my feelings more than my capture did." The war was over but the Scarecrow had assured him that he would be among the very last to be released, and he was.

Immediately Crowninshield thought of ways to discomfit the British. In all their history no one had made them more unhappy than Napoleon Bonaparte, now their prisoner on St. Helena in the mid-Atlantic. What could be better than to rescue the Emperor, set him loose once more? Captain Cocket was small fry. John got hold of a plan of "Longwood," Bonaparte's place of confinement. It was, he tells us, "an exact transcript of the plan . . . drawn out by young Las Cases [an Imperial companion in St. Helena] . . . which was intercepted." The document with Crowninshield's careful annotations — he provided a scale of English feet and one of "French feet," and we learn that a certain courtyard was "always muddy" — still exists. According to John's son, he attracted others to the scheme, only to be "frustrated" for undisclosed reasons, some of which may be imagined. Powerfully guarded by naval and military units, Napoleon was under the closest surveillance and could hardly do more than peer out at his red-coated jailers through a hole in the shutters. He was spied upon even when he took a bath. After a year or two of this the Emperor was glad enough to die of ulcers and lassitude and John Crowninshield went unavenged.

Like many other Americans of those postwar times, Crowninshield thought that his just due surely awaited him in the Louisiana acquisition. But in New Orleans he was to find only defeat and disaster. With the old honor, the old naiveté, he entrusted what remained of a fortune no sooner counted up than lost, to crooked New Orleans promoters in comparison with whom the Datoos of Sumatra were saints. What he intended as a steam-driven rum distillery ended in bankruptcy.

His health, never good after Dartmoor, failed and to a friend in 1825 he wrote that his "complaint was the dysentery, of six or seven years standing, reduced to the last stages of life; it was cured radically, by the most simple of all the old women's medicines . . . a bowl of *sour* milk porridge, with a lump of *Mutton tallow*, as large as a hen's egg boiled in it — if no *milk* is to be had, *water* is nearly as good." He went on to recommend as well the destruction of the pirates of Puerto Rico. Then the old elan flared again: Were there not "many rich Spaniards in the Pacific"? Perhaps he could be in the way of furnishing a few "small sloops of war" to someone, anyone. After all, was "there not money to be made"? He heaped abuse on the English, whose rulers were either "madmen or fools," and wished the United States Navy were stronger. It would be well, he said, to have a ship of the line so large it would barely fit into Boston Harbor, one that would have "a British 74 [a prize too] for a long boat." But for this Crowninshield, there was no further money to be made among the Datoos or His Majesty's merchantmen, and no one in the Pacific wanted his small sloops of war.

Around 1830 John set on foot a literary labor that was to consume the better part of his last years. The painstaking script, so small that one of the manuscript pages would occupy two if typewritten today, runs to almost three hundred thousand words. The never-published novel is entitled *Vindication of a Seaman's Character*. Solemnly assuring the reader that no word will "wound the pious mind" or "soil the chastity of principle," Crowninshield then embarks on a singular voyage.

The ship *Columbia* sails from Boston, presumably on a trading venture. Its captain is the soul of prudence, courage and skill, as are all

183

the officers and crew. Also aboard are a noble "full blooded and amiable African," an equally admirable American Indian, a "Rhode Island Travelling Pedlar," and a child stowaway named Little William, who has a widowed mother — no mean entrée into the hearts of these gruff, generous tars.

Columbia is the best of ships, the weather benign, and of profane words there are none. A drifting wreck full of skeletons is encountered; everyone, even *Columbia*'s manly Scottish doctor, is reduced to tears, and all fall to killing the sharks swimming about the wreck. Somewhat later, a corrupt governor (English, of course) and his black-whiskered pirate-cohort (who has the "step of a perfect dansing master") are foiled, given a good dressing down, and made to gnash their teeth and grovel. And when the villains assure *Columbia*'s captain that they will improve their behavior, he refrains from appropriating the vast treasure on board their black-painted ship. To make the villains' humiliation complete Little William refuses a parting gift of fifty dollars from the pirate captain, primly citing the advice of his mother about receiving stolen property. The buccaneer is utterly abashed, and *Columbia* sails on for a few thousand words or so in a sea of the highest moral dudgeon.

A slave ship is next seen and boarded. Having found the slaves happy, Little William distributes oranges to them and they are happier yet. Shortly, however, a terrible hurricane forces the captain to scuttle his vessel on an uncharted, uninhabited, half-enchanted island abounding with sweet water, game and fish, where splendid trees tower above shady bowers. Here they colonize ingeniously (shades of *Robinson Crusoe*), but it is Defoe with a difference: the captain gives "beautiful sermons from celebrated divines"; there are "manly athletics" (the good ship's doctor is an excellent foot racer, having learned to run fast in his native Scotland). In fact there are so many wholesome amusements, the blissful crew can hardly choose among them. Of the fair sex there is never a thought, and the rum stores go untouched.

And then without further ado, every variety of disaster rains down and an attempt to escape in an improvised vessel fails in a scene which the author believes equal to "the genius of Hogarth." Yet all is not lost. The captain establishes a barbershop; the newly appointed barber adorns the place with his coat of arms, "which . . . was the figure of a large hogs head, with prominant tusks & high branching ears, a very long face & brushy stif bristles, a monkey lathering it with a brush & shaving the bristles off with a razor in his right." While the castaways are agreeing that their new barbershop cuts "a perfect dash," a colonist pokes his head in one of the windows, whereupon the barber slams the window down on the colonist's neck and shaves the imprisoned face.

Such behavior is not without its consequences in John Crowninshield's demi-paradise, and within a paragraph or two the barber becomes "mopish" and hangs himself in the piggery out of remorse and the author's wish to have the demise consistent with the banker's coat of arms.

At this point all levity in the narrative ceases. There follow — immediately and unrelievedly — drownings, manglings, crushings to death beneath falling trees and barrels of rum, deaths from dysentery, yellow fever, and other awful diseases. Lengthy funerals of great drama are held daily. A ship sails tantalizingly by, and on. At this last, Little William, who heretofore has restricted himself to chasing goats about the island, erects a miniature gallows upon which, to the applause of his rapidly dwindling shipmates, he hangs in effigy the captain of the negligent vessel.

But it is no good. All perish except Little William and a seaman named Henry. Months, perhaps years, later Henry awakes to see a beautiful woman possessed of "a large share of phylosophy" cast away on the other side of the island with her two children and Jack, a very unemancipated black servant. They all join forces; Madam (for that is the only name Crowninshield gives her) and Henry become lovers but not before marrying in a prolonged and affecting sylvan ceremony — Spenser emended by a Yankee privateer.

Time goes by. Jack, the slave, amuses the newlyweds by disguising himself as a mountebank whenever possible — that is to say, when he is not coping with numerous and varied chores (no Crowninshield, however idle, ever believed in idleness). In the course of what may be years or decades, Little William marries Madam's daughter. They live happily and in the end are rescued, but not before finding an enormous treasure left in a cave by Spanish monks.

One closes the final page of these bulky tomes to rub one's eyes in fatigue and wonder. What is the flood of words all about? Clearly the *Vindication* vindicates nothing, and its happy conclusion seems to have been added reluctantly, almost as though by another hand. What the author really cared about was the way in which catastrophe obliterates the best of men. It had him, and long ago John Crowninshield had concluded that intrepidity and honor were never enough: "It was folly to calculate even on tomorrow."

His novel, the heart's cry of despair, rejects the human condition.

About the time of the Civil War, the onetime pupil of Miss Cushing and the *Jugendfreunde* of Henry Wadsworth Longfellow had reached certain conclusions about the human condition of Louis Thies. Clara's husband was, she wrote, "unfit to bear the slightest fatigue or annoyance," and "the least derangement" of his daily routine (which consisted of very little) "made him wretched." He also expected his wife to pay all the bills. Shunning household chores and the leaky roof of their Cambridge house, Louis made it clear to all that he was a European, a scholar whose sensitivity precluded "that mechanical ingenuity" which Clara thought "natural to every American man." Such deficiencies were of course supplied cheerfully enough by Clara, but she came to regret that she had no time "to meet the claims of society." Especially vexing was Louis's insistence on being read aloud to a portion of each day. Clearly he cared very little about such claims as society might make upon his wife; his own claims, especially those on her dividends, had best not be questioned. As to his business — the importing and selling of engravings — it brought in no money, was not even a pastime, and Clara found it "exceedingly trying."

And there were other demands upon her from her old mother and other poor relations. Under Clara's prodding, young Nichols had obtained a Revolutionary War widow's pension for her mother; it had not been enough. The poor relations seemed determined never to let her go. She could scarcely make ends meet. Would she be able any longer to afford such of her little charities as the Society for Employing Female Poor?

And what about young Louis and Clara? The latter was of an age now when chaperons were necessary and Clara, forgetful of an unchaperoned trip she had taken thirty years earlier, knew the girl could not go out in the world alone. Yet she could provide no advice, no encouragement; she was too absorbed in petty cares. Moreover, "the tone" among the young people of Cambridge was "very reprehensible." Who knew better than she that "if a young lady is social . . . and has not a large family circle, she must either go into the whirl . . . as most do or sit at home and feel unhappy."

Clara felt old and haggard but she must "command" herself. What was to be done? It was all money and that would go further in Europe where, she was sure, a more genteel life awaited her family. There was just one problem. If she sold up could it be that "Southern influence" might in some way or another interfere?

But the Confederacy was soon no more and on October 10, 1866, she packed up her family and left America forever. In a letter to her trustee she remarked that her husband's troublesome importing business would now surely cease; he could simply go out and buy engravings.

In Europe she feared a French invasion of Germany, which never came, but her sense of relief was short-lived. In July 1870, her son Louis, in whom she had reposed great hopes, died suddenly. A year later her husband, who seemed more enfeebled than ever, dragged himself from spa to spa in vain, and then was gone. For years Clara's letters were edged in black and all her attention was focused on young Clara, who married a German army officer, August von Ekensteen, in 1872. She was pleased by the match; she became a grandmother and never had she seen the Dresden autumn so lovely. At her daughter's marriage, she had been gratified that her Cambridge sewing circle ("The Bee") had sent a little gold thimble in a tiny box.

But that was all about Cambridge that pleased her. She commenced a running battle with its municipal tax authorities. How could they not understand that she was through with America forever? Nichols was flooded with advices and quotations from a book she had got hold of called *Business Law for Business Men*. Did not Nichols know the law of domicile? By this time she had concluded that her art collection — she owned paintings by Van Dyck, Correggio and Raphael — was all "dead capital"; a half century's dealing with trustees had made her sound very much like a lawyer.

In 1872, a good part of Boston and Clara's investments burned down but Clara took the loss stoically. In 1882 she was seventy-six and looked and felt as well as ever. Summers she spent by the seashore with her grandchildren, Clara and August. She was sorry that her "circle of old friends grows narrower each year." So did that of her family, for her son-in-law, Major von Ekensteen, took it into his head to die. Why were people always dying? A year or so before, he whose *Jugendfreunde* she had once been — the laureate Longfellow — had also died.

What really had their relationship been along the Rhine where Schiller and Byron cast their spell? We know that Henry Longfellow had gone alone to Switzerland leaving Clara to weep her eyes out in a Heidelberg pension and that he had lingered in Interlaken. His biographers are likely to tell us the poet was in Switzerland smitten with a debilitating Weltschmerz, and finding "emotional maturity." Perhaps so, but what is more surely known is that he met the very rich Frances Appleton and very quickly evinced a marital interest. The remainder of his life and all his works were accomplished in perfect ease and serenity. No longer had he the slightest use for any *Jugendfreunde*. Clara had figured in his life as a means to Europe, Harvard and, incidentally, Frances Appleton — and not at all in his poetry. Thereafter, Henry referred to her in a kind of "good old Clara" way.

But once she tried to set the record straight: "You always say that you are misunderstood, but I say that you have misunderstood me. I make only one reproach to you, and you are not to blame for it either, only your disposition. You lack constancy. If . . . any other person with whom I have passed so many intimate hours could forget everything so completely, I should surely be unhappy about it. This indifference of yours will not cause me any 'eternal' sorrow. But whenever I see you or write to you I must think of it and feel it too. Otherwise I have had no complaints. That I am right about this you will have to admit." Longfellow never admitted anything.

But that had been long ago; now all her thoughts were upon her little grandson, August. She thought he should best attend a Prussian military academy, although she herself did not wish him to be a soldier. August filled her long, solitary walks ("a withdrawal from the outward air was," she said, "a sore privation") with unease.

By 1891, the young cadet, who had in her opinion "no practical qualities," was subject to the temptations of garrison life in Metz. She concluded that August should never have gone into the army; it was too fashionable and the young man ran up debts and expected her to pay them. As if this was not bad enough, there were those in red-striped trousers at the Königsplatz who had determined to rid the Reichswehr of place hunters, especially those seeking status by association with an elite. At the same time it was decided, somewhat unmilitarily, to extract a certain intellectual capacity from the officer class. On all counts August von Ekensteen, whose principal ability lay in wringing a thousand marks or so from his grandmother, was doomed.

For a decade Clara devoted herself to the advancement of her grandson, a difficult task. Where was the appropriate place for the young ex-soldier? Germany, she thought, was "full to overflowing" and emigration "sustains the German Lloyd." Perhaps August's future awaited him in one of the German colonial possessions or maybe in Milwaukee in the United States. Had not other failed German officers done well in Milwaukee? The old woman queried her trustee Nichols and got back polite, fainthearted letters of encouragement intended to discourage.

In 1893, although she thought "he was . . . rather too old" for further schooling, she decided August just might do well in "Book-Keeping." Suddenly she changed her mind. It would be far better for August, who was still running up debts in her name, to raise coffee in

Mexico. Off she sent him to Guadalajara, where he found the climate "exquisite," but no job. From Dresden his old grandmother urged him to try San Francisco, California, but he chose instead to go to Boston and wheedle money out of Nichols. Soon he returned to Dresden, the last place he was wanted, and, somewhat wearily, Clara was reminded of a speech of Emerson's in which he had predicted that "the time would come when a child might come into the world to find every inch of God's earth already appropriated and that he was ousted out of every thing except the Air he breathed." Was this to be August's fate? Maybe it could be averted; he could study chemistry and then live in the south of Germany where it was cheaper.

But August von Ekensteen was not to go to the south of Germany. Having long since discovered that his pleas for money sounded more imperative if they came from abroad, he soon resumed his epic wanderings. From Australia he noted that employment possibilities were not promising. Yet again the old woman worried about her grandson and invaded her capital for his benefit.

Not quite as "elastic" as before, she found the trial of Zola in Paris upsetting, and was it true, she asked Nichols, that Harvard had a colored graduate? President McKinley's looks she rather liked and in June of 1900 she viewed a very satisfactory eclipse of the sun. Two years later Jane Warner, who was "the only one whose age approached mine within a decennium," had fallen asleep never to wake again. And now the hand of him whose father had been Clara's trustee before him trembled; "young" Nichols was old and worn out.

To Clara's delight, August came home in the fall of 1903, but he did so only to die, having found every inch of God's earth already appropriated. "His departure," she comforted herself, "has saved him from many trials and disappointments." Two years later she buried August's mother and once again her letters were edged in black.

In a letter to Nichols in April 1906, Clara worried about the eruption of Vesuvius and the earthquake in San Francisco. The poor souls. How glad she was that her August had not gone to San Francisco! By the way, how did her shares in the Boston and Albany Railroad stand? Maybe it would be best that he send her assets to Dresden forthwith,

190

where she would supervise them herself — she who had so long ago been the "Dutiful Ward" of his father. Nichols, exhausted, obeyed.

Since that night when ghosts and goblins had knocked upon the floor and upon her father's mind in Malden, Massachusetts, nearly ninety years had passed. She had been a child of four when an event occurred which was later recalled by Lieutenant Glieg of the British army: "When the detachment . . . entered his dining parlour, they found a dinner-table spread, and covers laid for forty guests. Several kinds of wine in handsome cut-glass decanters were cooling on the sideboard." Its tenant had been obliged to flee for his life and the soldiers, having taken their fill, fired the place. But it was to be rebuilt and house twenty-two more American Presidents in Clara's lifetime.

Almost a century old, she kept to her rooms, very much alone. What difference did that make? She had been alone before, perhaps always. Hers had been a long candle to burn. It went out without a flicker on March 12, 1907.

FIVE

"Crownie" and the Emperor of Japan

Frank Crowninshield (1872–1947)

The smile of the pretty, flimsily clad girl reclining on the grass was fixed enough but from time to time an odd expression seemed to interfere. Under his black hood, her beholder grew snappish and muttered instructions, which were acknowledged not by the girl but by the puppeteer-like gesticulations of a man perched in a tree. In either hand he held a thread attached to a nipple of the girl below and at last his patient manipulations were rewarded with the shutter's click. The silver-haired man now descended from the tree and advanced in an odd gait, at once mincing and strutting, his torso somehow arriving before the rest of him, to exchange effusive congratulations with both model and photographer. It was but another day in the life of Frank Crowninshield, who had determined that the girl's breasts sagged too much.

As perhaps may befit any tree-borne manipulator of nipples, "Crownie," as he was called, is not easily described. His obituary — the description he himself would have preferred (or would he have laughed at it?) — showed him precisely as he had always wanted to be: a bon vivant, a man of the arts, a polished speaker, a gentleman, and a founder of café society. Indeed, at his death in 1947, he was lamented by the New York *Times* as "the undiminished and suave apostle of gracious living, elegant manner and true urbanity."

Four years earlier he had received another accolade, one he prized above all. In a *New Yorker* "profile," he was flattered as the "Last of the Species." It is a little hard to say just what the species was, for those who knew him are at variance in their opinions and there are

195

times when one can scarcely believe they are speaking of the same man. To some he was all kindness and solicitude, to others he was a creature calculating and of depthless insincerity. Some admired his tastes in the arts. Others deplored him as a shallow dilettante. Was he a gentleman? Or was he but a social climber, an opportunist, and a ruthless one at that?

Perhaps no aspect of Frank Crowninshield has invited such diversity of opinion as his sexuality. The ladies loved him as "Bad Frank," and he relished the name. Some reliable acquaintances assert that he never had contact with any woman. Others equally worthy of belief claim that he had a woman a week. Was he homosexual? Some say yes, but more say that his homosexuality was so carefully sublimated that it did not really exist. Maybe he was neuter. Maybe he was all of these things. Maybe he was . . . what?

Certainly he is remembered by most for his magazine. On page after glossy page appeared all that was glamorous in the early decades of this century, and no sordid note was allowed to strike the eye. Such was *Vanity Fair*, a New York magazine dedicated to "the stage, society, sports, fashions and the fine arts," and the world of dreams. To many today, much of the sleekness seems irrelevant; it lacks, unabashedly, what is called "social consciousness." Yet one still turns the pages with pleasure. How is this? Is it possible that social conscience may become a trifle tiresome and from time to time be set aside?

But this is the art of conjurors and one such was its editor.

Francis Welch Crowninshield was in Paris in 1872 to the manner — but not truly the manor — born. His father, Frederic, a painter and the director of the American Academy in Rome, was a grandson of Benjamin Williams Crowninshield, privateer, but the riches of the War of 1812 had elsewhere devolved and the director was obliged to make do with his stipend and a small independent income. Frederic tended to be cross and fearful about money, and his watercolors, even the stained-glass window he designed for Emmanuel Church in Boston, brought in little cash. Frank, one of three children, was tutored by poor but cultured Italians hired from time to time by his father when he could afford them, and for a while he attended a convent school for girls in France. Who knows the effects, if any, of nunnery persuasions on a young man? Maybe there is more to be learned in such places than is generally thought. This may seem strange stuff of which to make New York's future arbiter elegantiarum and the essayist of *Ten Thousand Nights in a Dinner Coat*, but not really: genteel poverty is a potent breeder of ambition, more especially social ambition. Sparse though Crownie's education may have been, there was certainly no intellectual poverty in Frederic Crowninshield's household, where frequently Henry James and Henry Adams were visitors.

Family tradition, as recalled by a nephew, has it that at the age of ten Crownie's sense of savoir faire, for which he was later celebrated, was not highly developed. When one Italian afternoon a particularly tiresome old lady dropped in to visit his sick mother, Frank greeted her with, "Come in, come in, Contessa. Mama would be glad if a pig came to call on her."

Equipped with a kind of broad-wash education, a well-known name and no money, Crownie found himself in New York at the age of nineteen and desperately in need of a job. For him there would never be another American city; in New York he would live and die, and to it he brought a steely will to parlay his assets into something greater. The most important of these was a highly developed sense of class distinctions and of their pull on people. It was typical of the man to focus less on money than on such of its indicia as lay within his power to ape: a set of mannerisms he believed the social elite had — or at least ought to have. Now this kind of thing is familiar enough; it leads quickly into a kind of trafficking, and for the adroit, into creative mannerisms. Frank Crowninshield was one of the adroit, an advanced practitioner mostly for his own gain, sometimes for his own divertissement, sometimes just for practice, and frequently out of a compulsion so deeply seated as to be a neurosis.

His audacity has been recalled by Geoffrey T. Hellman in a 1943 *New Yorker* profile: "He presented a letter from William Dean Howells, a friend of his father's, to Major George Haven Putnam, head of Putnam's publishing house and bookstore. Putnam asked him what he wanted to do, and Frank . . . in whom the Crowninshield manner was already firmly ingrained, replied that he would like to read manuscripts, meet authors, and mix up in the publication end of things. 'Very sorry, but that's what I do myself,' said Putnam. A week later Putnam wrote Crowninshield saying that he regretted he couldn't offer him a position as head of the company but that there was an opening for a clerk in the bookstore at eight dollars a week."

Frank was delighted; he was in the world he wanted to be in. He soon found that young Americans of old family with continental backgrounds were not closely questioned, even by the Four Hundred. This phenomenon Crownie exploited as few have and shortly he assumed the form by which he is remembered. He wore a boutonniere day and night, and above it a long, spatulate nose debouched from among well-cut moustaches from which emanated every courtesy, every concern. Here surely was Edwardian grace, a jauntiness, the flavor of Europe; and the twinkle of the brown eyes suggested the lady-killer, maybe even an agreeably naughty one. This image he burnished and burnished again, even in the very hour he lay dying. A love of ostentatious wealth attracted him to the houses of the great, where his facile manners made him welcome. He was, it came to be said, "an American Beerbohm," "the Lord Chesterfield of Manhattan."

And indeed all his life he practiced the dictum of Lord Chesterfield with a will, flattering beautiful women for their wit, the ugly for their beauty, and doubtful cases for both. But possibly the great Englishman would have been appalled when years later, in 1914, in the first issue of *Vanity Fair*, Crowninshield editorialized: "For women we intend to do something in a noble and missionary spirit, something which, so far as we can observe, has never before been done for them by an American magazine. We mean to make frequent appeals to their intellects. We dare to believe that they are, in their best moments, creatures of some cerebral activity; we even make bold to believe that it is they who are contributing what is most original, stimulating, and highly magnetized to the literature of our day, and we hereby announce ourselves as determined and bigoted feminists."

Years later, in denouncing the proposed regulation of cosmetics by

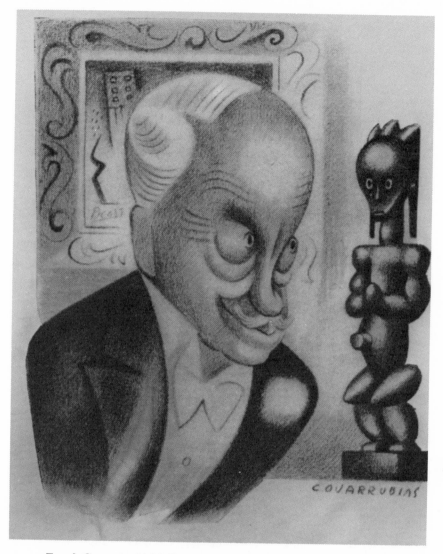

Frank Crowninshield. Drawing by Covarrubias; © 1942, 1970 by The New Yorker Magazine, Inc.

a Congress given to wondering, among other things, what was meant by "Ivory, 99⁴⁴⁄₁₀₀% pure," Crownie was to illumine his "noble and missionary spirit." To an appreciative gathering of the American Association of Advertising Agencies, he declared: "After a single hour's reading of the advertising pages, 10,000,000 American housewives, salesgirls, telephone operators, typists, bookkeepers and factory workers daily see themselves as 'femmes fatales,' as Cleopatra, as Helen of Troy, or even as Ninon de Lenclos, who, at seventy-five, was still deriving an ecstasy from her love affairs."

Such "dreams and illusions" were "the secret gardens into which they wander in order to escape the monotony of their work-a-day world and the banality of their well meaning husbands." The escape was best accomplished, allowed the dedicated feminist, with a "skin like a May morning, hair like a golden mist and a form that will dazzle all men and antagonize all women." This, he added, was miraculously and inexpensively available at the cosmetic counters of drugstores. It was to these (assuming that a few congressional vulgarians were gagged) his noble and missionary spirit would lead the unhappy women.

And Lord Chesterfield might have resented the comparison on another score. While both aimed at the seduction of the ladies, the Englishman had in mind, among other things, the pleasures of the flesh. Crownie did not. Chesterfield would have been startled had he known that his American counterpart was thought by some to prefer chubby young ganymedes whose discretion left the celebrated lady-killer image of their Zeus unclouded. Almost certainly he would have been confounded by the fact that homosexuals who knew Crownie could never agree on whether he was one of their fraternity or not.

Charm was his business and perhaps no man of his time was as relentless in its exercise as he; true, at times it failed him, but not often. No flattery was excessive: Crownie knew that even if it was recognized as such, the agreeable sensation of being paid attention to remained. About him there was a squidlike quality; when prodded, he exuded a cloud of charm, confusing and disarming his assailant. But behind the screen one senses the creature's sinuosity and resilience; the rubbery tentacles grope deliberately, delicately, in the murkiness. Of course he was a fraud, but when he so readily, so urbanely and so cheerfully admitted it, what could one do? There are, after all, few who sense that the self-deprecation of a snob is only another snobbery and those who do seem to easily tire of the game anyway. No matter: sincerity has never been the business of conjurors.

At the end of 1891, these qualities brought a raise of two dollars a week and a note of praise from Major Putnam. Crownie was meticulous in money matters all his life and retained this weekly account from the early days with the publisher:

$2.50 food
 2.50 artics [sic]
 1.30 Cavalleria
  .40 Bowling
  .25 Hair cut
  .25 carfares
  .10 stamp
  .10 shine
  .10 papers
  .50 Conway's versification
─────
 8.00

At Putnam's, Crowninshield developed, more than anything else, an interest in the physical appearance of books; content was not and never would be of much interest to the future editor of *Vanity Fair*. An intensely social creature, his solicitude for the ladies gained him access to many a town and country house. To the delight of society matrons he shunned male after-dinner conversation and billiards, choosing instead to amuse the ladies with a flow of wit, much of it at male expense. In time he would be asked to rearrange dinner place cards and suggest other little amenities; he early became, as he was to remain all his life, the extra man at dinners.

It is difficult not to attribute, at least partially, this kind of success to an atypical understanding of women — atypical, that is, from the ordinary male-heterosexual point of view. His exalted and often-expressed worship of his mother carried with it, of course, certain

Illustration from Frank Crowninshield's Manners for the Metropolis

Freudian implications. But these were easily dispensed with by pinching a matronly leg or two under the table, and perhaps — as was characteristic of him — he merely selected a posture, scattered enough evidence about to confound and raise certain difficulties for those who chose to question it.

Leaving Putnam's after four years to become publisher of *The Bookman* for Dodd, Mead, & Co., he from time to time interrupted his administrative duties to contribute an occasional piece of light social satire under the pen name of Arthur Loring Bruce. Many years later he explained that he had adopted the name out of fear of being embarrassed at the Knickerbocker Club, which he had recently joined and whose staid members he feared would not appreciate his quips. Under the same name he was to write a short book called *Manners for the Metropolis*, which concludes with the advice: "Always be half an hour late for everything. Nothing is so tedious as waiting" — except perhaps nowadays reading *Manners for the Metropolis*. We learn as well from the slim volume (in the chapter on dinners) that "when a lady beside you is so generously avoirdupoised or embonpointed that it is a physical impossibility for her to see the food on her plate, it is sometimes an act of kindness to inform her as to the nature of the bird or beast so hopelessly removed from her vision. This saves her the trouble of lifting it above the horizon in order to discover its exact species." And under "General Rules": "In motoring, avoid running over hens, dogs, and Italian children. They are almost certain to stick up the wheels."

The critical praise the book failed to elicit was supplied by Frank, if not by Edmund Wilson, to whom *Manners* was "a mixture of easy satisfaction at frequenting the then rich and ostentatious world of Newport, Long Island, New York, and of satire on that weekending, champagne-drinking and bridge-playing world."

If it was satire, the satire was of a nibbling, toothless kind; turning the pages of Crownie's book is (to use a simile that would have pleased him) like being at a cocktail party where a tray of canapés appears before you. You accept with pleasure or the appearance of it; instantly the food is offered again. You decline with thanks, and scarcely have your thanks been uttered when the tray is before you once more. A firmer refusal gets you nowhere; you cannot escape the pâté; it is as though the hostess cannot understand how it could possibly cloy. Most of what Crownie wrote was pâté, and at times it was worse, reminding one of cotton candy, the sweet fluff disappearing in one's mouth leaving only a nauseating residue which one longs to rinse away with some powerful astringent.

Characteristically, he had his book glossily and expensively bound and perhaps for this reason it found favor with the redoubtable Condé Nast, a man to be of great importance in Crownie's life. Nast was said to be a St. Louis (Missouri) Frenchman whose father, strangely enough, begat something called German Methodism in the United States. Nast never spoke of his childhood, was a financial genius and the millionaire publisher of *Vogue* and other magazines. According to a former lover, he was a niggardly tipper and "looked like a banker. He was about five nine, bald with a fringe of thinning gray hair at back and sides, small eyes behind rimless pince-nez, . . . a thin-lipped mouth turned down at the corners, a deeply etched line running from each side of his nose to his chin. He never slouched in public, whether at work or play, but always stood as if encased in a plaster cast from chin to toes. When seated, he didn't relax, lean back, cross his legs or put his elbows on the table. Even when playing golf there was a rigidity about him, while at parties, no matter how much he drank (champagne, whiskey, lethal mixtures like stingers and sidecars), he consistently displayed the vivacity of a stuffed moosehead. That steel backbone only unbent in private."

Evidently it frequently did, for we learn, a page or so later, in Helen Lawrenson's colorful memoir, *Stranger at the Party*, that Condé Nast "was cunt crazy. He loved to taste it, smell it, feel it, look at it, above all, fuck it." In Ms. Lawrenson's opinion and apparently not inconsiderable experience, he was the most rapt of fornicators. She also tells us he was a "kind, gentle, tolerant man." Less charitable are the memoirs of the late Edmund Wilson, who regarded the publisher as "the glossiest bounder I have ever known, who was incapable of saying good morning without a formally restrained but somehow obnoxious vulgarity." To Wilson, the most rapt of fornicators seemed socially uneasy, one who, although he sometimes moved among Astors and Vanderbilts, did so too peripherally for his taste and craved full admission into high society, perhaps through Frank Crowninshield.

In 1913 Nast asked Crownie to edit his new magazine, *Vanity Fair*, supposedly upon hearing Frank remark: "There is no magazine that is read by the people you meet at lunches and dinners. . . . Your magazine should cover the things people talk about — parties, the arts, sports, theatre, humor, and so forth."

Crowninshield was forty-one; he had found his medium at just the right time and right place; a few years later and he would not have become the successful editor of anything. The magazine must of course reflect what he called "the lighter vein." So did its offices. Typically Crownie would start his day by discarding the front pages of newspapers with a fine disdain; they would not be read; newspapermen were "muckers." He would then attend to his personal mail, first that of female correspondents. Before these envelopes were opened, they were sniffed and arranged in piles on his desk according to whatever associations were evoked by the particular perfume they exuded (he was an expert on perfumes and colognes). "This one," he would confide to his secretary, "is from a lady"; another must certainly be from "a chorus girl" and so on.

Next, he turned to whatever business letters he had received, edited them with a little gold pencil (even advertising circulars), and threw them away. There followed a time of divertissement, of relaxation. Calling in some of his staff, he would perform some simple sleight-of-hand — perhaps make a playing card disappear, or rap his desk smartly and propel a spoon into a water glass, or bark like a seal and stand on his head. Did anyone doubt he could write with his toes? He would remove his shoe and demonstrate.

Some mornings these feats would, to his delight, be eclipsed by a visit from the great Houdini or from John Mulholland, who frequently performed in his office; on others, a charming palmist would drop in.

"Crownie" in middle age. Courtesy of Wide World Photos

Palmists were always most welcome. After contemplating his collection of African masks, admiring them and causing others to do the same for a moment or so, and thus prepared and inspired, he who was something of a magician himself swung into his editorial routine.

There were plots to be conjured up for young writers. With an expansive wave of his hand he would point to some office prop. "Take that vase," he would say. "It is a rare porcelain and was formerly in a Buddhist temple in Burma. You steal it. Spies follow you. You smuggle it into Mexico. There you meet this young architect — you see, there's your plot!" The beneficiary would scurry off to a typewriter and the pleased editor would turn to his paintings and employees would notice a certain coldness on Crownie's part should their praise be less than effulgent. If he sought an opinion on whether the frame of a new painting was a little too wide or too narrow, it was best (knowing he had selected it) to say it was perfect, as a secretary was to later recall with rancor. For such time as an extraordinarily short attention span permitted, the gold pen pecked at manuscripts. A word would be scratched out, another substituted, scratched out, and finally the original replaced. Frank's own very favorite word was *serendipity;* he liked to see it in print whenever the context admitted, or could be made to admit, its inclusion. Satisfied, the editor would scour the latest copy of the *Harvard Lampoon* for undergraduate talent who might contribute to *Vanity Fair.*

And now more pleasant duties awaited him: little flowery notes to write to lady contributors and boxes of chocolate creams to send as accompaniments. To male contributors went telegrams (whenever possible he sent telegrams whether time was of the essence or not) of congratulation and encouragement. Just as charming were his letters of rejection. To Paul Gallico he wrote: "My dear boy, this is superb! A little masterpiece! What color! What life! How beautifully you have phrased it all! A veritable gem! — Why don't you take it around to Harper's Bazaar?" Editorial duties completed, Crownie might summon his staff (who might be shooting craps at their desks) for a rousing game of the Rape of the Sabine Women. At a signal the male employees hoisted the females over their shoulders and marched into the corridor; it was all so amusing. Never did he tire of it.

Those who performed the Rape of the Sabine Women were quite possibly as able assistants as any editor may ever have. To the magazine came Claire Brokaw (later Claire Booth Luce), Robert Benchley, Robert Sherwood, Edmund Wilson, Dorothy Parker, and Helen Lawrenson. Years later when she was Ambassador to Italy, Claire Booth Luce described how she got her job. Having been turned down flatly by Condé Nast at *Vogue* (she would, he had said, be married and off to Europe in six months), she was not disheartened. "Instead," she recalled, "he went off to Europe, and I walked into the *Vogue* offices, and occupied an unoccupied desk, writing fashion copy without pay." On his return, Nast, taken equally by her copy, her presumption, and quite possibly by something else, sent her next door to *Vanity Fair*, where there was a vacancy. "Frank Crowninshield, the editor, took one look at me and asked me to go home and think of 100 editorial ideas by Monday. 'My God,' he said when I returned with them, 'you must have had a man under your bed.' "

And there was the great "Colonel" Steichen, who headed the photographic staff and who, according to Helen Lawrenson, "managed to give the impression that a photographic session . . . was the equivalent of an investiture at Buckingham Palace." The Colonel regarded all other photographers as basely inferior but the "Baron" de Meyer, also on the staff, was in no way abashed. Had he not indeed pioneered the illumination of the faces of models by inserting light bulbs between their breasts? The Colonel had best be mindful of this.

At lunch, the bon vivant, boutonniere and all, frequently graced Schrafft's with his bevy of secretaries, where he steamed out their problems (he particularly liked to deal with problems of the heart).

There was also another kind of lunch. Contributors or staffers who wrote, illustrated or photographed in other than "the lighter vein" were marched off to the Knickerbocker Club, the Dutch Treat Club, or the Coffee House. About the latter Crowninshield purveyed the notion that it had been founded by him to advance the arts and particularly artists who might contribute to *Vanity Fair*. But the inspiration for the Coffee House had come about somewhat differently. Years before, he had wanted desperately to belong to the Century Club, which also tended to attract artists and which requited his attentions with a blackball. Wretched, he probed his many member friends. Who had the ignorant, depraved scoundrel been? They seemed more close-mouthed than was usual in such matters, but at length their reticence was penetrated; it was his father, Frederic, who had done the terrible deed. The Coffee House was the Century's surrogate and a filial response. Here his guests were flattered and exposed to the foibles of the very rich. These privileged few, said Frank, preferred to look at life from as cheerful an angle as possible, as he did. In the end he managed to imbue his listeners with the feeling that the magazine itself was a kind of exclusive club; "the lighter vein," they must remember, excluded carping over rates and salaries.

Setting aside whether habitual optimism — of the rich or poor — slides effortlessly into imbecility, one may think Crowninshield's wish (however he apotheosized it as deliberate choice) to deal only on one level, and that the most superficial life affords, was less choice than incapacity to do otherwise. This is what makes *Vanity Fair*'s undoubted quality all the more remarkable; it was achieved and sustained within the very severe limitations of an almost reckless insularity. For twenty-odd years a good deal of the best American writing appeared in the pages of Crownie's magazine, and formidable is the list of writers brought to public notice by its editor: Thomas Wolfe, Aldous Huxley, André Maurois, Edmund Wilson, Robert Sherwood, Dorothy Parker, E. E. Cummings, Robert Benchley, Noel Coward, Amy Lowell, T. S. Eliot, and Colette, to name only a few. Unsurprisingly, the wit, as Helen Lawrenson has pointed out, was highly mechanized; the pâté tray was passed and passed about.

Although Edmund Wilson thought the editor nearly devoid of what he called "journalistic decency," many of the magazine's contributors were genuinely grateful for his interest in their work and in them. A New York actor has remembered a backstage visit to Noel Coward's dressing room in Boston, where he was affixed with Coward's penetrating glance and "the famed staccato accents rapped out, 'Your Uncle Frank paid me the first dollar I ever earned in America. As I was almost starving at the time, I was positively enchanted to get it.' "

Another, although he privately thought Crowninshield was "too old to be an editor," wrote: *

> 1307 Park Avenue,
> Baltimore, Maryland,
> May 4, 1934.

Mr. Frank Crowninshield
Graybar Building,
New York, New York
Dear Frank:
   There is an outdoor picture at Scribner's showing the Fitzgerald family starting off on a surfboard ride. I have asked Max [his editor, Maxwell Perkins] to send you a glossy, if it has not already been sent out in the general publicity. Otherwise, you will have to wait ten days, at the end of which time I am transfering my wife from one hospital to another and we will have a few hours in New York during which we can have a new picture made, if you will send at once the name of a good *cheap* photographer in New York.
>   Thanking you for thinking of us.
>   Best wishes always,
>   Scott Fitz

Fitzgerald, on the verge of a great triumph and amid desperate melancholies, boundless expectations, nagging debts, and the third mental breakdown of his wife, would receive more than a photograph: the commiseration and encouragement of Crowninshield.

Frank's celebrated lunches were not dispositive of all problems. One was Dorothy Rothschild, who came to work at *Vanity Fair* as a young girl. In 1920, now known as Dorothy Parker, she was the drama critic on a magazine whose editor did not want drama — and friends and admirers — criticized. Dorothy, however, had panned more than praised. Crownie began to feel the heat, notably from a shrill and angry Billie Burke. He set up an elegant luncheon at the Plaza; the table was bedecked with red roses and Dorothy was plied with the enameled smile, some gossip, and the tinkling little jokes that tumbled from Frank's pink face. He massaged his moustaches, shot his cuffs, and extolled

* Letter © 1976 by Frances Scott Fitzgerald Smith.

Dorothy's merits, finally telling her that she was to be replaced by the more understanding P. G. Wodehouse. Now Dorothy had never been much fooled by Crowninshield anyway, and had overheard his abject apology to Billie Burke. Over the table Frank rambled on; Dorothy was, he had always known, extremely witty. Did she not remember — he did — when she was, obscurely, Rothschild? Would she be a contributing editor? How this would please him; he was counting on it; it would make him the happiest man on earth. Amid these effusions and the roses, Parker calmly ordered an expensive dessert and resigned.

Poor Dorothy — he had done so much for her. Why couldn't she understand? Besides, she knew nothing of the theatre anyway — probably wouldn't know Aristophanes if she saw it, silly girl. But immediately two of his prize discoveries (Crownie never realized that anyone could tire of being his discovery), Robert Benchley and Robert Sherwood, resigned in sympathy. Evidently they could not understand, either. Oh well, shortly the delightful Wodehouse would set all to rights.

But Wodehouse did not. "This left the *Vanity Fair* office empty," Edmund Wilson recalled, "except for Crowninshield's woman secretaries; and I was called on to fill in, and was first tried out on reading manuscripts. Benchley and Dorothy joked about my being a 'scab,' but were kind about showing me the ropes. . . . Very soon I became aware that, except for the woman secretaries, whom Crowninshield knew how to charm, the people who worked for 'Crownie' were not very much attached to him. Benchley came from Worcester, Mass., and there was something 'la-dee-da' about Crowninshield that offended his New England taste. He told me how Crowninshield had watched from a window some parade of American troops, and commented on their sloppiness and lack of good form in comparison with the soldiers of other nations. I was somewhat shocked by what I thought his lack of manners when, having taken me to lunch at the Coffee House, a little lunch Club, . . . he explained to the men on his right, telling me to turn away and not listen, that Benchley had absurdly 'got excited' about their treatment of Dorothy Parker."

Frank's concern for fine books was limited to the glossily embossed spine of *Manners for the Metropolis*. "The most shocking thing" Wilson ever saw him do — "an incident that I never quite got over — was the result of our needing for some reason to print the text of a letter of Voltaire's. He sent down to Putnam's bookstore below us and borrowed a volume of an expensive and splendidly printed edition of Voltaire, then simply cut out the pages with the letter and sent the volume back, knowing that this would not be detected."

Another source of editorial unease to Crownie was Amy Lowell: she could withstand any bombardment of endearing little notes and boxes of bonbons. He begged her to submit her work and she, wanting the publicity, did so. But the relationship had become uneasy when in 1919, in response to a returned proof, she wrote to Crowninshield: "I have naturally put the words back to what they were, and I shall be awfully obliged to you if you will suggest to the erudite persons who run these things that I have a predilection in favor of having my poems printed as I write them."

Now the "erudite" person was, as Miss Lowell knew, Crownie himself. For once, his editorial cogitations had not consisted of crossing out this or that word, toying with a dozen synonyms or so, and finally replacing the word he had deleted. Although Miss Lowell promptly received a properly penitent note, it failed to appease: "Never, in the course of my whole career," she snapped back, "have I had an editor change a word before."

And there was something else bothering Miss Lowell about *Vanity Fair* and its editor. Crownie sought to have her sign away all rights of republication for twenty-five dollars. "You are," said the angry poet, "so far as I know, the only publication with which I have ever dealt, and I have dealt with most of them, who make this stipulation." Frank hastened to explain in a little note more charming than legally accurate, but it was no good. No Crowninshield balm, much less a box of chocolates, would in the future soothe Miss Lowell. What she wrote for *Vanity Fair*, she complained, were "scraps which leave nothing behind," yet they consumed her time. The poor woman did not realize that scraps which leave nothing behind were precisely what Crownie prized and nothing more.

About this unpropitious time, he set about explaining to her, with what he imagined was boundless tact, his new and racier editorial policy. But Miss Lowell tore away the gossamer; to her, *Vanity Fair* was already "a social whirlpool" in which one spun uselessly about like a piece of flotsam; it was too heavily dominated by the "sex question" and, she snarled, sex was not quite what Frank Crowninshield thought it was. Moreover, she felt that a kind of historically recurring decadence was upon the magazine. The decadence was, she declared, a "visitation," whether from on high or below she knew not.

She wished to escape. "I know," she wrote, "that no matter what I did or tried, or what you did or tried, my articles would swear with the policy of the magazine and be a cause of struggle and more or less distress to you and to me. . . . I'm getting rid of a problem and you're getting rid of a problem." But, historical decadence or no, Crownie was not through yet. Intermittently, the rubbery and resilient tentacles emerged from the foaming whirlpool; she thrust them off one after another until at last he disappeared in a cloud of ink forever.

It was far better to deal with the likes of Edward Estlin Cummings, author of *The Enormous Room*. Not only was "E.E." a "dear boy," he was greatly pleased to have the seventy-five or one hundred dollars *Vanity Fair* paid for his little articles. Theirs was a lasting friendship sprinkled over the years with such quintessential Crowninshieldiana as:

May 9, 1931

DEAR E.E.

Where are you? I want very much to talk to you over the telephone or to meet you in the flesh. All good wishes to your *Cher Maître*.
Yours ever,
Frank Crowninshield

Although Cummings, whose poetry was heavily dependent on punctuation for its effects, disliked Crownie's meddling with his colons and commas, the two met often enough to enable him to renovate his captions and assuage his feelings. And, unlike the terrible Amy Lowell, "E.E." was responsive to editorial suggestions. Here is one such plot suggested by Crownie:

Gladys Vanderdecker brought up as a girl at Newport; has a governess, also a maid, caviar, and clotted cream on the oatmeal. Her debut while Gladys Twombly at a big dance at the Ritz. They have a house at Aiken, house at Newport, house in New York, a smart hotel in Paris, visits to London, Rome, and a really roomy house on Long Island (72 rooms) near the Piping Rock Club. She is always with her father and mother. Father keeps inheriting more money and getting richer and richer. Their opera box, the large dinners at home (40 people) five formal dances at their house every winter and, of course, luncheons, bridge, and a private car. She is the slave of society — pampered, waited on, petted, but miserable.

She reads, in the Illustrated News about a girl who found happiness while working as a mill girl. An unhappy love affair with her father's chauffeur gives Miss Vanderdecker the idea of becoming a mill girl. She takes a room on the East side of New York and becomes a mill worker on the river front. She becomes acquainted with the head waiter at an automat, a very handsome man. True love. They are married. The arrival of a little one, and another, and another and still another. Her husband buys a restaurant of his own. She becomes the cashier. One rainy night an old and bedraggled man, soaked with rain, appears at the door. She is about to turn him out into the street. 'Good God, it is my father!' He has lost all his money in Petroleum Preferred, etc.

Then — some clever and ingeni[o]us denouement.

Although Miss Lowell would have retched, "E.E." was of different stuff; he was even moved to poetic raptures by the editor of *Vanity Fair* on April 24, 1943: *

Dear Mr. Crowninshield —
your good and generous letter's as welcome as the
gay and miraculous truth for which it stands; that
any-or-this unworld may murder-or-measure its
selfless to nine millionths of one-to-the-minus-N
inch, but no individual possibly ever has been or
shall ever impossibly be divided

Patchin is happily still a peaceful and otherwise
nowhere off West Tenth Street between Greenwich

* Letter © 1976 by Nancy T. Andrews.

and Sixth Avenues: at numero quatre, rez de chausée,
le feef o'clok (served by a beautiful admirer of
yours) awaits his presence; the better the sooner
               — sincerely
                  eec

No "E.E." Cummings was Edmund Wilson, who quit *Vanity Fair* when Crownie refused to give him a small weekly raise. Wilson was receiving less than the men's fashions writers and resented it. The author of *Memoirs of Hecate County* and *Axel's Castle* thought the editor of *Vanity Fair* shallow in the extreme and Wilson "never knew anyone who talked as much as Crowninshield [did] about being and behaving like 'a gentleman' and . . . who exemplified this less in his own relations. This has made me suspicious ever since of people who talk about 'gentlemen.' I think it ought to be a warning to be careful and hold on to one's wallet. The career of Frank Crowninshield, I suppose, did have its pathetic side: there was the 'gentleman,' the personality to which he aspired and which he rather too ostentatiously acted, and the treacherous opportunist who so often destroyed these pretensions." Moreover, Wilson was revolted by Frank's "not very attractive habit of seizing you by the arm in a way that seemed calculated to establish some kind of affectionate ascendancy." In spite of these just-above-the-elbow clutches, Wilson did not believe Crowninshield was homosexual. In his turn, Crowninshield thought Wilson's literary ability was limited to book reviewing and seemed genuinely surprised at even that talent.

But such contretemps were nothing compared to the terrible struggle with Condé Nast, which began as early as 1915 and lasted for years. Although Nast had agreed to give Crowninshield a free hand with *Vanity Fair*, he tried to renege when Crownie insisted on reproducing such artists as Matisse, Van Gogh, Modigliani, and Rouault. The most rapt of fornicators was scandalized; the paintings were distorted, confusing. He straightened his "steel backbone" more than ever: they were, he said, decadent. What would the advertisers think? Didn't Frank know how expensive it would be to reproduce the trash in four colors? Not only was Crowninshield ignorant of art, he was insane. There were vitriolic scenes between the two men. Nast suspected that Crownie, who owned a number of Impressionist canvases, was really using the magazine to tout them and inflate their value.

Frank had always traveled in Europe whenever he could, and he was accustomed to seek out and befriend young artists of promise there. Some, like Segonzac and Despiau, became protégés, close friends. In 1912 he was, as he called himself, a kind of "unofficial press agent" for an exhibition of the more advanced European painting in New York. But he had been considerably more than that: he had made all the arrangements, overcome very substantial resistance, and Picasso, Van Gogh, Despiau, Matisse, Lachaise, Laurencin, Pascin, Epstein — the list is almost endless — are largely American household words through the good taste and persistence of Frank Crowninshield.

True, Crownie made some mistakes and his more than occasional efforts to convert mediocrity into genius in the pages of *Vanity Fair* were once assayed by the likes of Westbrook Pegler. Invoking an afterlife for the editor, he wrote in his syndicated column: "Mr. Crowninshield's spook . . . would curl his lip over the rim of his glass for a little sip, dab the moisture off his moustache with an elegant sweep of his flowing white sleeve and say, 'Have you seen the new sculpture of this man Mike Hogan, the Kansas City ashman? Really lovely, really charming in its way. A new thing. He works in chewing gum, matchsticks and hair-combings.' Mr. Crowninshield is always discovering a new painter who does it with a mop on isinglass or a sculptor who models in mayonnaise."

Even so, one has the feeling it might have been better to err with Crowninshield, isinglass and all, than hit the mark with Westbrook Pegler.

In 1922 Crowninshield felt he could afford to give a little party, which may well have been the foundation, as he later claimed, of New York café society. If so, today's jet set is in his debt. For at the time it was generally thought that the old guard would not mix easily with writers, actors and painters at a social gathering. What fearful consequences awaited him who dared, for example, give a party at which he would introduce Mrs. William Astor to Gypsy Rose Lee amid the chic and a few improvident artists who would have to rent tuxedos if they wore them at all? Crownie dared, and it was a great success — due to a remarkably insightful selection of the more malleable elements of both camps. Once his guests were assembled, Crownie moved among them effecting introductions with a charming little phrase here and another there, in exorcism of social tension. To their pleasure, the guests found their disparities could be accommodated; could the differences have been more imagined than real? One almost sees the deft, nearly subliminal, wave of the birch wand and all was, at least for the moment, transformed. Mrs. William Astor and Gypsy Rose Lee found they were sisters under the skin, albeit one showed a little more than the other.

"In the old days," he later recalled, "society was so snobbish and narrow and limited that artists and writers and playwrights were not sought after. Finally it was discovered that they were more amusing, so the narrow society began breaking its neck to get into what was the forerunner of café society. It became chic to go to Alma Gluck's, Stanford White's, Bessie Marbury's, Augustus Thomas's, Elsie de Wolfe's." It was, he said, "a very charming society," and so broadened, it has remained.

Naturally those who formulate chic are the most chic. For the next twenty years "Bad Frank" was in extraordinary demand at any New York party worthy of the name. Geoffrey Hellman's 1943 *New Yorker* profile was not larger than life: "Sit long enough at the Café de la Paix in Paris, Shepheard's Hotel in Cairo, or the Raffles in Singapore, the adage used to run, and you will see everyone in the world go by. America's closest approach to a pre-global-war Shepheard's, Raffles, or Café de la Paix is Frank Crowninshield, a man whose juxtaposition to celebrities over a period of five decades has been extreme. Unlike the Café de la Paix, Crowninshield has not lost his title; the Crowninshield circle . . . is still agreeably crowded, its polish maintained in part by Crowninshield's undiminishing liveliness as a toastmaster. A partial inventory of the people whom Crowninshield has introduced at banquets includes Charlie Chaplin, Clare Booth, Kirsten Flagstad, Jackie Coogan, Edna St. Vincent Millay, Walter Damrosch, P. G. Wodehouse, Geraldine Farrar, Grace Moore, Charles Dana Gibson, Otto Kahn, George Bellows, Lanny Ross, Edward Steichen, Gloria Swanson, Ely Culbertson, Gene Tunney, Hugh Walpole, Hendrik van Loon, Efrem Zimbalist, President Theodore Roosevelt, Robert Frost, Heywood Broun, John Sloan, Van Wyck Brooks, Nelson Rockefeller, Irvin S. Cobb, Paul Whiteman, and George Arliss. 'Crownie has introduced everyone in this country who has ever been introduced, and in many cases he has introduced them to each other,' a friend of his once said."

Frederic Bradlee, Crownie's nephew, has preserved his favorite among his uncle's toasts, one given at the Dutch Treat Club: "Gentlemen. Once upon a time there was a little colored girl named Eliza who died and went to heaven. She was met at the pearly gates by Saint Peter, who said to her: 'You're in heaven now, Eliza, and you're an angel in good standing. Go and pick yourself out a nice pair of wings.' So Eliza did, and in no time at all she was flashing about doing arabesques and entrechats and I don't know what all. She became, in fact, so confident that presently she thought she'd show off a bit before God. Now God and His Son were seated on Their golden thrones enjoying an afternoon nap — when Eliza came zooming into view. God awakened and watched her in mounting astonishment. At last He shook His sleeping Son and exclaimed softly and reverently: 'Jesus Christ, can that girl FLY.' Gentlemen — Amelia Earhart."

While a black-tied listener or two might think the celebrated Crowninshield approach a trifle studied, even rococo, clearly it was caviar to the general.

It should not surprise that the glass raised to the pleased aviatrix was full of water. Like his great-grandfather, Benjamin Williams Crowninshield, the toastmaster to ten thousand toasts was a teetotaler — with perhaps a difference or two. All his life he was fond of telling this story: When he was ten years old, his grandmother, a Bostonian, had taken him to a meeting dedicated to the damnation of Demon Rum. In the course of these solemnities, the speaker enjoined all those who pledged themselves never to take a drink to stand up. The boy saw his grandmother rise, and because he had been taught, he said, to stand when a lady did, he did so. True to his pledge he never touched a drop, but nevertheless, as became so studied a bon vivant, he was an authority to be reckoned with on liquor, and even more on wines. He seldom lost an opportunity to recommend this or that claret for its matchless bouquet, this champagne for coming from the right part of the right bank of the Rhine, and so forth. Now this kind of thing has its attractions, but there were those who felt that Crowninshield was laboring under the sort of disability a deaf music critic or a virginal Don Juan might have. Even more malign were those who suspected that he might not trust his behavior after a belt or two. But who were they? Probably muckers.

But from time to time, Crownie did lapse from his "elegant manner and true urbanity," and a nephew has recalled one or two of these incidents. Once Crowninshield "took my then sister-in-law and myself to lunch at the Colony restaurant. At a nearby table he spied his old friend Mrs. William Randolph Hearst. 'Millicent, my dear,' he intoned vibrantly across the room, 'how lovely you're looking. Oh, say, Millicent, I'd like you to meet my little grandniece-in-law. You have a bond in common, you and she. You see, she also is a long-suffering, dedicated newspaperman's bride. And I thought possibly you might give her a few pointers.' The subsequent hush in the restaurant was a little gray eternity that still now and then haunts my slumbers." The worldly editor of *Vanity Fair* had forgotten that for some time Hearst's paramour, Marion Davies, had assumed some of the duties of the "long-suffering, dedicated newspaperman's bride."

On another occasion the famous cartoonist Rube Goldberg asked how things were in Stockbridge, Massachusetts (long a Crowninshield summer spot), and Crownie had unhesitatingly replied, "Terrible, nowadays it's nothing but Jews." Such slips were not entirely malicious; and they make the man more believable: brisk puffs of wind dispelling for the moment the effluvia of pâté.

More often than not he showed a great deal of insight. One evening he insisted that his nephew repeat the toast with which Tallulah Bankhead had introduced a new bridegroom at a party. He was, she had declared in more earthy language, an accomplished fornicator and a peerless sensualist. The nephew, aware of his uncle's predilection that erotica be cast in Victorian — or at least Edwardian — language (a woman with big breasts, for example, had to be "generously avoirdupoised or embonpointed"), speedily did so: "This is my new husband, everybody: he makes love to me like Casanova and he titillates me like the Marquis de Sade." Crowninshield's reply was instant: "Oh, poor darling — I'm afraid that means he does neither."

The year 1925 found Frank Crowninshield at the zenith of his powers: he was what he wanted to be: wanted everywhere. But his boss, Condé Nast, was not, and Nast had made his yearnings known to his editor. With his customary confidence, Crownie set out to rectify what he assured Nast was a temporary oversight on the part of certain of the Four Hundred. Was he not, after all, the arbiter elegantiarum in such matters? If high society would not accept Nast, Frank would create another, an elite within an elite, that would.

To achieve this end, it would be advisable, he counseled Nast, to subject the social lions of New York to a kind of refining — after which the name of Condé Nast would surely stand prominently. Incidentally, this sort of thing took money. Nast shrugged his shoulders; what was that?

Crownie's crucible would be a very smart supper club with a very limited membership to be called The Embassy. Together, he and Nast carefully thumbed the *Social Register*, culling the names of the chic who might fear exclusion from a club which, avowed Crowninshield, would without a doubt elevate New York night life to that of Paris and London, perhaps beyond. The Embassy membership list was then further reduced by the names of those who, however chic, had in one way or another furnished some indication they would be likely to object to Condé Nast. All went well enough until the purpose of the business was nosed out by a couple of powerful dowagers. The Embassy, and presumably the elevation of New York society, collapsed in ruins. It was one of Crowninshield's few misadventures; thereafter, the rapt fornicator nursed his wounds with parties of his own. In his mentor's estimation, all that could had been done; a little sleight of hand, yes, but he was no Houdini.

By 1930 a strange change was coming over the offices of *Vanity Fair*. There were still the delightful games, the Rape of the Sabine Women, little jokes, and lunches at the Coffee House and Schrafft's. But the staff found on their desks each morning little slips of paper which showed precisely how late each had been in arriving at his or her job. What had happened to the days when Robert Benchley excused his tardiness by saying, "I got up early, but on my way here I was attacked by five lions"?

Equally new and unwelcome was a men's-wear department, although Crownie had always insisted that gentlemen never needed to be told how to dress. The new department's two luminaries warred with one another, the younger accusing the older (who wore heavy false eyebrows glued on with a substance that gave him a peculiar smell) of being "just an old queen." The older retaliated by calling his associate "just a little fairy."

Crownie, try as he might, could not rid himself of either the obnoxious little slips of paper, one of which was daily upon his own desk and which he dumped into the wastebasket, or the new staffers that had been imposed on him by his employer. The spell Crowninshield had cast over Nast appeared to be weakening. Once the two had shared an apartment but Nast now irritably dismissed his editor's drolleries, which had formerly been so consumingly hilarious. Frank found it more and more difficult to appeal to, much less manipulate, the gentlemanly instincts which he had managed to persuade Nast that Nast had. What had happened? Could not Condé appreciate the lighter vein? Condé was a boor.

Boor or no, Nast did read the front pages of newspapers. Bellboys played the stock market in frenzied speculation and then all collapsed; the very fabric of America seemed rent forever. Schoolchildren fainted from hunger, there were defenestrations, and Wall Street brokers walked the streets like zombies. The Middle West was plagued with terrible dust storms and the doors of houses were chalked by beggars to signify the kind of reception those who came after might expect. To Crownie's disgust a popular tune, "Brother, Can You Spare a Dime?" was to be heard everywhere; he could not escape it. Social tensions were aggravated as never before. Men were picked up by the police for no other reason than that they were unshaven, and labor organizers hummed "The Internationale" and "Solidarity Forever." In Detroit, Henry Ford pondered briefly whether to hire blacks or goon squads and decided upon the latter.

Closer to home, *Vanity Fair* had never made any money. Its circulation had never risen above ninety thousand and to Nast's distress it required constant transfusions of cash from more successful operations like *Vogue*. Nast's thin-lipped mouth turned ever more deeply down at the corners; advertisers evidently could no longer be moved by yet another Crowninshield persuasion to continued optimism; neither could Nast.

To Crownie, these concerns were all so squalid. Besides, who, really, was that vulgar Alf Landon whose followers wore yellow sunflower buttons to church? What was he to think of Al Capone in his wide-shouldered suits or Franklin Roosevelt in his braces chatting before the fireside? In Europe there was Hitler, "an unattractive son of a bitch," who knew nothing of art. If only the German dictator would encourage his "cooks to make the best mousse, the best pâtés" and forget everything else. Yes, surely that was what should be done. Maybe Hitler could also "build a little theatre" and put on plays. If he did not, where would all this lead? At times over Maryland terrapin at the Knickerbocker, massaging his moustache and rolling his eyes in agony, he feared the worst: even the rich might be inconvenienced.

Before long it was Crownie who was inconvenienced. One August day in 1935 he sought such solace as he could from the miserable Condé Nast and his dreaded balance sheets by donning his baggy plus-fours and having a round at the Links Club. There his jabbering, ineffectual game, fun as it was, was interrupted by a throng of noisy newspapermen, some with cameras. Why could they not leave a gentleman alone on the golf course? Was not the Links a private club? But the "muckers" cornered him. Why had he, they demanded, precipitated an international crisis to the distress of the Secretary of State, Mr. Cordell Hull? It was all so silly; he had never really paid any attention to a *Vanity Fair* cartoon depicting the Emperor Hirohito drag-ing off the Nobel Peace Prize on a gun carriage. Couldn't they under-stand it was simply part of a series called "Not on Your Tintype — Five Highly Unlikely Historical Situations by One Who Is Sick of the Same Old Headlines?" It was all so innocent. Hadn't his magazine agreeably spoofed Admiral Byrd and J. P. Morgan in like manner? These two had never objected; they thought it was all good fun, gentle-men that they were. What, really, was this all about?

But those who made the headlines Crownie pointedly never read yet was sick of, sensed a rare quarry at bay: a snob who despised his har-riers. He was fair enough game. The desperate man tried in vain to appeal to that notion of Edwardian gentility he had given a merchan-disable form.

But no sympathetic Edwardians confronted Crownie that day. Much mauled, he extricated himself and returned to the office, only to be greeted by a Mr. Kuriyama, who, although his coat was cut much too short to be a gentleman's, was the emissary of Emperor Hirohito. This tight-lipped presence encouraged no invitation to admire an African mask or two or even observe a rousing game of the Rape of the Sabines. Decidedly, Frank's caller was not in "the lighter vein" nor one who gave the slightest indication of any interest in a charming little lunch — maybe eggs benedict — anywhere. For perhaps the first time in his life, the hard, brown, birdlike eyes of Crowninshield had met their match.

The editor gave it his best. Surely Mr. Kuriyama was aware of the many times his Emperor had been publicly depicted as bellicose, straining for conquest? Kuriyama shrugged; there was nothing wrong with that; such stuff was agreeable enough and not the reason he was there. Indeed, had the Emperor been drawn dragging off the Nobel Peace Prize on horseback, Mr. Kuriyama would not have called on Mr. Crowninshield at all. The problem, one of the utmost gravity, was the depiction of the divinity in a menial act; Crowninshield had mortally insulted the eighty million subjects of the Emperor, among them, in-cidentally, the man before him. What clever and ingenious denoue-ment, wondered Crownie, could be put to all this? But for once he was

DRAWINGS BY
GROPPER

JAPAN'S EMPEROR GETS THE NOBEL PEACE PRIZE

The controversial cartoon of Hirohito, from Vanity Fair, *August 1935. Copyright 1935, © 1963 by The Condé Nast Publications, Inc.*

at a loss. Mr. Kuriyama hastened to assist and Crowninshield wrote out an abject apology, which was then suitably emended by his caller.

The Japanese had been even worse than Amy Lowell, maybe even as bad as the struggles with Nast over French art, and in truth the end was near. The following year the most rapt of fornicators concluded that the revenues of *Vogue* would no longer support *Vanity Fair,* which was liquidated.

A "born courtier" who lacked "an appropriate court" was how Edmund Wilson summed up Frank Crowninshield. Yet his magazine had been his court, and although sometimes elbowed by Condé Nast,

224

he had been its king. As the end drew near he had difficulty in accepting it and frenziedly dispatched were more little notes, florid telegrams and boxes of chocolate creams. Geoffrey Hellman has described one of the last days of the reign:

> A new assistant editor, who had arranged for Helen Hayes to come into the Nast studio the next day to have her picture taken for *Vanity Fair*, went into Crowninshield's office to report this fact. "We want to take a picture of Helen Hayes," the editor, an earnest young lady, began, "and — "
> "Archie, take a letter," said Crowninshield to one of his two secretaries.
> "Helen, my dear, you know how long I've loved you from afar . . ."
> "Jeanne, take a telegram to Miss Hayes," he said to his second secretary.
> "As an old slave of yours, dear Helen, will you pose . . ."
> "Adele," he said to another secretary, who happened to walk into the office, "call Miss Hayes at the National Theatre in Washington — "
> At this point the new editor found her tongue and informed Crowninshield that everything was set for Miss Hayes to pose the next day.
> Crowninshield looked at her blandly. "Archie," he said. "Go on with the letter. . . . you know how long I've loved you from afar, and I hope now that you will do us the honor of posing for *Vanity Fair*. Yours ever, in admiration, Frank. Cancel all that."

For most of his years with the magazine Frank lived in an apartment with his brother Edward, an interior decorator and dope addict. Edward, whose name his brother pronounced as "Ed-Ward," spoke in a nasal New England twang and was at one time a satyr of sorts (he favored society beauties, among them Edna Wallace Harper, famed as a "Gibson Girl"). Without elegance or seeming affectation and a very clever junkie, he cloaked the habit in a down-east pragmatism so well that few suspected it. Always in need of money and rarely employed, he suddenly acquired a new and well-received interest: antiques. He went among his pleased friends and relatives admiring this and that piece of furniture. To spur on this laudable turn of events he was given several pieces for his collection, whereupon he sold all. Frequently Edward ran incredible temperatures, and Geoffrey Hellman recalled that "one morning, when the two men were at the Stock-

225

"Crownie" in October 1942. Courtesy of Wide World Photos

bridge Golf Club, Harrie Lindeberg, the architect, found Edward sitting on the porch, his feet on a stool and an ice bag on his head, complaining loudly. Lindeberg stuck a thermometer in Edward's mouth, pulled it out after a minute, and set off in alarm for the locker room, where Frank was dressing. 'Edward has a temperature of a hundred and four!' he said. 'Oh, it often goes up to a hundred and six,' said Crowninshield."

Finally very ill, Edward implored a niece to make sure he was embalmed twice and so often did he repeat the request that at last she lost patience. Embalming was expensive, she told him. "You ought to count your blessings if we do it once"; shortly he was embalmed. Once. Although Edward had been an inconvenience and an embarrassment, Frank was loyal and cared for his troublesome brother through thick and thin.

Crownie was now alone. Among his thousands of acquaintances he had no close friends, for he kept everyone at a distance and unburdened his soul to no one. Instead, he held himself in readiness to hear the difficulties of others and assist in any way he could. One form of Crowninshield assistance was hardly that. He had a lifetime habit of officiously loaning small sums and almost instantly demanding repayment, a custom particularly embarrassing to those who had, with reason, construed the offer as a gift. No sooner had this notion been formed than Crownie disabused them.

At seventy he lived with his cats, his paintings, his African masks and more dinner invitations than ever. Trim and jaunty, he played golf, swam daily, could still bark like a seal and stand on his head, and was a familiar figure at his clubs. But were the clubs really what they had once been? Certainly Maryland terrapin was no longer as it had been. As to café society, it had, he regretted, "drifted into barrooms and night clubs and lost its chic," but the idea of café society "was all right" except for the café. "What actually ruined the whole goddam thing was alcohol and noise." He much preferred the Cavendish Club, which was "dedicated to the axiom that all bridge players are not created equal." There he would chew furiously and almost swallow his elegant moustaches, glare at his partner, snarl at timid bidders, and sometimes reduce the ladies to tears.

In 1943 he needed money. His art collection was his one asset and was sold at the Parke-Bernet for a little over $180,000. He had been especially delighted that some of the highest bids were for works by such old friends as André Dunoyer de Segonzac and Charles Despiau. All along he had been right. To those who told him he had invested well, he shrugged; his collection was only what anyone of taste and determination might assemble on an editor's salary.

Old age seemed to relax his mannerisms somewhat; they had served him well and perhaps now they could be set aside. He thought of his life: "I have been thinking a little of weaknesses, failures, and vulnerable points. The first, I suppose, would be snobbery — a too great interest in the world of high (and rich) society. Second, my failure to establish, firmly, any business or periodical, literary agency, etc. Third, a perhaps preposterous liking for the new, as against the old, in painting, music, architecture, night clubs, dances, food, and women. Fourth, there is my almost inhuman avoidance of alcohol. I am probably the only man you ever met who has never so much as drunk a glass of wine, whiskey, beer, claret, white wine, cocktail, etc. I suppose, too, that I am vulnerable as regards the matter of sincerity, since I am always making new friends, acquiring new fads, going to new places and trying new restaurants, tailors, authors, shaving creams."

There was now less of the new than the old: quip after quip to be scribbled to almost anyone. To a young cousin at the Foxcroft School who he sensed felt fat and unattractive, he wrote cheery cards, little notes of encouragement. She was Little Red Riding Hood, he, of course, the Wolf. Then he was Romeo, begging his Juliet, "Don't tell me about any more of your love affairs" (he knew there were none). Next he was Anthony (he hoped "not adverse") and how he wished he could have seen "Cleo dancing those old waltzes at Newport with what is left of the prosperous and rich." And he whose romantic tendencies had always been much speculated on advised: "Don't get confused about men. You are too young to decide on a man who may not be the right one for you at all. Don't take the first egg on the buffet, wait, and wait and wait! You may like the sardines better, or the shrimps, or the anchovies!" It was all very kindly, very encouraging.

And although "doddering," he was still "a doting admirer" and pained by her "affaire de coeur." But he forgave her for he surely knew:

Early to bed
And early to rise,
Makes a girl puffy under the eyes.

In April 1947, he wrote her: "I have been ill for three months. Two months in a hospital with an operation that resembled a picture puzzle — several pieces missing — other pieces misplaced." But he was still able to conjure up a rival: "Last night, I had a very strange dream. I was at the seashore and there was a storm on the ocean. There was a man apparently drowning in a boat, I launched a dory and went out to rescue him. But, when I saw it was Richard Sears, I turned back and let him drown."

By July 22, 1947, Anthony had returned; with Cleopatra he would go to the Nile for a weekend but she must be careful of that silly asp.

The temptation to dismiss this kind of correspondence as so much more Crowninshield tinsel is, of course, compelling but perhaps better resisted. It seems rather the delicate extension of the healing hand to a troubled heart; it was therapy, and to few of us is given so deft a compassionate touch, much less to guise the surgeon's steel so well.

Nearly blinded by morphine and beyond any steel, Crownie set about the last of his editing — his enormous Christmas list and a list of his pallbearers. But both were set aside the moment an opportunity arose to clown with his nurses. As death neared he seemed to clutch more closely, as may a dying field marshal his baton, his own birch wand — "the lighter vein." A last scrawl directed that his doctor be sent a bottle of the champagne he himself had never tasted; nothing but the best would do.

The last of the species?

Alas, his is not one in the slightest danger of extinction; for he was a kind of P. T. Barnum: a dealer in illusion, and like any good showman, he never for a moment believed very much of what he did or said.

Frank Crowninshield had been preceded in death by the most rapt of fornicators five years before. In late life Condé Nast had acquired a singular distinction which no man deserved more than Crowninshield: the cross of the Légion d'Honneur for advancing French art in America.

No matter. It is distinction enough to have plucked one's own essence from a favorable if short-lived ambience itself partly of one's own creation: to lunch with the Queen of Spain, dine that evening with Gypsy Rose Lee, and in the bargain mortally insult the eighty million subjects of the Emperor of Japan.

SIX

"Keno," His Queen, and a Minotaur

Francis Boardman Crowninshield
(1869–1950)
and
Louise Evelina du Pont Crowninshield
(1877–1958)

Flowing, diaphanous caftans she favored for herself. Black she could endure not — and would reprimand the young or old females who dared wear it in her presence: "Please go off and change." Her maids wore uniforms of flowered print. No male indoor servant would she tolerate; maids would do well enough for her and the gentlemen too. She was redheaded, weighed over two hundred pounds, and had arms that looked as though they could scarcely be encircled by a yard-long measuring tape of the sort seamstresses use. The vast figure wore bracelets of diamonds so large they looked unreal, like stringed ice cubes. When she eased herself into a chair, two or three yapping, bad-tempered Pekingese would jump in her lap, and glare out from among the enormous sheltering arms and the tortured chiffon.

From large froglike eyes she surveyed her entourage with equanimity; she was all kindness, all concern, and it lay within her power to grant great favor. It would, of course, be necessary to dance to her gavotte. Those who did not? Well, they could be banished from her court forever. For she was the "Queen." Her name was Louise Evelina du Pont Crowninshield.

Shortly at Peach's Point, Marblehead, luncheon would be served in four courses on oriental Lowestoft over which her subjects would pay the homage of mannered, guarded conversation occasionally rent by ear-piercing screams. Bobby liked to shriek unpleasantries only dimly understood by those who heard them and not at all by himself. No regal displeasure feared he: Bobby was a macaw.

These sounds reached irritatingly outside to a terrace where a soli-

233

Francis Boardman Crowninshield — "Keno" — at the wheel of Cleopatra's Barge II

Louise du Pont Crowninshield — "the Queen" — wearing a diamond brooch in the form of the Crowninshield coronet

tary figure, in blue-blazered self-exile from the rich fare of the dining room and its guests, sat before a chicken sandwich and a large picture puzzle. Somewhat earlier he had shunned the cocktail hour for a couple of whiskeys drunk neat and standing up in the pantry. Why, he wondered, did the Queen always have to include fairies or arty types at lunch? And that Englishman! They all wore lace on their drawers too. When would these people, some of whom even liked that man in the White House, Roosevelt, ever leave? Not soon, he thought, for this afternoon there might be as many as six tables of bridge. But his picture puzzle was large and challenging; so he would kill the afternoon since he could not kill a few of the Queen's luncheon guests.

As for the dogs — Nomo, Fou-Fou, Noel, Ting-a-ling and Kai-Shek — only Kai-Shek, who slept in his master's room in a little wicker basket, was worth his salt. The rest slept with the Queen. He must remember to make sure Kai-Shek got some ice cream when the hubbub subsided. The short, barrel-chested exile on the terrace, who presently addressed himself to the hundreds of bits of colored pasteboard spread out before him with a lisped oath and the prayerful hope that no one would disturb him, was "Keno," husband of the Queen and the last of the Crowninshields. He had wished himself aboard his yacht where his superiority was evident but she had wished him otherwise. It had never done him much good to expostulate with his enormous wife ("Goddamit, my dear"), for Louise had always known exactly what she wanted.

So had her antecedents. Long ago, in December 1799, when it had so rejoiced Keno's great-great-grandfather, old George Crowninshield, to see his *Belisarius* "beet" *Essex* in a "fare Tryall" out of Salem Harbor, another ship was nearing Newport, Rhode Island. It carried thirteen members of a French family called du Pont and a quarter of a million francs in a small, heavily guarded chest.

Pierre du Pont and his brood, after narrowly escaping the guillotine of Robespierre only to find themselves lodged in one of Napoleon's prisons, had chosen 1799 as a propitious year in which to shake the dust of the Old World from their feet. As G. C. Zilg has recounted

235

in *Behind the Nylon Curtain:* "Landing amid the harsh New England winter, . . . du Pont led his shivering clan to the first lit house they saw. The elder du Pont rapped heavily on its door, but failed to summon any answer. Instead, through the windows teased a full dinner neatly laid out on a table awaiting the return of the family that had gone to their worship, as was the custom of churchgoers of that time. While the American family unsuspectingly folded their fingers in humble worship of their God of Wrath, the du Pont family broke into their home and ate their entire meal."

One of the uninvited was the Père's son, Irénée, who knew how to make gunpowder. In Delaware, along the banks of Brandywine Creek, Irénée set to work. An early customer was none other than the United States, for Thomas Jefferson was an expansionist, whose activities were likely to require no little gunpowder. Irénée built a new house for his wife Sophie, a stone mansion called Eleutherian Mills where heirs, enriched by successive wars, inbred. The year 1812 turned a handsome profit; the Mexican War was comfortable enough and the Civil War brought a flood of gold. In the 1850's, Henry, the Queen's grandfather and the shrewdest, most able of Irénée's sons, became uneasy at Delaware's vulnerability and teased the South with innuendos of support which shortly vanished beneath a flood of gunpowder contracts from Washington.

Henry du Pont liked hard work; he liked to waken his sleeping workers with huge greyhounds, and he liked the trowel he carried about with which he dug up weeds wherever he found them. The war, which had brought millions to the du Ponts, also brought him the rank of general: Lincoln had appointed him to conquer southern Delaware and Henry's bluecoats had done so. What Lincoln had not known was that General du Pont had captured Delaware for the du Ponts, not the Union. It has so remained.

Tall and choleric, Henry had a blazing beard that led him to be called the Red Fellow. He wished simply to be the most powerful man in America and wiled away his long winter of discontent after Appomattox by destroying his rivals, who were spun into his Gunpowder Trust. From this tangled web a bristling and voracious du Pont monopoly was to emerge. Henry was loath to delegate authority to any other of the large and fecund tribe; the rest of the du Ponts did as the Red Fellow said and the brightest of them did it in a hell of a hurry.

If Louise's grandfather did not become, as he had wished, the most powerful man in the country, he was something very close to it. In a long life only once did he err. When in 1866, a Swede, after much tinkering, divested a new explosive called TNT of some of its more touchy qualities, Henry du Pont was unimpressed. What could be wrong with the black powder he and his father before him, Irénée, granulated along the Brandywine and which he had in too-ample stocks? For years Henry fought off Alfred Nobel in every way possible and his skepticism found comfort when he learned that Nobel had merely packaged TNT with dirt and called it dynamite. Only when sales of du Pont blasting powder (it had but a twentieth of the explosive power of dynamite) sagged badly did Henry shake his red beard in dismay and commence manufacturing dynamite.

From such a sire sprang Henry Algernon du Pont, Keno Crowninshield's father-in-law. A Union officer in the Civil War, he had, among other exploits, managed to burn the Virginia Military Institute and its valuable library to the ground. The short, dapper little colonel with the sprightly waxed moustache concluded that his military services would best be crowned with the Congressional Medal of Honor, the highest award a grateful United States government bestows and then usually posthumously. Although du Pont sent out feelers of such candor and immodesty as to have a certain charm, somehow the decoration was not forthcoming. He kept after it. In fact he kept after it (or rather after the Congress) for thirty-four years.

At war's end, the Colonel's job with the Red Fellow was to extract rebates from railroads carrying the produce of the Brandywine, a task which prepared him to become the family's political arm in the United States Senate after a series of political contests that would have made Jacob Crowninshield blush with shame. About Colonel du Pont there was nothing devious; "me or nobody" was really the only plank in his campaign platform. He cared nothing for election scandals; he simply purchased his Senate seat. When from time to time some newspaper blasted him one day and praised him the next, everyone knew why: an overnight purchase by the Colonel, who was to acquire another title, the Junker of Delaware. He disliked weakness in any form and he believed he saw it all about him in every form.

In the councils of state, the Junker of Delaware battled the administration's attempts to escape the du Pont toils by building its own powder plants and extolled the virtues of Teddy Roosevelt's Big Stick, in which he foresaw a sale or two of gunpowder. From the breastworks he threw up on Capitol Hill against such weaknesses as munitions taxes, antitrust legislation and women's suffrage, the Colonel would sally forth in quest of the Congressional Medal of Honor.

Louise's father loved the Senate, its rough-and-tumble cabals, and reminded his colleagues that he was the least progressive senator in the history of the United States, which none doubted. By the way, he would ask, how was that House bill coming along? Who, he demanded, were the obstructionists? The House bill authorized the award of the Congressional Medal of Honor to Colonel Henry Algernon du Pont, U.S.A. Didn't his enemies realize that his legendary military ancestor was the Roman General Pontius Cominius? Such timid souls as Woodrow Wilson and Senator La Follette would never defeat the Colonel.

And they never did. But in 1916 he was not reelected to office. Unhorsed and unhappy, the bewildered man looked about him. It was incredible. What had happened? Stunned disbelief gave way to anger; he had been thrown out of the office he loved by those he thought loved him, the du Ponts. Had he not even rewritten the state constitution for his family?

But the Colonel had forgotten when boasting "me or nobody" that in truth it was the du Ponts or nobody. Things had changed since the autocracy of his father, and certain of Henry's crudities — especially those senatorial — were no longer acceptable in Wilmington, where corporate images had to be fashioned, refashioned, and polished again and again. Disgusted, the Colonel beat a retreat to his vast estate at Winterthur with its one hundred and fifty rooms and five hundred acres of gardens. He was seventy-eight; he was very, very rich and his lapel, which now bore the blue and white ribbon of the Congressional Medal of Honor, would never again be without it.

In 1898 war had been declared against Spain. The du Ponts happened to have a new kind of gunpowder on hand; it was smokeless or nearly so, and dispelled forever were the gray palls that had hung over such places as Antietam and Cold Harbor. Moreover, the presence of a weapon was no longer as obvious to the enemy as before and the new gunpowder was quickly adapted to the rifles carried by the ordinary footsoldiers.

One of these was a rather unhappy Rough Rider without a horse who sweltered in the Cuban heat in a heavy woolen uniform in 1899. Francis Boardman Crowninshield, although he did not know it as he dutifully lugged about his 30/40 Krag rifle and cartridges filled with du Pont's new smokeless, was to be the last Crowninshield.

Frank had come to the United States Army as has many another young American: he had had nothing else to do. Born in 1869, he was one of the great-grandchildren of Benjamin Williams Crowninshield, Secretary of the Navy in 1812. After graduating from St. Paul's School in Concord, New Hampshire, Frank attended Harvard, where he gave evidence of a certain testiness and received no degree after four years of study. How was it that a gentleman, and a rich one, need study?

Nor was the Spanish-American War the glorious thing he had hoped it would be. He saw little action, never succeeded in landing himself a horse, received neither promotions nor medals, and instead came down with a case of yellow fever. Apparently, Crowninshield's sole gain from Cuba was the permanent incorporation into a somewhat limited vocabulary of the word *bully*. The war had been a far more agreeable thing to the du Ponts of Delaware, for the cartridges Frank's rifle had fired had been sold to the United States at a profit of 320 percent.

Returning to Peach's Point, Marblehead, on the North Shore of Massachusetts, the former Rough Rider recuperated by the sea at surely one of the most attractive places on the east coast of America.

A lush bluff atop the granite overlooking the Atlantic, it was as close to Salem as Crowninshields dared return. The tip had been purchased by Miss Evelina du Pont of Wilmington, Delaware, who invited her niece, Miss Louise du Pont, for a visit.

By the fall of 1899 Frank was finding reasons to run down to Delaware and he hoped her family would not object to his writing "so soon after the last time," for she was his dearest "little girl," his "Precious Puss," and "Ittles." Crowninshield, however, found fault with the Colonel's champagne, which was stored in a huge wine cellar in such quantities that a considerable portion of it was always turning bad. The Colonel always served Frank the bad stuff. Nevertheless, the couple was shortly engaged, Crowninshield vowing, "I'm never going to allow myself to die or you either."

At the wedding in June 1900, the in-laws viewed one another with understandably mixed feelings. Louise's only sibling was small-boned, effeminate Harry, who had an incurable speech defect. He mumbled so oddly that it took one's entire attention to understand what he was trying to say. Particularly difficult were mealtimes: he always stared straight ahead making lip-reading impossible. Once at a masked ball in Florida he slipped a paper bag over his head, and the ladies he danced with who didn't know who he was thought the strangely thickened speech from the paper bag to be that of a drunk, which he never was.

As a boy at Groton, the Colonel's son had been regarded as a "pill," the pathetic butt of cruel jokes. The unhappy child hated the school; its obligatory sports dismayed him and he in turn dismayed the Junker of Delaware, who willed that Harry stick it out. That he did so was due to the kindness of certain of the Groton authorities, who deliberated at length Harry's one tearful request: that he be allowed to have a little plot of ground in which to plant seeds. Now this kind of thing sat as ill at Groton then as it has since: it was out of the question. However, a gardener with a greenhouse lived not far from the campus and the little pariah was allowed to spend his free hours there. They were conclusive and Harry du Pont was to become perhaps the greatest horticulturist in America; his marvelous gardens at Winterthur were done to perfection.

But the gardens are not truly his monument. Harry had dared, at a time when the country had long looked to Europe or Asia for superiority in the decorative arts, to collect Americana as none had before. Across the continent, can be seen above the Pacific headland the works of another collector who was du Pont's contemporary, William Randolph Hearst. You may wander from room to room and as splendid as it is, you could well be in Europe — nothing American meets the eye. At Harry du Pont's Winterthur you see what we were and not so very long ago. It is also possible that one Winterthur is enough. The place consumed most of his time and money; to perfect his museum was his obsession and in old age he scattered pans about the floor of his winter house in Boca Grande, Florida, rather than spend any money on roof repairs. He personally examined the guestbook at Winterthur. If some visitor whom he knew neglected to sign it, the Groton misfit could wax unpleasant.

Yet for all his knowledge of Americana, du Pont was not infallible. When a young couple was to be married he asked them their choice of a wedding present and was told they particularly lacked a dining-room table. Harry directed them to his vast warehouses of early American furniture and at length a table was selected. In the course of transporting the prize it became necessary to turn it over. Then they discovered the stamp: "Made in Sweden."

At Boca Grande he roughed it in a tiny wooden house — once that of a local fisherman — where he liked to give luncheons for twelve or eighteen. One was invited for one o'clock precisely. Many found it advisable to walk around the block consulting their watches and bumping into others doing likewise so as to arrive at the appointed hour. So it was that all arrived at once, when a footman, gloved and in full livery, opened the door into a hallway so narrow and so nearly filled by himself that it was hard to get by him. Drinks were served from a tray and hastily gulped down; luncheon was served. In a dining room not much more than ten feet by twenty, the guests were packed at the table. A clap of the majordomo's hands summoned more liveried footmen (their black-and-yellow banded vests made them look like wasps) in such numbers they could scarcely move to serve. The settings would be exquisite, perhaps red lacquerware, and of Harry's own placement. But ample time to contemplate them there was not, for the various courses were whisked in and out with amazing speed, the footmen tumbling over one another. Without air conditioning, or even a fan, the temperature could reach ninety degrees. Luncheon over, all trooped up a narrow flight of stairs to a room where Harry's shell collection was housed in glass cases. Over coffee, Harry would remark that shelling wasn't the fun it once had been; the beaches were too much picked over. Postprandial amenities lasted only a few minutes and the guests were politely and firmly ushered out. Those who lingered were very likely to have Harry tell them: "Please go home."

Food had to be sent down by rail from Wilmington in wicker hampers and once Harry ordered twenty-four lamb chops and invited twenty-five guests. He of course got his chop and one of the ladies an empty plate. An immediate neighbor offered to give her hers but the lady declined saying, "I live here and understand it all very well."

The master of Boca Grande could not bear to meet one of its natives on the street and when this appeared likely he would engage in complicated circumventions and so avoid his subjects. Some of them, to his discomfort, were an old Boca Grande family named Du Pont. They were black, and Harry, who had absolutely no sense of humor, insisted more adamantly than ever on "du" rather than "Du." To write the name otherwise genuinely angered him all his life.

The bridegroom had a sister and two brothers who may have puzzled Harry every bit as much as he did them. There was Benjamin, who of all the Crowninshields most closely resembled Benjamin Williams Crowninshield, privateer. Short and colorless, he was never to marry; attended by a manservant named Max, he traveled about Europe buying antiques. Always neatly but never expensively dressed, only once was he ever seen to take more than a solitary cocktail and that on the occasion of his successfully removing his domicile from Massachusetts to Florida after protracted resistance by the former. Massachusetts had taxed his unearned income ferociously and long enough in Benny's view; they would gain nothing by his death.

Although a resident of Florida, he kept a very small house near Peach's Point which was crammed with oriental porcelain and other antiques; there were unopened barrels of the stuff lying about and in a tiny kitchen he would help Max prepare meals.

Benny's last years in Florida were reflections on his life's triumphs — the cordon bleu from a French cooking school he had attended and destructions of large and audacious tropical bugs. Horrified of insects of any kind and at length failing to poison them, he set about rooting out the vegetation on his patio. It happens that the houses of Boca Grande depend heavily on plantings for their charm; in time his patio — without a living thing — assumed the odd antiseptic sterility of the man himself.

His securities investments were enormously successful; never a speculator, he always bought high-grade stocks and then simply waited. When he died a large strongbox was found to be so full of stock certificates that the lid could no longer be closed.

Benny never gave offense in his life but his death made a certain bank unhappy: his checking account was so enormous that it constituted a large part of the bank's assets. That institution chose to resist the transfer of the cash to a Florida executor, and the Commonwealth of Massachusetts clamored for a share of Benny's estate — to no avail.

In vivid contrast to Benny was his brother, Bowdoin ("Bowdy") Crowninshield. A frantic and indefatigable satyr, anything in skirts would do for him. He was to lose his money, marry among others a drunken Nova Scotian woman, and generally annoy everyone as long as he lived. His new sister-in-law, Louise, was at once treated to some Crowninshield family fireworks. No one had ever liked Bowdy's salty wife, and his brothers and sister decided to put him in Coventry permanently, which worked well enough until their mother died in 1902. Then they decided to exclude the offending Bowdy from the funeral and a very Crowninshield stratagem was decided upon. They hired a policeman to stand at the door of King's Chapel to keep him away.

One of those who hired the policeman was Bowdy's only sister, Katharine. When her Crowninshield temper surfaced, she lay down on the floor and grew rigid. The habit angered her husband, a physician of competence; he would pick her up stiff as a board and plunge her into a bath of cold water. This remedy the good old doctor swore by; it always worked, said he.

Strangely, a bathtub (one in the Parker House across the street from King's Chapel) got Bowdy out of Coventry in 1912 when his wife got drunk and drowned in it. The hatchet (among the Crowninshields, burying a hatchet had more often than not been a matter of in whom to bury it) was, after a fashion, laid aside.

The newlyweds lived in Boston at 164 Marlborough Street, where Frank remained alone when the Colonel frequently and imperiously summoned his daughter to Delaware, but a flood of little letters followed her. In these he described his days — persons, places and things were "happies," "goodies," "funnies," "nicies," or sometimes "badies." There were also a great many "cleavers" (all his life he never learned to spell *clever*). He had no job (he never did have a job) and found employment in walking with Our Son, a Pekingese, on Boston Common, and in worrying about how to conceal the purchase price of this or that new car from his and Louise's friends. No one must get the wrong idea; that would not be a "nicey."

Clearly 1903 was a "badie." In that year the Boston police complained that Francis Boardman Crowninshield had been "riding and driving" a motorcar in excess of the speed limit, eight miles an hour. In municipal court, he was found guilty as charged and fined a dollar or so. Frank refused to pay, hired some lawyers, and appealed his case to the Superior Court of Suffolk County, demanding a jury of his peers.

Anyone at all familiar with the County of Suffolk will recognize this as a mistake, or at least a waste of money. At the trial his peers (Frank did not think they were) stared briefly at the indignant Brahmin and his battery of Yankee lawyers and decreed: guilty as charged. But Crowninshield was not through yet. He instructed his counsel to bring the matter before the Supreme Judicial Court, the highest in the Commonwealth. There, before some testy and puzzled judges who felt that their time was being absorbed by trivia, Frank's lawyers admitted that their client had indeed been "riding and driving" faster than eight miles an hour but, they argued, Commonwealth Avenue was not a public way and the speed limit applied only to public ways. A great many old deeds were unearthed as showing some evidence that the city of Boston's legal title to one of its major thoroughfares was possibly clouded. But it was no good; Frank's appeal, surely the most expensive from a traffic ticket ever recorded, was dismissed. When one examines the old docket papers, one is struck rather forcibly by the young man's conviction that the ordinary rules did not apply to him. Indeed, Francis Boardman Crowninshield felt simply and sincerely that he had been given a first-class ticket through life; it remained only for him to sit back and ensure that the steward was on his toes.

Perhaps awed by the Brandywine and all that went with it, Keno set about in 1905 to enhance the prestige and honor of the Crowninshields. In all he caused three books about them to be privately printed, which must stand as some of the most expensively bound bowdlerizing ever done. His technique (ghosted by a compliantly prudent ghost) does not depend on the warping of facts but on simple and ubiquitous exclusion. Nevertheless, he prided himself on his historical accuracy and never for a moment considered omission as distortion. Should some ancestor turn out to be not quite what he had hoped and too difficult to be transformed, he or she was given no existence at all.

He had printed a journal his father had kept at Harvard in 1856, when, Frank thought, "the multitude of present pressure groups so busily engaged in sucking our life blood, were not even imagined." Also he wrote in his preface to the journal, a collection of astonishing banality: "There were fewer subnormal and irresponsible citizens" in those "glorious old days." He had forgotten what a singular pressure group the Crowninshields had once been. Certainly he had forgotten, if he had ever known, that his ancestors had been "leveling Jacobins" — members of what had passed for a commune in Salem in 1800. Behind the Rough Rider "bullys," one senses an old-womanish quality of selective and barbaric prudery. So sensitive was he that when *Vanity Fair* carried a story about Dick Crowninshield, the assassin, he canceled and never renewed his subscription, and one wonders about his strained quality of manliness much as one does about that of Ernest Hemingway, whom Keno much admired. Although gruff old seadogs of the sort he liked to think he was become less believable when they have very rich wives, fondle yapping Pekingese, lispingly insist on fresh mangoes for breakfast, Frank did have the Hemingway urge to simplify what is not really very simple. Unfortunately this kind of thing is particularly subject to evaporation and in the end one is left only with a residual, glucose sentimentality every bit as cloying as the *Vanity Fair* pâté of his cousin Crownie.

In truth, the last of the Crowninshield line had become effete. Divorced for a century from money-making and its vulgarities, his insulation from the forces of life was further buttressed by a du Pont. He could at once remember his great-grandfather, Benjamin Williams Crowninshield, with pride and loathe the bar sinister of commerce. Of "King" Derby and "his boys," he chose simply not to know.

His passion for collecting family memorabilia, especially ship pictures, led him in 1914 to dispatch the correspondence of his great-grandfather for the edification of the United States Navy. Strangely, the authorities made no disposition of these documents. A year or two went by and although he received one or two polite bureaucratic notes from Washington, it began to appear to Frank that the naval authorities were not properly grateful. The short-tempered man grew angry; he wanted his great-grandfather's letters returned to him. Another year passed and they were not. He demanded them once more and received a letter in which the Superintendent of Naval Records explained that although a "diligent search" was being made, he keenly regretted that some of the manuscript material had been evidently mislaid.

Keno was furious. Who in hell did they think they were, anyway? Some months later his letters were returned along with their probable disposition:

February 15, 1917

MY DEAR MR. CROWNINSHIELD:

There are returned to you all the MSS papers, three hundred and two in number, of your worthy ancestor, Hon. Benjamin W. Crowninshield, Secretary of the Navy, 1814 to 1818.

These papers were kindly lent by you for examination by the Department in 1914. The accompanying calendar of them may be of use or interest to you.

Mr. Stewart, Superintendent of Naval Records and Library, who received the papers has prepared this calendar and suggests the return of all the MSS. He considers them as historically valuable and interesting and expresses the hope that they will some day be safely deposited in a Naval History Building where the brave story of the early naval history of the country may be preserved.

Thanking you for your courtesy and consideration regarding these papers, and trusting that you will find them conveniently arranged and indexed for your own examination, I am

> Sincerely yours,
> Franklin Delano Roosevelt
> Assistant Secretary of the Navy

Who was this Roosevelt anyway? Probably a Jew. Clearly only a Jew would refuse to aggrandize the Crowninshields. Little did Frank know that a long and fateful relationship had inauspiciously begun — or that a first-class passenger might possibly be inconvenienced, even rudely jostled.

As a child he had sailed his father's boat, the *Effie*, a shallow centerboard sloop of forty feet, and had annoyed its owner by constantly firing off its small brass cannon. Then there had been the Scotch cutter *Madge*, the *Witch* (his first very own), and the *Tomahawk*, which he had raced in various regattas. A first-class sailor, he brought *Tomahawk*, on her maiden voyage from City Island, New York, to Marblehead without tacking. In 1907 and 1908 he had sailed with the Eastern Yacht Club against the Germans, first at Marblehead and then at Kiel with good results. Going on to Spain, he won many a race for the King of Spain's Cup, but Keno had resented his trophies, which "were little larger than ladies' thimbles, too small in fact to be suitably inscribed." Affronted by the offerings of Alfonso, he made inquiries of the Spanish Foreign Minister in Washington with the usual Crowninshield tact, and although "he expressed the greatest astonishment," the Spanish ambassador "was utterly unable to explain."

At Winterthur there was one who contemplated Crowninshield's doings with less astonishment than dismay: Colonel Henry Algernon du Pont. The hero of the Civil War had never understood his son-in-law. He was a nice enough young man; his Spanish-American War service had been acceptable enough, although he had not been an officer or seen combat. Why, wondered the Colonel, had Crowninshield never finished at Harvard? It nagged at him that his son-in-law carelessly forgot to file income tax returns and he had had to see to it. What really were Frank's plans? There was nothing wrong with yachting but the former United States Senator from the Brandywine did not feel that was quite enough. True, the young man had money, but what was that? He too had always had money, now maybe a hundred million, but all his life he had worked ferociously; money had nothing to do with that.

And why had his daughter given him no grandchildren? It was not a very du Pont thing to do. Perhaps the Colonel was mindful of his grandfather's counsel on the family's arrival from France: "The marriages that I should prefer for our colony would be between cousins." Maybe he should have married off his daughter to one of her cousins. The very moment the Colonel's heart stopped, she would be very rich. His thin lips pursed. Was Crowninshield a fortune hunter? The golden harvest from the banks of the Brandywine was du Pont money; du Pont, thought the Colonel, it must remain. What must be done? He huddled with his lawyers, who drafted an arrangement whereby Louise would have only a life estate; on her death all would revert to where the Colonel wanted it to go — to the du Ponts. Neither she nor Frank Crowninshield would have the slightest control over the matter. But what annual income should he leave her? Never should his daughter want for anything. Let her have something like two million a year after taxes and if she needed more, it would be there. In no way whatever would any principal ever fall into Crowninshield hands. Such were the Colonel's deliberations and they were not very different from those of another Crowninshield in-law, "King" Derby.

All his life Frank Crowninshield loathed the British as much as had his great-great-grandfather, George. Now Anglophobia is common enough among Americans but what was distinctive about his was its ubiquity; it was very much on his mind always. He could, for example, readily convert a conversation having very little to do with the English into a kind of tirade. In his lifetime it had been a very long time since the British and Americans last faced one another in the cypress swamps of New Orleans, yet Crowninshield took the greatest of pains in assigning a historical basis to his dislike. That he knew very little history troubled him not at all and almost surely he would have denied that his Anglophobia was perhaps traceable to the sort of Englishman who used to appear frequently at the houses of the great in, say, Newport and on the strength of a long-bankrupt title ask to be put up for three weeks or so.

Whatever the reason, it became aggravated by World War I, and to understand the misfortunes of Keno one must know that of all American cities Boston is the most Anglophile, the most emulative of the English, and that Crowninshield was extraordinarily socially sensitive. Boston clubs are made up almost exclusively of upper-class Anglo-Saxons, and the Somerset Club, located on one of the city's most attractive and historic streets, is quintessentially Boston in this respect. It was founded we are told (among its founders was his father) in 1851 as a place where gentlemen could pass an evening without listening to abolitionist talk. Perhaps. What is certain is that it never existed to hear Anglophobic talk either.

But one pleasant day in May 1915, Frank lunched there when the news of the sinking of the *Lusitania* sent a thrill of horror through the members. Someone recited the death toll — 1,100 civilians, including 128 American citizens, some of them women — and the U-boat had attacked without warning and without effort to rescue the victims. Suddenly the buzz of consternation was broken by the lisp of Frank Crowninshield. He wished, he said, there had been no survivors at all; moreover, the Germans ought to sink more ships like the *Lusitania*. In fact, he wished he had been the torpedoman.

Within twenty-four hours a purse-lipped committee met and unanimously decided to ask Crowninshield to resign; he did. But there was still more awaiting the Anglophobe — a sharp slap on the wrist from

Louise and difficulty with a second organization, one somewhat differently constituted from the Somerset Club.

At the portals of Peach's Point one November day in 1917 there appeared one Grady (who managed the Marblehead baseball team in the summer); Thomas Swasey, Adjutant of Post No. 2 of the Grand Army of the Republic; and Mr. George Nichols. They were, it was explained to the irritated Keno, a committee of the Young Men's Christian Association, which had come to collect funds to improve the amenities of American soldiers overseas. Scarcely had the dignitaries made known the purpose of their call than Crowninshield, "mad all over," rounded on them. Not one red cent would he give "to help the boys in the war"; the United States government be damned.

The astonished committee withdrew, licked its wounds, and called a vengeful meeting that evening of young Christian men and those who approved of their works. Mr. Grady telephoned Keno to invite him to the proceedings and Crowninshield declined with an oath worthy of his great-great-grandfather, old George. At this, shaking with rage, Grady addressed the large and indignant crowd. Was Crowninshield a German spy? Was he not married to Louise du Pont? Just what were his connections with the "du Pont Powder Company" anyway? Were the du Ponts not merchants of death? Of course they were. How could it be otherwise, asked the manager of the Marblehead summer baseball team. The G.A.R. Adjutant and Mr. George Nichols followed Mr. Grady to the floor, heaping fuel upon the fire. The crowd warmed; in fact, it did more than that according to the Boston *Herald* of November 16, 1917: it talked of "mobbing Crowninshield" and "some arose and advocated that he be tarred and feathered." But cooler heads prevailed. The matter, they said, was best referred to the United States Department of Justice. And so it was, but nothing ever happened.

To Keno's further distress, Colonel du Pont was hardly in agreement with his son-in-law. Before 1914 business had been bad. To Wilmington it now appeared that the British might be customers. Were they willing to subsidize du Pont powder-plant expansion? The British were willing but they allowed that they would become unhappy should the beneficiary of their subsidy sell munitions to their enemy, the Germans. Impossible, cried the du Ponts, how could one even dream of such a thing? Privately, however, a du Pont wrote that should the Kaiser match the British largesse "we would be willing to sell." But, he cautioned the tribe, it would be indiscreet to let the United States government know of any such arrangements. As for the ban a wary Congress was considering on the sale of munitions to belligerents, they would do business out of powder plants in Canada. Before long, however, a more judicious view of the great European struggle was assumed. British generosity toward du Pont expansion took the form of notes, not cash. By 1915, two years before America entered the war, the du Ponts were uneasily fingering nearly fifty million in British notes. What if England should lose? The British had been looking less for gunpowder than a partner and they had got one. So it was that Keno's father-in-law had become, for the nonce, an Anglophile.

The war also had another consequence for Frank and Louise, one which although the subject of much gnashing of teeth in Wilmington was to be a blessing in disguise. For years the government, restive at du Pont munitions profits, had been brandishing a bugbear; it had threatened to make its own gunpowder. Although the menace was largely hollow, what would happen to the "armorers of America" if it was not? The du Ponts adjudged the risk too great. What were they to do with their nitrocellulose? So it came about that the heirs of the fierce old Red Fellow were to make stockings of nylon for ladies.

In 1921, powder-making having ceased on the Brandywine, Colonel du Pont set about restoring Eleutherian Mills, the stone house his grandfather Irénée had built in 1803. It would be a gift for Louise: "The two original marble steps, worn by the feet of so many generations of the family, are in position at the entrance door and give out a certain flavor of dignity and antiquity which no modern structure could possibly have. When one considers that the same steps have been used by your great-great-grandfather, Du Pont de Nemours . . . by your great-grandparents, Irénée and Sophie du Pont, as well as by your grandparents, whom you knew personally, and lastly, by your mother and myself, these steps must have associations which will be very dear to you."

She could remember 1890 when a nearby powder mill had exploded, blowing men and machinery across the river and into the mansion's gardens. Powder-mill hands called this sort of thing "going across the creek."

Promising her father that she would live in the ancestral home for at least a couple of months out of every year, Louise Crowninshield set about furnishing it with American antiques and a garden of classical ruins. Years later, when she died, her collection was regarded as the most outstanding of its kind anywhere and is now a museum, a monument to good taste.

But Keno never much liked the place, of which he owned nothing, Louise reminded him, except "your clothes and the pistol you sleep on." Once he complained to a friend that even the cattle there were more comfortable than he was.

For the remainder of their lives, Frank and Louise spent the winter in Boca Grande, the spring at Eleutherian Mills and the summer at Peach's Point, following the sun in perfect ease and luxury. None of their houses resembled the huge palaces of Newport, for neither conspicuously spent in that way. What struck one most, whether in Delaware, Florida or Massachusetts, was a certain casualness; some priceless object was juxtaposed with a very ordinary, very comfortable chair of the sort which sent Harry du Pont into a frenzy. Priceless or no, china, glass or furniture were all subject to the hazards of daily use. Always there were shrilling Pekingese — generations of them — and the yet more raucous Bobby, the macaw, who was to survive them all. The pets defiled Aubusson rugs and delicate brocades as the occasion suited them.

The giver of life had a way of assigning proper orbits to those around her. As long as these paths were followed one basked in the benign rays; deviation cast one into darkest night, and a long-ago guest remembers a luncheon at which a waitress inadvertently failed to serve him some dish or other. He was young and did not wish to embarrass the waitress, yet Louise was staring at the empty plate before him. She

The Crowninshield house at Eleutherian Mills. Courtesy of Eleutherian Mills Historical Library

assumed he did not like the food and he never forgot the look in her eyes — the fierce glare of the Red Fellow — when she sharply reprimanded him; the Queen intended that her meals be eaten. It was part of the gavotte.

Because she was without malice or suspicion, Louise expected the best of people and only by the most compelling evidence was convinced, and not always then, that things were not as she thought and wished. She disliked drunkenness, preferring to think a guest was unwell. Once a very sodden young man turned green and vomited in his soup and it was only when, a moment or two later, he commenced to eat it again that Louise concluded that the young man was other than unwell. Promiscuity, however blatant and prolonged, was recognized only with the greatest reluctance and disbelief.

She loved children and their amusements, which were apt to correspond with her own view of life. Young brothers, sisters and cousins were marshaled to parties and games and made to like one another. A favorite game was played at the seawall at Peach's Point. The children were given a fishing pole and instructed to lower line and hook to see what they could catch. A servant was concealed below and each fisherman reeled in a handsome present.

Another class of guest at Marblehead, Eleutherian Mills or Boca Grande also liked the fishing: the sycophants, who found Louise an easy mark. These wanted most usually a college education for some exceptionally gifted son or daughter, or perhaps a new car for themselves. Antique dealers cast their bait before Louise, whose zeal often exceeded her knowledge of their wares. She was frequently stung in very substantial ways, much more than her brother, Harry. But when one spends tens of millions on antiques, as she did, such swindles are unimportant.

Her size made all sports save one impossible for her. She loved to swim, dog-paddling about in sometimes nothing more than a huge straw hat. The sea was good for both "pleasure and business" but a flood of houseguests ashore were wont to pollute her salt-water pools by too much "business." She is said to have determined that the children were at fault; she would embarrass and punish them. A substance was placed in the pool which would, upon contact with uric acid, turn bright purple. Louise and Keno watched as houseguests, young and old, splashed merrily about. At once, purple streams issued forth from a couple of Boston's best old dowagers in tank suits; the children had been innocent; thereafter their elders swam more for pleasure than business.

In no way whatever was she self-conscious. An elderly lady has recalled a party Louise gave at the Ritz Hotel in Boston over fifty years ago. Trained seals were the featured entertainment. When it came time for them to perform, the ballroom became crowded and in order to see better Louise climbed upon a delicate gilt chair. Slowly eyes turned from the seals to fix upon Louise, to wonder whether the chair would collapse under the great weight. It did not. Many remember her swims in the raw, her vast breasts ballooning in the water.

At about the time Keno had been pilloried by the Marblehead Y.M.C.A., there lay a-building at the shipyard of Nathaniel Herreshoff a schooner yacht for Frederick Jacob Brown. Constructed of high-grade steel, she was 80 feet on the waterline, 109 feet on deck, 24½ feet in width, 15 feet deep and powered with a 150-horsepower engine, which in calm, smooth water gave her a speed of six knots. Because a power windlass on deck hoisted both anchors and sails, the yacht required only a captain, a mate, an engineer, a boatswain, two quartermasters, some deck sailors, a chef, his assistant, and a couple of stewards. Herreshoff had not built her for racing but she was very fast, very comfortable, and very beautiful indeed.

There were ample quarters for both officers and men; there were two double and two single staterooms for the owner and his guests. The dining room or main cabin was chandeliered and expensively paneled. But most striking of all was the purity of design, for which Herreshoff was famous.

Much as had Kamehameha fallen in love at first sight with the "Harlequin of the Mediterranean," Keno knew he must have the *Mariette*, for so Frederick Brown had named his schooner. Why not? Had not Colonel du Pont at last joined the Red Fellow at Sand Hole

Cleopatra's Barge II. *Courtesy of the Peabody Museum of Salem*

Woods, the final resting-place of the house of du Pont? In 1927 Frank bought her, renaming her *Cleopatra's Barge II*. Possibly excepting Louise du Pont, the yacht was to become the most important thing in Keno's life. He had her hull painted a gleaming black with a gold stripe and for a decade and a half sailed the sea with his Queen.

From Marblehead, the *Barge* and her guests would sail to New London for the Harvard crew races, thence to see the start of the Bermuda Race, and on to Newport. Those "aft" (the ladies) would go ashore to do a little "antiquing." Once, at Rockland, Maine, Louise spent $175,000 in a single afternoon at a single shop. Its owner, Dave Rubenstein, was never again to hear her name without a film of perspiration forming on his upper lip. Understandably Louise's affluence sometimes provoked a different kind of reaction. There was the scion of a successful retail merchant who fled an unenthusiastic Boston elite to patronize the arts in New York City. He liked to display his collection in his plush apartment and was particularly fond of a complicated system of illumination whereby he contrived great dramatic effect. Behind a kind of screen, in oil on tempera and invisibly lighted, were wall to wall the seven deadly sins. To visitors he would point out Gluttony, a mass of obscenely spilling flesh. "That," he would say, "is Louise du Pont Crowninshield." He hated Boston.

Frank hated the notion of "exchanging a lot of real money for antiques" and much preferred to "movie" when ashore. And if the day were good, he would "mud up some perfectly good water-color paper."

And so it went — to Bar Harbor, to Northeast Harbor, and back to Newport. Once Frank left the flagship of the N.Y.Y.C. and its commodore; the whiskey was too ordinary. There was a sail to Brenton's Reef to see the start of the Astor Cup and then to Marblehead and the Eastern Yacht Club's annual regatta. Sometimes the water would be "full of holes" and the auxiliary engine was, to his remorse, put into play.

There were dog days of endless rubbers of bridge and days when he could only amuse himself by killing the flies which flew aboard while the *Barge* sailed near the shore. Louise "warred" with antique dealers, only to return late in the afternoon with the "plunder," some-

U.S.S. Crowninshield, *a four-stack destroyer, about 1930. Courtesy of the United States Navy*

times "well stung." Frank loathed "Maine days" of foghorns, fog and a flat calm and was happiest when the sun was out, there was a full-sail breeze, and the *Barge* would behave like a "real Cleopatra." At times like these, he would take the helm himself.

From time to time he would spot *Crowninshield*, a United States Navy destroyer. She was a four-stacker, one of the first prefabricated ships and designated "134"; the sight always filled him with pride. At last his family was being accorded the recognition it had so long deserved. Let Grady of the Marblehead baseball team and the ungrateful Franklin Roosevelt put that in their pipes and smoke it!

To Long Island, to Hampton Roads, to the Patuxent River for luncheon at Coleman du Pont's estate, and on to Annapolis where he viewed the Naval Academy, noted with rancor the presence of flying boats, and swatted the "cursed flies" with a towel. Chesapeake Bay he hated; it was full of flies and fishnets. Back to Maine, to Northeast Harbor, where Louise "annexed" two Willard banjo clocks. Always "Neptune" was aboard and "libations poured in his honor."

But there could be problems even on *Cleopatra's Barge II*. In July of 1930, he had a "beastly tooth" which bothered him all day. Once there was a near collision with another yacht, an incident he elaborately diagrammed in the *Barge*'s log in a way careful to absolve himself of any blame. And at Newport that "little bum schooner" *Osprey III* ran her generator before daylight, thus obliging the *Barge* to change her mooring to escape the noise. Later on, the movie ashore had been a poor one.

Frank always followed the most elaborate rituals of yachting courtesy. He never failed to signal whatever yachting squadron he was with for permission to leave and he never failed to note when the signal was not answered. And sometimes he found "hayseed Coast Guardians," who obstructed a favorite race, but his testiness was once relieved by "a wonderful drunk . . . who amused everyone to tears."

For some reason he always had trouble at Hampton Roads, where there were "uninteresting people and places." But this was nothing compared to the flies of the Patuxent River in June of 1931: "We beat to windward some 25 miles; we were never within three miles of land; and yet when we came to anchor we must have had several thousand, and before night, ten thousand at least. With four swatters in continuous action we could only hold our own and it was not till well after sunset that we made any real progress. They came in steady streams from aft forward. We shut all skylights and ventilators, just to keep afloat, and Oh! God, how they did bite! They are truly the curse of the Chesapeake." He vowed never to go there again.

But that summer had a very pleasant moment. In July, at Marblehead, "all of us, and a lot more, were on board at 9.30 to see the old frigate *Constitution* enter the harbor. She passed us soon after eleven amid a great booming of guns, much cheering, etc. She was a great sight. F.B.C. lunched at the E.Y.C. to meet her officers. At six o'clock by special invitation we inspected the ship. I presented her with letters to my great-grandfather, Benjamin W. Crowninshield, from Isaac Hull, William Bainbridge, and Charles Stewart, her best-known commanders. Captain Gulliver gave us a special photograph of the ship. We had a stand-up dinner of twenty afterwards on board."

Yet Frank had scarcely savored his triumph when the unthinkable happened — Franklin Delano Roosevelt was elected President of the United States.

Summer was "King's time"; after it came "Queen's time." Estuarine, so low-lying its dead must be buried elsewhere, and where the mangrove march to the sea, Boca Grande is famous for the tarpon, an inedible fish prized only for the tenacity with which it yields up its life, and for gently shelving beaches that cast up exotic sea shells — the Angel Wing, the Bleeding Tooth, the Banded Tulip and the Lion's Paw. At a certain time of the year blue-headed dragonflies hover in millions above the purpling sea grape, when at sunset the day blazes to an end.

The island, with a population of about three hundred, is without the pretension of much of Florida. There are a small hotel, an abandoned railroad station, and a few stores of the necessary and practical sort. Its one or two bars — resembling neither the supposed interiors of Benedictine wine cellars nor some Polynesian fantasy — are agreeably simple bars where reasonably priced drinks are served with dispatch. People do not dine out much except at one another's houses. Night life is to be found in an old barn with a floor of powdered shells where a movie is shown once a week. The theatre lacks any sanitary facility. One fends for oneself outdoors.

For years the place could be reached only by rail or water and the class of tourist who mostly likes to display himself to other tourists does not find his way to Boca Grande often; another class is likely to be dissuaded by a toll bridge run by the United States Army Corps of Engineers. Those who do are likely to wander about for a few moments and leave without knowing that its difficulty of access is no accident and that Boca Grande until very recently was — and perhaps still is — the smallest, most absolute of du Pont fiefdoms.

For forty years or so Louise and Frank wintered here with their dogs, macaw and the more indispensable chauffeurs, maids and retainers from Eleutherian Mills and Marblehead. With her husband very much in the background (perhaps only another retainer), the Queen exercised her feudal prerogatives and obligations.

Among the island's blacks there was a custom of "giving children around" when one family had too many to support. These arrangements could be confusing, yet Louise knew the real parents of every single child. No one will ever know how much she did for them but it is certain that it was a great deal. Each child on the island always received a Christmas gift and their parents enjoyed a different kind of largesse: she is credited with ridding them of the venereal diseases they had long come to accept as the natural consequence of life.

In time she came to be regarded as a fairy godmother whose wand dispelled many a problem. People in desperate need are not inclined to reflect (at least not for a time) on the evils of paternalism, and they repaid her in the only way they could. At the poolside cocktail hour they would appear to sing their soft, melancholy spirituals.

But fairy godmothers had best have a practical turn of mind. Once an Irish maid, Margaret, interrupted the Queen at lunch to say that Annie-Mae wanted to talk to her. Louise ignored Margaret, who promptly returned to repeat Annie-Mae's request. "Tell her I can't be bothered, I've got guests," replied Mrs. Crowninshield. Later she went out into the kitchen, whereupon Annie-Mae sobbed out, "Miz Crowninshield, I done shot my husband dead." Without a moment's hesitation Louise asked, "Are your people still in Georgia?" Yes'm, they were still in Georgia. "Have you got any money?" asked her employer. No, ma'am, she had none. Louise glanced at her watch: at 2:15 the only train would be leaving. "Go immediately home, Annie-Mae, speak to no one and don't leave your house." The girl was whisked away on the train. As for the local law-enforcement authorities, Louise tossed her red head in contempt. The deceased? "He was no damn good, anyway." She had known how to deal with the matter; she always knew what she wanted to do.

With the autocratic, fierce energy her grandfather, the Red Fellow, had brought to the Brandywine, she built in Boca Grande a health clinic and a school, and was astonished when the community praised her; like any good feudalist she had always understood its complicated system of rights and duties.

Keno, who mostly liked to amuse himself by painting quite good watercolors at Boca Grande (he signed them with the family crest which had been contrived by an earlier yachtsman, one who had had a passion for the Princess of Wales), was enjoying his summer cruises less and less. By 1933 Frank found very few yachts in New London, only a fraction of the fleet generally there in past years. Nonetheless "lots of bottles were opened and emptied" and Keno won five dollars from an Eli who never paid him. Nor was he pleased a few days later when "a G.D.S.O.A.B. of a steamer had pumped out her tanks and, as was unavoidable, the whole ocean smelt like a tanker or that other place which ends in double *l*," or when a lady clogged the *Barge*'s necessary with a peachstone.

He was also disturbed by "unmoral" gangster movies (they should never have been allowed) and by the Coast Guard, which in "a regular Coast Guard operation" had delayed the *Barge*'s departure for a half hour after the Harvard-Yale races were over.

Monday, September 10, 1935, was a good day, for "our radio announced the death of Huey Long, who certainly got what was coming to him. O.K. I calls it." Friday, however, was as "cold, calm, and gray a day as ever came over the horizon. The wind — whenever there was any of it — which wasn't straight up and down was always dead ahead. We did our best to make her go. Set and re-set everything we had in the way of fore and aft canvas, but to little effect. To everyone's disgust we finally had to fall back on gasoline, and made Boothbay at 6.30 P.M. Our only pleasant remembrance was the appearance of an old grandfather whale who came up and grunted several times close aboard. The Bar Harbor provision man supplied us with no end of bad fish and meat, all of which had to be put over the side. We were cheered up and dined principally on Old Fashioneds and the wine of France — the only good thing, to my way of thinking, in that G.D. country."

The year 1936, he feared, would be "the last year of yachting in all probability unless the people vote right in November and defeat Roosevelt." Aboard *Cleopatra's Barge II* he listened to the Republican National Convention until 1:30 A.M. and "heard the unanimous nomination of Langdon [sic], who is to try and save America from the domination of that Gang of Reds who call themselves Democrats, headed by Franklin D. Roosevelt." A day or two later he was pleased with the results of the first Schmeling-Louis fight; Louis lost. But within a week or so his pleasure was dampened by "a typical Roosevelt outburst" (Roosevelt's speech of acceptance). Yet for a while he thought the "chances of turning out our crooked government excellent."

"Nineteen thirty-seven — The year of Our Lord, and the 6th in the misrule of F. D. Roosevelt." The *Barge* commenced her summer of cruising, "antiquing," and "movieing" as usual with flags flying. Yet in the Rappahannock River it was too hot, "hotter than that place toward which this country and most of us, thanks to the leadership (if you can apply such a word to such a person) of F. D. Roosevelt is headed." Besides, he was obliged to pick the *Barge*'s way through the fishing boats in the mouth of the river. In Chesapeake Bay the usual flies and fishnets angered him, "the two F's . . . the only things comparable to the former are Roosevelt Dollars, billions and billions of

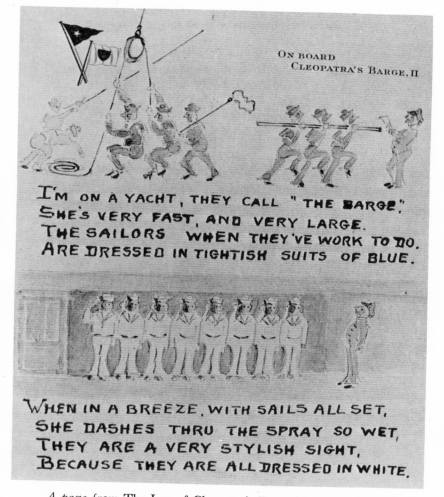

A page from The Log of Cleopatra's Barge II (1928–1942), *published in 1948. Doggerel by H. K. Milliken*

The crew of Cleopatra's Barge II

them." At Newport he criticized the British America's Cup entry, *Endeavor*, for its cocksureness and for delaying the race "ostensibly to remove a supposed lobster pot from its keel."

As if flies and Englishmen were not enough, on a warm day in Delaware, Franklin Roosevelt, Jr., married Ethel du Pont. Keno was now a kind of Roosevelt relation and the very thought of it made him speechless with fury. How could such a thing have happened?

But by the following year he had recovered sufficiently to log painstakingly at Eggemoggin Reach:

A POEM OF THE DAY sent to us

Brutus and Arnold and Franklin D
Sat in the shade of an Old Apple Tree
Their conversation took a turn
As to which was the most traitorous worm

It is I, cried Brutus, I betrayed my friend
I double crossed Caesar clear to the end
I won his trust and the histories say
His final words were 'et tu brute'

Not bad said Arnold, but listen awhile
Your horse and buggy record makes me smile
You fooled only one man, but look at me
I sold out a whole blooming Armee.

Then up stepped Franklin haughty and sure
You boys are like an amateur
When I took charge in thirty three
A great nation placed her trust in me.

I promised this and I promised that
I calmed their fears with a 'for-our-side-chat'

267

"Keno," His Queen, and a Minotaur

I scattered billions both right and left
And that 'my friends' is no small theft.

I told them all to feel at ease
I had them chanting there A.B.C.'s
I promised them I'd soak the rich
Aint I the lyingest S'o a Bitch?

I promised a land of milk and honey
Where every person would roll in money
I promised this but what did they get
Only a bigger and bigger debt.

They called me the great humanitarian
(I should have been in a sanitarium)
Blue buzzards were plastered on every pane
And new born babes proudly bore my name

Beware of Wall Street I dinned in their ears
Put your trust in me and have no fears
I'll keep you safe from every harm
To Hell with all work plow under your farm.

They believed in me all husbands and wives
But the damned little pigs all ran for their lives
They alone knew they were no longer free
As I killed them off with the greatest of glee.

I fooled those Yoekels both old and young
Me the greatest scroundrel still un-hung
I've ruined their Country My Friends and then
I place the blame on nine Old Men.

Brutus stood there all filled with awe
And Arnold sat with falling jaw

—◆●►—

Then up spoke Brutus, We've had our fling
Get up there Arnold Salute your King!

Then came 1939. The *Barge* started her annual cruise with a visit to City Island, New York, and the World's Fair, where Keno dined at the Danish Exhibit on "no end of little bits of made-over meats buried in poisonous-looking green and yellow sauces, dashes of this and that, and God knows what. All of which come under the heading of the stuff we put in pails and hand over to the garbage collector." Nor did he find impressive the du Pont exhibition to which the Queen had dragged him because it featured a new kind of ladies' stocking. Hardly any money in that sort of thing, thought Keno.

By June the flat, calm gray days were no longer "regular Maine weather," they were "regular Roosevelt weather" and "what, pray, could be worse?" Only "doldrums 'a la' the New Deal" in New London. To make things worse, a bridge had been built across Eggemoggin Reach. "We," he lamented, "in the olden days, used to come through Egamoggin and enjoy sailing through that most interesting reach. Now, alas! it is no longer possible to have that pleasure, thanks to our beloved President, who, in order to assist his re-election, in the good American way, has seen fit to spend some millions of other people's money building a bridge across it, which no one wants and very few use. A regular ROOSEVELT proceeding." He changed shipboard games, abandoning crossword puzzles for a new one, Chinese Checkers.

All the news seemed to be bad. The New York Yacht Club cruise "thanks to our beloved President and his G.D. high-jacking practices," was a ghost of its former self. "Like everything else which comes in contact with him, it withers and dies." Off Fisher's Island, the army artillery practice was an outrageous irritant: "Doubtless, Roosevelt, so desirous of starting another war to help him get another term, ordered the shooting. So discourteous to the New York Yacht Club."

On Saturday, September 3, 1939, at Provincetown when Crown-inshield appeared on deck before breakfast, the captain gave him "the sad information, just picked up on the radio, that England had declared war on Germany. All of which goes to show that though we possess ninety per cent of the fools on this earth, we don't own all of them. The water being fifty-eight and dirty we did not go in."

The end seemed near, yet *Cleopatra's Barge II* swept out of City Island as gaily as ever the following year, and at New London, Harvard won the big race. Frank was pleased. But Newport was practically devoid of yachts; the cursed war had seen to that. Roosevelt had "crucified" yachting; moreover the millionaire whose wife was worth many more was furious when he had to pay $3.85 "per" for Jamaican rum.

As Crowninshield prepared his yacht for sea in May of 1940, his two bêtes noires set about a piece of business. From their beleaguered island, the British were begging Franklin Roosevelt for old U.S. Navy destroyers. F.D.R. balked: the U.S. Navy, he replied, was spread out over two oceans; besides the Congress might not like it. Privately, he remarked that any transfer of U.S. naval ships to Britain might antagonize Hitler.

All through the summer Winston Churchill pursued "our best friend" and cautious ally: "I know you will do all in your power, but I feel entitled and bound to put the gravity and urgency of the position before you."

Once again F.D.R. equivocated. It was, he said, against the law to deliver American ships to belligerents. Why could Winston not be content with sympathy and good wishes?

But, the Englishman countered, did not his friend realize that the British fleet had been historically a shield for American security? What if Britain were to collapse? If it did, the British navy might be surrendered to Germany and the United States would become a second-rate naval power.

Perhaps so, thought Roosevelt, but what would America receive in exchange for her ancient destroyers? How about some U.S. bases on British territory? This way he could make the deal more palatable in the United States.

But Churchill cabled back: "Our view," he said, "is that we are two friends in danger helping each other as far as we can"; any swap must not, of course, resemble a swap, he admonished. America would get no British territory for her old destroyers.

What was Roosevelt to do now? He proposed that in exchange for the destroyers (he was by no means sure he could persuade the Congress to release them), Churchill guarantee that the Royal Navy make its way across the Atlantic to America if Great Britain should fall.

The Prime Minister flatly refused. Had he not already told the House of Commons that if an invasion succeeded, "our Empire beyond the seas, armed and guarded by the British Fleet, will carry on the struggle"? In short, the British had no intention of guarding American shores, destroyers or no. He now instructed the British Ambassador to "discourage any complacent assumption on the United States' part that they would pick up the debris of the British Empire by their present policy."

Now this was hardly the language of two friends in danger helping each other as much as they could, but the Americans, at least for a time, struck an obdurate stance. Could not Churchill pledge the future of his fleet in the event of England's collapse, maybe even withdraw his statement to the House of Commons? If not, could he kind of act like he was, even if he wasn't?

Back came a bold and negative reply, and once more Churchill fell to conjuring up the specter of a British fleet in German hands.

Roosevelt succumbed, but there was still the Congress and in it were powerful isolationists who feared that the business would lead to war. Besides, how could the U.S. Navy simultaneously plead for money for more ships and give away most of its destroyer strength? Franklin was unhappy; he was about to buck for a third term. Didn't Winston know this was going to be difficult?

But Churchill knew his business. "You know well," he wrote the President on August 15, 1940, "that the worth of every destroyer [privately he thought them so much junk] you can spare to us is measured in rubies." He wanted a partner.

For those on board *Cleopatra's Barge II* on Thursday, September 5, 1940, off Marblehead there was a fast sail, a good lunch and a very satisfactory slaughter of flies. But even so, it was the unhappiest day of Crowninshield's life. In the early afternoon he spotted some vessels moving out of Boston Harbor into the Atlantic at flank speed. Curious as always, he picked up his binoculars for a better look. The ships were the first U.S. Navy destroyers on their way to Winston Churchill. Keno peered again and gasped in horror. Was it possible? It was; one of them was *Crowninshield*, the very vessel his "dear little niece" had christened years ago and now given over to the "only country on this earth which has ever abused us." It was, he said in one of his few similes, an Athenian maiden sent to be devoured by the Minotaur.

But while *Crowninshield* with the stamp of an English king upon her shaped her course much as had *America IV* more than a century earlier and he penned his fury in his log, he did not know that the entry was to be his last, the last in all the logbooks of all Crowninshield ships that had ever been. The following season he prepared his yacht for a season that never was. The country was at war.

Now minotaurs are apt to be careless, even of first-class passengers, and another Athenian maiden was necessary — Keno's very own. Shortly he was informed that the Coast Guard had requisitioned *Cleopatra's Barge II* for offshore patrol.

For a few weeks the splendid yacht plied Atlantic waters, presumably in search of enemy submarines, and in 1943 she was returned to her owner, but Keno refused to accept her. His captain, Lawson, told him, "It would have made you cry could you have seen her." Frank refused to see her and wept not. The old Crowninshield litigiousness swelled again. He summoned his lawyers but the last of nearly three centuries of Crowninshield lawsuits was not particularly successful. Nor could it have been: the *Barge* had been his very ego and the courts afford no remedy for damage of this sort.

About this time a luncheon guest at Marblehead arrived to see his host, oblivious to all, reading and rereading a letter. From time to time he glanced blankly at his guests, who were now arriving in numbers. "Louith, Louith, where are you? Come down here. Who are theth people? I don't know who they are." His trembling hand clutched the United States government's award, a few thousand dollars, in his view

272

outrageously inadequate. He sold the *Barge* to a man who renamed her *Gee Gee* and the name made Keno almost retch to hear it. Many years later after more names and owners, the yacht found her way to Captain Boudreau in the Caribbean and a Panamanian flag.

It is perhaps as well that Keno chose not to have his beautiful yacht back again, for in the postwar years a revolution was sweeping the sea. The great unwashed, having acquired two automobiles and a house in the suburbs, became the owners of millions of small boats. Soon they were choking the harbors he loved so well, polluting those pleasant out-of-the-way spots where the *Barge* had paused to allow Louise a swim in the raw, a good lunch, to see and be seen by only a few fishermen or by another yachtsman whom of course he knew. Frank would have found undesirable the new class of sailors who mostly rely on gasoline engines, something he hated and used only when absolutely necessary. Their manners, their ignorance, would have appalled him. From time to time the U.S. Coast Guard, whose own bumblings he had despised, comes upon a plastic boat rocketing about whose crew does not know how to navigate or to swim.

Indeed there would be little room for *Cleopatra's Barge II* whether off Cutty Hunk or Chesapeake Bay, nor very much room for Frank himself; the world had changed. To him the sea had been a place for those who fished in it and for those who were gentlemen on it for pleasure. By no means did Frank ever for a moment think the former vulgar; he admired them as members of a kind of nonegalitarian fraternity.

It happens that the intrusion into what he thought a sacred province had been in no little way brought about by the du Ponts of Delaware, whose products are to be found aboard every "stinkpot." Although Crowninshield — in his darkest mutterings — saw clearly enough that their middle-class owners would, in addition to being a squalid nuisance afloat, destroy him as a class, a steadfast one-dimensionality prevented his understanding that the du Pont dividends, which had kept him afloat, were almost exclusively derived from pandering to his enemy. It would have puzzled and angered him to consider — as they have in Wilmington ever since Irénée built his gun-powder mill — that dividends are yielded up not so much out of the formulation of the needs of the millions as they are from creating needs, real or imagined.

He never owned another yacht, instead amusing himself with huge picture puzzles and watercolorings, and one of his days was brightened when he learned of the death of his old antagonist, Roosevelt. "Thank God," said he. "Now I can get a decent meal."

At eighty his thoughts sometimes turned to *Crowninshield* but he never knew what became of her. It was just as well. In 1940 the British renamed her H.M.S. *Chelsea* (names of towns and cities common to both Britain and the United States were tactfully chosen), and the groaning, creaking destroyer plied Atlantic convoy routes under the Union Jack. On April 6, 1941, she rescued the twenty-nine survivors of S.S. *Olga*, which had been sunk by German aircraft, and a year later she attacked a surfaced submarine, which dived and escaped. But Winston Churchill complained to Franklin Roosevelt of the destroyers' "many defects" and "the little use we have been able to make of them so far." Moreover, the sailors of the Royal Navy, used to hammocks, had to spend stormy sleepless hours in the bunks with which *Crowninshield* and her sister vessels were fitted.

In November 1942 Churchill passed her off to a yet poorer relation, the Royal Canadian Navy, which returned her to the British, without gratitude, the following year. For a few months the antique rusted at Londonderry in northern Ireland and then was packed off to the Soviet Union as part of some understanding or other. As *Derski*, she sailed the Black Sea until 1947, when the Soviet navy, modernized by captured German and Japanese vessels, had no further use for her. Whatever service the relic, named after what had once been a great capitalist family, performed for the Union of Soviet Socialist Republics is known only to the Russians. One's inquiries go unacknowledged; the Soviets, it seems, do not put much emphasis on individual ships, and moreover the victories of World War II are ascribed to the Red Army.

Whatever the case, the Russians sent their *Derski* back to the Brit-

A cannon from America IV, *as displayed at Peach's Point, Marblehead. The cannon has since been stolen. Courtesy of the Peabody Museum of Salem*

ish in June of 1949, when a P. W. MacLellan, her last owner, bought her from His Majesty's government. Barely able to move under her own steam, the last and weary voyage of *Crowninshield* ended on a Scottish scrap pile on the river Clyde.

Francis Boardman Crowninshield survived the destroyer by a few months. The Queen, always an indefatigable traveler, sensed there were many trips he chose not to make. On such occasions she took pains to ensure that guests were invited to pass the time with him wherever he was. At Eleutherian Mills she left him with suitable companions when she went away for a few days; Keno never liked to be alone. On the evening of her return, all enjoyed a good champagne supper. In the morning a maid, having knocked on Frank's door without response, asked the houseguest in an adjacent room to see what the trouble was. He entered; the last Crowninshield had died in his sleep.

Although Frank was eighty-one, Louise was stunned. He was buried at Eleutherian Mills, where he had owned nothing except the pistol he slept on, to lie with the Red Fellow and Colonel du Pont. It was perhaps better that he predeceased her; his dependence had been too great for him to have gone it alone.

She hurled herself anew into her charities; she continued restoring such remarkable houses as the Lee mansion in Marblehead, Kenmore in Virginia, and the Gardner-Pingree house in Salem, where Captain White was murdered. A hundred other activities also demanded her time and money.

In Boca Grande in 1958 she became seriously ill, and in so small a place everyone knew it. One evening her chauffeur and general factotum pushed her to the beach front, where she sat quietly and watched for the last time, tears streaming down her face, the sun sink into the Gulf of Mexico. Her farewell came next day when her private car was attached to the daily train. A crowd had come to say goodbye and unassisted she walked to the rear platform of the private car, quipped with friends and weeping blacks below, and waved, smiling and tearless, as the train pulled slowly away.

A resident recalled: "We sat on the lawn beside the road and I heard a sobbing sound as someone approached on the sidewalk. I saw it was a colored woman of mature years who had worked for Louise over a long period. I asked her what made her so sad and she said she had been to say goodbye to Mrs. Crowninshield. She said how wonderful she had been 'to my people and to your people,' and then added, 'I think when her time come there won't be room on her crown for all the stars. They'll have to put some on her robe.' "

The train rolled northward to Boston where she lay in a hospital, pillowed, sedated, and consumed with cancer. Yet the vast bulk was strangely undiminished. The curator of a favorite museum came to tell her that a certain painting could be acquired. Without hesitation she groped for her checkbook; yes, it must be done. To a young man with her niece, she extended a still formidable hand; how she was looking forward to the wedding! It had taken place some hours before but the dying woman took only seconds to regroup: "You take care of her and I'll take care of you." She then gave a kind of sign, rolled over and faced the wall; she wished the visit concluded. Louise du Pont Crown-inshield had always known what she wanted.

After her funeral in Wilmington, those concerned immediately repaired for a reading of her will — if not a French custom, a du Pont one. A paragraph disposed of "my little dogs" but not Bobby the macaw. Nonetheless someone took him and for another ten years he lived on to shriek what sounded mostly like telephone numbers. Another omission was to stun the black servants in faraway Boca Grande; some had served her all their lives and none received a cent. All knew that what had been hers would revert to the du Ponts and heads nodded in the soporific heat of the tidewater plain. But still there was page after page of bequests — this vase — that chair — to be droned out by a lawyer.

Suddenly, at the description of some artifact or other, an odd but imperative voice broke the somnolence: "No, she can't!" As quick as a thrush, Harry du Pont was on his feet. "It's mine," he said.

L'Envoi

———◄•►———

With trepidation, one seeks out "a certain pond, called Spring Pond," for after nearly three hundred years the fate of ponds in Massachusetts mill towns is foregone. A gas-station attendant shrugs his shoulders in determined parochialism. No, he does not know where Spring Pond is; it may be over in Peabody, in which case the notion he could be of any assistance whatever is an affront. Finally, a half-mile away, one turns up a graveled road and, suddenly, there is Spring Pond and it is, when a low and soft mist clings to it, a thing of great beauty. Seized years ago for a municipal water supply, it has remained uncontaminated; no houses are allowed to be built near it, and it is a very quiet place. Gray birches overlook great boulders lining its banks, one such stone bearing vividly in green the legend "Don loves Diana," and among fallen leaves there glint ubiquitous aluminum beer cans. Yet all is as it was in Dr. Kronenscheldt's time, when he and Cotton Mather sat here admiring the fireflies on summer nights, pondering witchcraft and the Evil One. Beyond the birch once grew the pine of English kings.

In the mist among the boulders one thinks of George and John Jay, of "King" Derby and his wooden hermit, of powder mills along the Brandywine, of the Bonapartes, of the Datoos of Sumatra, of a silken noose of death, of "Roosevelt" weather in Long Island Sound, of Clara's disconsolate walks, of Sundays of ten tables of bridge at Peach's Point, of Crownie aloft in his tree, of *America IV* under sail in the English Channel, of wind in the rigging, of ebb and flow, and of prayer and curse.

How is it to be summed up? Surely the Crowninshields had something in common, and if one could but find it, a comparison could be set on foot and cudgeled about for a paragraph or two. But they did not.

It is enough to say they were extraordinary. Anything more comes too perilously close to an attempt to portray the human condition, something mercifully beyond reach.

A pair of black duck glide by; shortly, irrevocably, the mysterious waning of a sun neither benign nor indifferent will commit these fiercely beating hearts to a journey serene because beyond understanding.

References

CHAPTER ONE

Most Crowninshield family manuscript materials are in the Peabody Museum of Salem and the Essex Institute. The former has upwards of eighty boxes of various writings, but the most significant collection, consisting of several volumes of journals and letters, and about thirty-two boxes of other writings (there are roughly four to five hundred writings per box) are in the Essex Institute. It is awkward that the material is not under one roof and that neither library has to date been able to index its collections systematically. This mass of paper has attracted only specialized scholars — particularly those concerned with the East India trade — and, as far as I know, no inquirer with more general interests.

Particularly abundant is material relating to the late eighteenth century and the early years of the nineteenth, for these Crowninshields were a chatty bunch. But their letters, often cryptic, are difficult to read and once read, it is hard to tell what it was they were chatting about. To catalogue such letters according to the categories "personal" and "business" is to honor a convention the Crowninshields, like others of their time, were not much concerned with.

Over the years the donors of manuscripts have made various attempts at deletion. The mutilations seem to have arisen from an anxiety to attribute the sentiments of a later time to those who never felt them. A case in point is the good soul — probably around 1900 or earlier — who took it upon herself to expunge any allusion to

281

Crowninshield slave-owning. But happily this kind of thing has never been very thoroughgoing; occasionally one sees in the margin of some tainted document: "no one must see this." Much in the material is likely to remain obscure. An example is some truly frenzied letters of George Crowninshield, Jr., a tirade against someone or something, but one cannot find out the cause of the outburst. To me the most pleasing of family letters are those of his father. Although old George was scarcely literate and seldom scrawled more than a few lines, he cannot ever be misunderstood.

After the War of 1812 Crowninshield correspondence — I feel — becomes progressively mannered and loses the delightful candor of an earlier time; one wonders what someone so essentially concerned with substance as old George Crowninshield was would make of a speech of, say, former President Nixon.

Obviously I have had to consult many other sources. Particularly useful have been the hundred-odd volumes of the Essex Institute Historical Collections. *The Diary of William Bentley*, admirably edited in four volumes by Peter Smith in 1962, has also been very valuable. In it one sees Dr. Bentley (a Crowninshield adherent) reluctantly yet finally lose patience with the family. The works of the historian James Duncan Phillips have great merit but one feels he was not quite fair to the family; Mr. Phillips died in 1954 a Federalist. Many more sources were consulted but I cannot say any has been so contributory as to be cited here. Salem newspapers of the early nineteenth century were violently partisan and must be treated with caution.

To the extent witchcraft is dealt with, I have heavily relied on the records of the Essex County Superior Court. John Randolph's speech is from the records of the Eighth United States Congress.

I am greatly in the debt of the Essex Institute and the Peabody Museum for the many courtesies extended me during the year and a half it took me to examine their materials. I must single out Mrs. Arthur R. Norton, the reference librarian at the Essex Institute, who has assisted me in my many tiresome inquiries with unfailing patience and good humor.

◄●►

CHAPTER TWO

This chapter is largely based on manuscript material in the Peabody Museum, more particularly the diaries of "Philosopher Ben," a cousin of George Crowninshield, Jr. In 1913, Francis B. Crowninshield emended them in a book privately printed in Boston; it is necessary to read the unexpurgated diaries to understand what really happened. *The Diary of William Bentley* (1962), cited among the sources for Chapter One, has been very valuable for this chapter as well.

Those who care to see what the interior of George's yacht looked like may do so in the excellent reconstruction at the Peabody Museum of Salem.

CHAPTER THREE

Materials relating to the White murder are in the Essex Institute. Several accounts have been printed of the affair; one such, published by another Crowninshield, reappeared in *Vanity Fair* by Cleveland Amory and Frederic Bradlee (New York: Viking, 1960).

CHAPTER FOUR

In 1956, Mr. Andrew Hilen, a prominent Longfellow scholar, edited the diaries of Clara Crowninshield for the University of Washington Press. The originals are now at the Houghton Library of Harvard and nothing has been lost in Mr. Hilen's emendation. In his book he gives us a biography of Clara, and while understandably enough the fact of her illegitimacy is stressed, one regrets this thorough scholar has overlooked the murder of Captain White and its effects on Clara. Other papers relating to her were for a time not to be found. They are now at the Peabody Museum through the good efforts of Walter Muir Whitehill, Mr. Atherton P. Loring and Mr. Hilen.

———— ◄●► ————

CHAPTER FIVE

Frank Crowninshield — although a public figure for many years —
was essentially a very private man. Oddly, although he died in 1947,
the evidence about him is far staler than that about some of his ancestors who have been dead for a century and a half. In death he is
nearly as elusive as he was in life. Once someone undertook to write a
doctoral thesis about the man but, as I understand it, gave it up. I have
relied somewhat on Geoffrey Hellman's *New Yorker* profile (September 19, 26, 1942), which later appeared in *Mrs. de Peyster's
Parties*, written by Hellman for the Macmillan Company, although it
suffers from having been largely written inter vivos in a style someone
— I believe — has called neo-sycophantic. Almost all of the people
who knew him with whom I talked expressed a wish not to be identified. Family informants, with exceptions, have been so guarded —
and in some cases puzzled — as to be of no great use. Very kindly the
Houghton Library of Harvard allowed me to reproduce certain of his
correspondence with E. E. Cummings and Amy Lowell. My sister-in-
law, Mrs. Karl Riemer (a cousin of Crowninshield's), has permitted
me to reproduce some of her correspondence with him. Mr. Frederic
Bradlee of New York was good enough to give me the letter from
Scott Fitzgerald.

CHAPTER SIX

This part is based mostly on the recollections of those who knew
Mr. and Mrs. Crowninshield and on mine. With few exceptions they
have asked that they not be identified and their wishes must be hon-
ored. I have quoted from *The Log of the Cleopatra's Barge II*, which
Mr. Crowninshield had privately printed in Boston in 1948.

Index

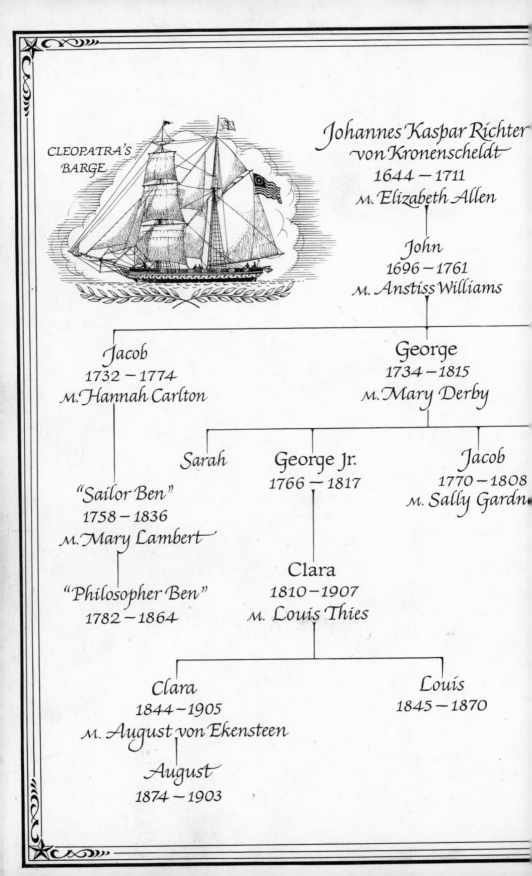

CLEOPATRA'S
BARGE

Johannes Kaspar Richter
von Kronenscheldt
1644 — 1711
M. Elizabeth Allen

John
1696 — 1761
M. Anstiss Williams

Jacob
1732 — 1774
M. Hannah Carlton

George
1734 — 1815
M. Mary Derby

Sarah

George Jr.
1766 — 1817

Jacob
1770 — 1808
M. Sally Gardn

"Sailor Ben"
1758 — 1836
M. Mary Lambert

"Philosopher Ben"
1782 — 1864

Clara
1810 — 1907
M. Louis Thies

Clara
1844 — 1905
M. August von Ekensteen

Louis
1845 — 1870

August
1874 — 1903